VCs

OF THE FIRST WORLD WAR

THE WESTERN FRONT
1915

VCs
OF THE FIRST WORLD WAR
THE WESTERN FRONT
1915

PETER BATCHELOR AND CHRISTOPHER MATSON

First published in 1997
This edition first published in 2011

The History Press
The Mill, Brimscombe Port
Stroud, Gloucestershire, GL5 2QG
www.thehistorypress.co.uk

British Library Cataloguing in Publication Data.
A catalogue record for this book is available from the British Library.

ISBN 978 0 7524 6057 4

Typesetting and origination by The History Press
Printed in Great Britain
Manufacturing managed by Jellyfish Print Solutions Ltd

CONTENTS

ABBREVIATIONS

ADS	Advanced Dressing Station
ASC	Army Service Corps
BEF	British Expeditionary Force
BVM	British Victory Medal
BWM	British War Medal
CAMC	Canadian Army Medical Corps
CEF	Canadian Expeditionary Force
CFA	Canadian Field Artillery
CG	Coldstream Guards
CIB	Canadian Infantry Brigade
CO	Commanding Officer
CRE	Commander Royal Engineers
CSM	Company Sergeant Major
DCM	Distinguished Conduct Medal
DFC	Distinguished Flying Cross
DLI	Durham Light Infantry
DSO	Distinguished Service Order
EEF	Egyptian Expeditionary Force
GC	George Cross
GG	Grenadier Guards
GSO	General Staff Officer
HLI	Highland Light Infantry
IG	Irish Guards
IOM	Indian Order of Merit
KOSB	King's Own Scottish Borderers
KOYLI	King's Own Yorkshire Light Infantry
KRRC	King's Royal Rifle Corps
MC	Military Cross

MG	Machine-gun
MID	Mentioned in Despatches
MM	Military Medal
MO	Medical Officer
OCA	Old Comrades Association
OCTU	Officer Commanding Territorial Units
OTC	Officer Training Corps
QVR	Queen Victoria's Rifles
RAMC	Royal Army Medical Corps
RB	Rifle Brigade
RE	Royal Engineers
RGA	Royal Garrison Artillery
RIF	Royal Irish Fusiliers
RNWMP	Royal North-West Mounted Police
RSF	Royal Scots Fusiliers
RWF	Royal Welsh Fusiliers
SAA	Small Arms Ammunition
VAD	Voluntary Aid Detachment
VC	Victoria Cross

ACKNOWLEDGEMENTS

We would like to thank the staff at the following institutions for their help and patience during the research for this book: The Commonwealth War Graves Commission, Maidenhead; the Imperial War Museum, London; the National Army Museum, London; the Public Record Office, Kew; and the Royal Artillery Institution, London.

We have used Gallahers cigarette cards for the majority of the men's portraits. The artist's impressions of the actions are drawn mostly from *Deeds That Thrilled The Empire* (Hutchinson, n.d.). Other illustrations have been obtained from the following: *Bravest of the Brave*; Pearse and Sloman, *History of the East Surrey Regiment* (Medici Society, 1923); *Illustrated London News*; Merewether and Smith, *Indian Corps in France* (John Murray, 1929); Hammerton, *I Was There* (Waverley, 1938); *Lincolnshire Echo*; *Sentinel*; G.H. Woolley, *Sometimes a Soldier* (Benn, 1963); Creagh/Humphries, *The VC and DSO* (Standard Art Co., 1924); J. Smyth, *The Story of the Victoria Cross* (1963); *The War Budget* (The Daily Chronicle, 1914–18); Hammerton, *The War Illustrated* (Amalgamated Press, 1914–19); other photographs are provided by the Maple Leaf Legacy Project, Jim McGinlay at The Scottish Memorials Project, Nottingham and Nottinghamshire Victora Cross Committee, Dr. Judy Landau and Dave Stowe. Our thanks are due to Eric Gee for producing the scaled maps from various sources that we supplied. We have also received considerable assistance from the following individuals who have all helped in various ways: the late Edward Campbell, David Empson,

Derek Hunt, Maurice Johnson and Steve Snelling. Our special thanks to Gerald Gliddon for his invaluable guidance and encouragement. We should also like to thank Brenda Gullett for word-processing the manuscript and to Pauline and Tim who helped her. Our wives Jean and Gill deserve special mention for their unfailing support.

INTRODUCTION

The war was not 'over by Christmas' as the 1914 slogan had proclaimed and by the end of that year the BEF were in the stalemate of trench warfare and fairly disillusioned about the prospect of a swift victory. The British troops had suffered badly in the early campaigns and by January 1915 were holding about 30 miles of actual trenches, a small fraction of that held by their French allies. Reinforcements were needed and General Sir John French, C-in-C of the BEF, felt under pressure to carry out some sort of offensive operation. This was prompted first by the withdrawal of German divisions from the Western to the Eastern Front and the fear of a decisive German victory over Russia, and secondly by the need to boost morale among his own troops.

Joffre, French's counterpart in the French Army, also wanted the British to take a greater part in the drive to oust Germany from conquered areas. Initially, to facilitate French Army plans for action in the New Year, Joffre demanded the relief of French units north of Ypres by British troops so that French troops belonging to the same Army group were not separated by British units.

Sir John French had an initial meeting in January 1915 with Joffre to air his proposals for offensive action. His idea of a swift knock-out blow using overwhelming numerical superiority and a short, heavy artillery barrage to precede the attack at Neuve Chapelle fitted in well with Joffre's plans and showed a willingness on the part of the British to take some of the burden of the war. The battle was to be a British 'show' with limited French artillery in support. Forty-eight battalions on a narrow frontage were to be launched against a mere nine German battalions opposite. Morale among the attackers was high; the promise of victory, given the favourable odds and the elation created by the heavy barrage on the enemy positions, gave the troops confidence. Initially, despite setbacks on each flank, the main thrust of the attack was successful and broke through the lines. All the ground won in this battle was taken in the first three hours. The tragedy was that there was no swift follow-up of the advantages achieved. The 'rolling-up' of the line from behind was not realised. Neuve Chapelle was to be the first of a number of British actions that year in which the Germans seemed to learn lessons more quickly than the British Command.

The same principle as employed at Neuve Chapelle was used again with minor modifications in the later offensives of Aubers Ridge and Festubert but without the success realised on the first day of Neuve Chapelle. Prior to these two battles the British attacked successfully at Hill 60 on 17 April. German determination to protect the gas cylinders secretly laid in readiness for a general attack against Ypres and the need to retain the vantage point of the hill for artillery spotting in bombarding the Ypres area, led to savage fighting and outstanding bravery on both sides, resulting in the awarding of several VCs including Woolley, the first Territorial VC, before the British were finally driven off the hill.

During the fighting on Hill 60 the Germans launched a general offensive against Ypres on 22 April using poison gas to open the way forward. The brunt of the attack was borne by the Canadians whose steadfastness and courage in the face of this new weapon is commemorated by the monument at Vancouver Corner near St Julien. Canada's first VC of the war was won on the opening day of the Second Battle of Ypres.

Operations quietened down after the battle for Ypres and the British prepared a retaliatory attack at Loos, using chlorine gas for the first time. Loos was a bloody failure but the high rate of casualties sustained in the battle confirmed for Joffre, finally, as the earlier efforts had promised, a real British commitment to drive the Germans from French soil. General Sir John French's handling of the Battle of Loos culminated in his ignominious removal from command, just as General Sir

Horace Smith-Dorrien was ousted from command by French during the Second Battle of Ypres. General Sir Douglas Haig took command of the BEF at the end of the year.

An important contributory factor to the lack of British operational success in 1915 was a shortage of artillery shells. Always a problem, the situation became critical during the Battle of Aubers Ridge, after which French 'leaked' information to the press regarding the lack of artillery support owing to the shell crisis.

The second year of the war gave many opportunities for men to show courage 'beyond the call of duty'. Sixty-seven VCs were awarded on the Western Front in 1915, of which twenty were posthumous. Just under a third of the recipients were officers. There were a number of 'firsts' in this year, some of which were used usefully for propaganda at home. The first Irish VC of the war, Michael O'Leary, was made much of, being lauded, paraded and used in recruiting drives to inspire others to the Colours.

Territorial units, originally intended purely for home defence, were now given the opportunity to volunteer for overseas service. This enabled Geoffrey Woolley, who had volunteered on the day war broke out, to transfer to a unit with better prospects of going to France. His ambition was realised and within months of arriving he had earned the first Territorial VC of the war.

As one might expect, the VCs came from all walks of life and those who came home found equally varied fortunes in their post-war lives. John Smyth recognised the exclusiveness of the award and helped found the VC and GC Association in 1956; they held their first reunion at the Café Royal, London on 24 July 1958.

The book is arranged in broadly chronological order, though we felt it better to include men within the context of particular battles, and as a result a few men are not in strict date order. Although we have consulted numerous sources we would be grateful for any further information that readers may have. One thing that struck us during the writing of this book is that however much we try to empathise we cannot understand fully the grim conditions these men endured and fought in. The courage, determination and sacrifice of their generation must never be forgotten.

M.J. O'LEARY
Cuinchy, France, 1 February

The year 1915 opened in northern France with the opposing forces facing each other in water-logged trenches and fortifications, separated by a narrow strip of no-man's-land. At Cuinchy, immediately south of the La Bassée Canal, the British line formed a salient from the canal on the left, running east towards the Railway Triangle (formed by the Béthune–La Bassée railway and the junction of another line towards Vermelles), then south to the La Bassée–Béthune Road, where it joined French positions (see map on page 18).

There had been a number of German attacks in the Cuinchy sector during January, culminating in a large-scale offensive on 25 January when the enemy penetrated into the above salient, forcing men of the 1st Scots Guards and 1st Coldstream Guards (CG) (1st Bde) back to partially prepared positions 500 yards west of the Railway Triangle. The Germans renewed their attacks on 29 January but were repulsed with heavy losses.

During the evening of 30 January the 4th (Guards) Bde moved forward to take over the front line, and 2nd CG, 2nd Bde, took over the thousand yards of front line in front of the ruins of Cuinchy with 1st Irish Guards (IG) in support. 1st IG were allocated positions east of the La Bassée–Béthune Road and in the centre of its line was a collection of huge brick stacks, originally 30 feet high. There were nearly thirty of these stacks, five held by the British and the remainder in German hands; converted for defence, they were connected by a complex system of trenches and saps. Apart from these stacks the area was flat and difficult to defend; the only raised areas were the canal and the railway, because it ran on a 16 ft high embankment, separated from the canal by a tow-path.

The right of the German line rested on the Railway Triangle. A little over 200 yards to the west was the area known as the Hollow: a narrow 20 yard wide strip lying to the south of the railway embankment. At the western end of the Hollow was a canal lock, which was crossed by the railway via a girder bridge, and about 60 yards east was a brick culvert through which the tow-path was reached. No. 4 Coy, 2nd CG, held the left of the line with its flank on this culvert. In the early hours of 1 February, a German attack was directed at the CG which forced No. 4 Coy to retire to a barricade erected in the Hollow.

A British counter-attack was organized and at 04.00 hours fifty men of CG supported by No. 4 Coy IG attacked along the tow-path, and the Hollow. This attack was halted 30 yards short of the enemy position near the culvert. The Irish Guards lost all the officers from No. 4 Coy. 2/Lt Innes, No. 1 Coy IG, was ordered forward to take command of the survivors of No. 4 Coy and to withdraw them to the railway bridge, leaving a party holding the barricade in the Hollow. Innes himself stayed at this barricade.

Orders were issued by 1st Bde to retake the lost position at 10.15 hours and after a 15 minute artillery bombardment the counter-attack began. Fifty men of CG led the assault followed by thirty men of No. 1 Coy IG under Lt Graham; the men carried *filled* sandbags, spades and two boxes of bombs as their task was to consolidate the position once it was captured. No. 2 Coy IG maintained covering fire and 2/Lt Innes, with his small party, was ordered to maintain his position. As the CG advance faltered, 2/Lt Innes was ordered to lead his men forward, which he did 'in a very bold manner'.

L/Cpl Michael O'Leary, 2/Lt Innes's orderly, was with his officer in the Hollow. On the command to advance, O'Leary ran quickly on, outdistancing the men with him, mounted the railway embankment, fired five times at the German machine-gun crew at the barricade, and killed them. At a second enemy barricade, 60 yards further on, another enemy machine-gun was preparing for action. The ground between the two positions was too marshy for a direct approach so O'Leary again climbed the railway embankment and ran towards the Germans. He was seen by them and as they attempted to turn the machine gun towards him he shot three of its crew. The remaining two Germans immediately surrendered, not realizing that O'Leary had now fired all the cartridges in his magazine. He then returned to the original line with his prisoners. According to a witness, 'O'Leary came back from his killing as cool as if he had been for a walk in the park'.

The IG Battalion *War Diary* says, 'This was a fine piece of work and he [O'Leary] has been recommended for reward.' O'Leary's reward was the Victoria Cross which was gazetted on 18 February and he was presented with it by the King at Buckingham Palace on 22 June 1915. His VC, the first won by a member of the Irish Guards, was the first to be won on the Western Front in 1915.

The third of four children, Michael John O'Leary was born on 29 September 1890 at Kilbarry Lodge, Inchigeela, 10 miles from Macroom in County Cork, Ireland. His parents Daniel and Margaret ran a small farm where Michael worked after attending Kilbarry National School and at the age of 16 he joined the Royal Navy. Attached to HMS *Vivid* he served for some years before being invalided out with rheumatism in the knees; he returned to work on his father's farm for a few months before enlisting in the Irish Guards on 2 July 1910.

He was placed on the Reserve after his three years' Home Service with the 1st Battalion and applied to join the Royal North-West Mounted Police (RNWMP), Canada. On 2 August 1913 he was engaged, as constable no. 5685, for a three-year term in the RNWMP at Regina, Saskatchewan. He soon displayed his courage, taking part in a two-hour running

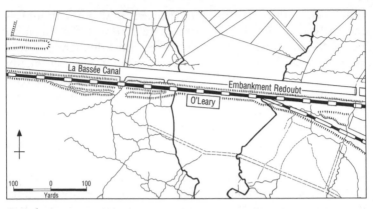

Cuinchy area

battle with two gunmen; after their capture, he was presented
with a gold ring which he wore for the rest of his life.

He was granted a free discharge from the RNWMP on
22 September 1914 in order to rejoin the British Army.
Returning to England, he was mobilized on 22 October,
going to France on 23 November to join his battalion, 1st
Irish Guards. After only a short time in France, O'Leary was
Mentioned in Despatches for gallantry, and was promoted
lance-corporal on 5 January 1915; on 4 February he was
promoted sergeant in the field after his VC-winning action.
An item appeared in the *New York Times* of 28 May 1915
reporting that an artilleryman serving at the front had written
to a friend, 'Sergeant Michael O'Leary, V.C. was killed in the
last battle'.

O'Leary's bravery captured the public's imagination
and a large reception was held in Hyde Park, London, on
Saturday 10 July 1915. Thousands of Londoners turned out
and accorded him a hero's welcome. Among other tributes
the *Daily Mail* published a poem about him, a ballad about
his exploits was performed before the King, and a short
play was written by George Bernard Shaw. On his return
to Ireland, O'Leary was greeted by crowds at Macroom but
when his father, a strong nationalist, and a prize-winning
weightlifter and footballer in his youth, was asked by a

reporter to comment on his son's courage, he replied, 'I am surprised he didn't do more. I often laid out twenty men myself with a stick coming from the Macroom Fair, and it is a bad trial of Mick that he could kill only eight, and he having a rifle and bayonet.'

After receiving the award of the Cross of St George, 3rd Class (Russia), in August, O'Leary was commissioned into the Connaught Rangers as a second lieutenant on 23 October. On a recruiting drive in Ballaghaderrin, Ireland, he was jeered by Ulster Volunteers, an incident which led to questions being asked in the House of Commons on 6 December. Serving with the 5th Bn Connaught Rangers in Salonika, O'Leary was again Mentioned in Despatches, and after a posting to Macedonia retired from the Army in 1921, his final service being at Dover with the 2nd Battalion.

Leaving his wife Greta and two children in Ireland, he returned to Canada in March 1921, reputedly to rejoin the Royal Canadian Mounted Police (the name of the RNWMP since February 1920), but for reasons unknown he did not do so. Instead, he first gave lectures on the war and then spent a brief period in a publishing house before joining the Ontario Provincial Police during 1921 as a licence inspector for the enforcement of prohibition, a post he held for two years. His wife and twin boys having joined him, O'Leary was then appointed sergeant of police on the Michigan Central Railway, stationed at Bridgeburg, Ontario, at a salary of £33 per month.

As he later informed a *Daily Mail* reporter:

> I was with Michigan Central for two years. Unfortunately on the railway I came into contact with bootlegging and smuggling interests . . . A detective has to take bribes to keep his mouth shut or else people are out to get him.

O'Leary was arrested in 1925, charged with smuggling an alien into Buffalo, USA, from Bridgeburg; after a delay of some months the court acquitted him of the charge. In the autumn of the same year he was again arrested, charged with 'irregularity in a search for liquor'. He spent a week in an

American jail but was again acquitted at a later trial. He was
not reinstated in his job by the Michigan Central Railway.

After he had been unemployed for several months, the
authorities at Hamilton, Ontario, advanced the money
(£70) for passage to Ireland for O'Leary and his family
and in October 1926 his wife and four children sailed from
Montreal, on the *Letitia*, for Ireland, where an uncle had
promised to look after them. O'Leary stayed in Canada
having been promised a 'suitable position' by the Ontario
Attorney General and worked in Hamilton for a time, during
which period he suffered several bouts of malaria, contracted
in Salonika. Finally, he left Canada. The British Legion heard
of his parlous state and employed him for some time as a
packer in its poppy factory in England.

In 1932, while he was working as a commissionaire at
the Mayfair Hotel, Park Lane, London, he took part in the
'Cavalcade Ball' held there in aid of the 'Journey's End' home
for disabled officers; together with A.O. Pollard VC, he
served tin mugs of rum to the distinguished audience.

He continued working at the hotel until called up from the
Reserve of Officers in June 1939 and went to France with
the BEF as a captain in the Middlesex Regiment. He was
invalided back to England before the evacuation at Dunkirk,
transferred to the Pioneer Corps and put in charge of a
prisoner of war camp in the south of England. Discharged
from the Army on medical grounds in 1945, he returned
to civilian life as a building contractor, in which trade he
worked until his retirement in 1954.

He attended the Victory Parade in June 1946 but at the
1956 Centenary VC Review held in Hyde Park, London, he
was impersonated by a man in a bathchair.

O'Leary lived in the same district of London for more than
thirty years, originally at Southborne Avenue, Colindale, but
in later years at Oakleigh Avenue and Limesdale Gardens,
Edgeware. He died at Whittington Hospital, Islington, on 1
August 1961 after a long illness and was buried at Mill Hill
Cemetery, Paddington. After the funeral service at the Roman
Catholic Annunciation Church at Burnt Oak, the coffin was
saluted by Guards officers as it left the church and it was
accompanied by a 'lone piper' through the cemetery. Six of

O'Leary's seven children were at the funeral, including twins Daniel and Jeremiah, both winners of the DFC in the Second World War.

In July 1962 O'Leary's medals – VC, 1914 Star and Bar, BVM, with MID, BWM, Cross of the Order of St George, 3rd Class (Russia), Coronation Medals for 1937 and 1953, and Defence Medal 1939–45 – were presented to the Irish Guards by his family. Although O'Leary also wore his 1914 Star with a Bar, and always claimed that he was entitled to do so, his military records show he arrived in France one day too late for such entitlement.

THE BATTLE OF NEUVE CHAPELLE

10–12 March

On 15 February Sir John French asked the First Army Commander, Gen. Sir Douglas Haig, to draft a plan for an offensive with the line La Bassée–Aubers Ridge as its objective. Haig's subsequent plan of attack was for the Meerut and 8th Division (Indian and VI Corps respectively), to break through the German line at Neuve Chapelle between Port Arthur and the Moated Grange, and to fan out to right and left; the Lahore and 7th Divisions would assault on either side of the breach. The Cavalry Corps would then ride through to the Aubers Ridge and wheel right behind the enemy line, with supporting infantry consolidating along the Ridge. An artillery barrage was planned to precede the infantry attack: the German wire and breastworks were to be bombarded by nearly 300 field guns and howitzers, and the enemy batteries shelled by heavy artillery.

When the artillery bombardment began on 10 March the enemy wire and breastworks were largely destroyed, leaving significant gaps in the defences. Eight battalions advanced at 08.30 hours and in less than half an hour a breach some 1600 yards long was made in the enemy line. Problems arose on both flanks; on the right the 1/39th Garhwalis advanced in the wrong direction and attacked undamaged German defences, and on the left a 200 yard long stretch of the German breastworks was left untouched as two siege batteries had arrived too late.

The centre battalions were ordered to advance only 200 yards beyond the enemy breastworks and wait while the village was subjected to further shelling. This delay took away some of the advantage gained by the surprise attack. During the bombardment the Germans occupied some of the recently constructed machine-gun strongpoints (*Stützpunkte*) which were located 1,000 yards to the rear of their breastworks, and positioned 800 yards apart to cover much of the flat ground.

Having advanced through the village, the leading battalions were ordered to wait until both flanks of the attack could advance; consequently, the battalions supporting them could not advance as planned, causing a bottleneck west of Neuve Chapelle as several battalions were held up in the traffic jam.

As both Corps HQ were some 4 to 5 miles from Neuve Chapelle and separate from each other, up-to-date information took some time to reach the Corps Commanders, Rawlinson and Willcocks. It was not until early afternoon that Rawlinson became aware of the situation of his forward battalions and he ordered a resumption of the attack in conjunction with Indian Corps. However, the orders took three hours to reach the front-line battalions and so the attack did not take place until it was nearly dark. It failed.

A further attack was ordered for the next day. Due to poor artillery support, the gunners were unable to register their shots in the mist, and this, combined with the fact that the Germans had brought up reinforcements during the night, meant that this attack was also not successful.

The Germans launched a counter-attack early on 12 March, superseding a planned British attack ordered for that morning. The enemy attack was halted, with very heavy losses inflicted on the attackers. Because of poor communications, Army HQ received little accurate information about the German attack for several hours, and at 15.00 hours Haig, convinced that the Germans were 'much demoralized', ordered both Corps to 'push through the barrage of fire regardless of loss', and ordered 5th Cavalry Bde to move forward in support. Again the orders took some time to reach the battalions concerned and those which attacked were repelled with severe casualties. The action was called off later that night.

British casualties for the battle exceeded 11,600, with German losses almost as high. Virtually all the ground gained had been taken in the first three hours, and despite the unwieldy nature of the British force (under two Corps Commanders) operating in a relatively small area, and the poor and confused communications, the Battle of Neuve Chapelle was nevertheless significant for it proved to the French that the British *were* capable of attacking and were not just a defensive force.

GOBAR SING NEGI
Neuve Chapelle, France, 10 March

The Garhwal Bde (Meerut Division), comprising the 2nd Leicester, 3rd London, 2/3rd Gurkha Rifles, 1/39th and 2/39th Garhwal Rifles were ordered to carry out an attack on the south-western sector of Neuve Chapelle. The start positions ran from Port Arthur for about 500 yards along the Estaires–La Bassée Road where the battalions designated for the attack moved up during the early hours of 10 March (see map opposite).

On the left of the Brigade was 2/39th Garhwal Rifles under Lt-Col. D.H. Drake-Brockman; their assembly position was to the left of the road which led to the village of Neuve Chapelle. The defences projected in a small salient and Drake-Brockman observed that the ground in front of the main German line sloped more steeply in front of a ditch close to the La Bassée Road. Consequently, he ordered a passage to be cut in the breastworks and a shallow trench to be dug on the eastern bank of the ditch, which offered some cover to the front companies before the attack. The battalion moved up to the front line and at 05.15 hours Nos. 1 and 2 Coys filed out to the shallow trench.

The artillery bombardment commenced at 07.30 hours, the flight of howitzer shells clearly visible up to the point of impact in the German trenches. Promptly at 08.05 hours

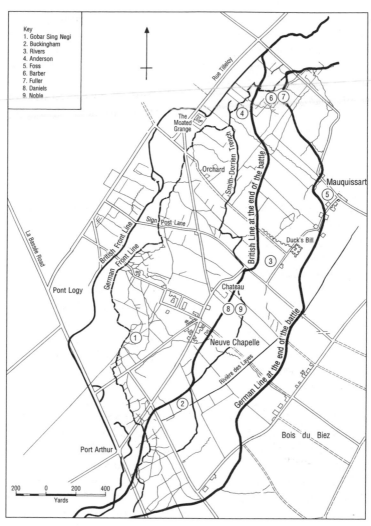

Key
1. Gobar Sing Negi
2. Buckingham
3. Rivers
4. Anderson
5. Foss
6. Barber
7. Fuller
8. Daniels
9. Noble

Rue Tilleloy

The Moated Grange

Orchard

Smith-Dorrien Trench

British Line at the end of the battle

Mauquissart

La Bassée Road

Sign Post Lane

British Front Line

German Front Line

Duck's Bill

Pont Logy

Chateau

Neuve Chapelle

Rivière des Layes

German Line at the end of the battle

Port Arthur

Bois du Biez

200 0 200 400
Yards

Neuve Chapelle

the leading companies doubled across the intervening space between the lines. No 1 Coy, on the right, advanced on an orchard, which ran at right angles to their line of attack. They found the front line empty but captured a machine-gun and some prisoners in the second line; the third line was also easily taken but in the subsequent advance to a trench behind the orchard, several men were killed by an enemy machine-gun positioned to the left.

No. 2 Coy, on the left, had a longer approach to the first-line trenches as the German line angled back sharply from the orchard so that the men on the far left of the battalion had almost twice as much ground to cover as those on the right. Parties from No. 2 Coy eventually worked up to the German front-line trench but met considerable opposition. It seems that either the artillery bombardment was less effective in this area, or the longer approach gave the enemy sufficient time to man their defences.

The British line bent sharply north-east some 200 to 300 yards from Pont Logy, and so one part of the German front line, held by *12th Coy, 16th Regt*, was not directly attacked by infantry, for both the Garhwal Bde, on the right, and the 25th Bde, on its left, were advancing roughly at right angles from the breastworks, on a line that met at a point behind the enemy main line.

No. 2 Coy split up and those on the left began to clear the trenches. A section under Naik (Cpl) Jaman Sing Bisht drove a party of Germans up the trench towards No. 1 Coy, forcing many of them to surrender. For this action the Naik was later awarded the Indian Order of Merit, Second Class.

The most prestigious award of the day, however, went to 1683, Rfn Gobar Sing Negi, a bayonet man with the bombers of No. 2 Coy, who was awarded a posthumous Victoria Cross. In his book *The Royal Garhwal Rifles in the Great War*, Drake-Brockman described the action thus:

> . . . the other half [of No. 2 Coy] remained on working up the trench towards their left to gain touch with the British regiment on the right. It was in one of these parties bombing up the trench to the left, whose commander

had been killed, that one of the party, Rifleman Gobar Sing Negi, had the initiative to assume command and carry on bombing and rounding up prisoners and working up the trench. This action also drove others of the enemy into the hands of the British unit on our left. A machine gun detachment was thus captured. He, gallant fellow, was unfortunately killed later on, but I am glad to say he was awarded the Victoria Cross for his great gallantry that day . . .

The Garhwal Rifles moved on and linked up with British units on their left, clearing the remaining Germans out of the buildings in the eastern part of the village. A position east of the village was established in support of 2/3rd Gurkhas and the battalion remained in these trenches for the remainder of the day. Their total casualties were relatively light: 3 Indian Officers and 57 other ranks killed, 2 Indian Officers and 71 other ranks wounded; they captured 3 machine-guns, 3 officers and 187 other ranks. Some of the prisoners were identified as men with whom the Garhwalis had fraternized on Christmas Day 1914.

The battalion suffered over thirty casualties on the 11th, although it was not actually involved in any attack, and later moved to billets near Croix Marmeuse where it remained throughout the next day before returning to billets at Zelobes on the evening of the 13th. Negi's VC citation was published in the *London Gazette* on 28 April 1915.

Gobar Sing Negi (Gabbar Singh Negi) was born on 7 October 1893 at Manjaur village, near Chamba, in the State of Tehri, part of the original Kingdom of Garhwal. The son of Badri Sing, he enlisted in the 39th Garhwal Rifles in October 1913.

This regiment was formed in 1887, and first became known as the Garhwal Rifles in 1892; the second battalion was created in 1901. Originally composed of hillmen who had previously served in Gurkha regiments, the Garhwal Rifles wore Gurkha-style uniforms and carried the kukri.

Gobar Sing Negi's Victoria Cross was sent by the War Office to the India Office on 28 July 1915 for presentation to his next of kin. It was acquired (as was the Victoria Cross of Darwan Sing Negi, 1st Bn) by his regiment, and a duplicate was sent to his widow. A painting by J. Princep Beadle, entitled 'Neuve Chapelle, March 10th 1915', shows members of the Rifle Brigade and Garhwal Rifles moving past ruined houses; this painting was later purchased by Lt-Col. Drake-Brockman.

Since 1925 the Gabbar Singh Negi Fair has been held annually on 20/21 April (depending on the Hindu calendar) and organised by members of his family. A strong Indian Army presence including bands, athletic displays and recruiting rallies attracted many villagers from some distance. In 1971 the Garhwal Regiment adopted the Fair and an impressive memorial was built. During the last few years the military interest appears to have waned but the family has continued the tradition with a procession to the memorial followed by a ceremony and wreath laying by family members including Gabbar Singh Negi's grandson, Kamal Singh.

On 6 November 2002 HM The Queen unveiled the Commonwealth Gates at the Hyde Park Corner end of Constitution Hill. Comprising four stone gate posts, two each side of the road, each surmounted by a bronze urn and a domed pavilion (or chattri) on the north side of the road. Country names, India, Pakistan, Bangladesh, Sri Lanka, Africa, Caribbean and Kingdom of Nepal are inscribed on the gate pillars. The names of 70 Victoria Cross and George Cross winners, including Gabbar Singh Negi, are inscribed within the domed roof.

On 10 June 1970 the *New Delhi Evening News* ran a story about the fate of VCs awarded to Indian soldiers, and pictured the widow of Gobar Sing Negi wearing his medals, including the Victoria Cross. The newspaper, questioning what would happen to this award, seemed to be unaware that she was almost certainly wearing the replica VC.

Inscribed upon the Neuve Chapelle Indian Memorial at Port Arthur are the names of all members of the Indian Corps killed in France who have no known resting place. The names include Rfn Gobar Sing Negi VC, together with 140 other members of his battalion.

W. BUCKINGHAM

Neuve Chapelle, France, 10/12 March

The second Victoria Cross won at Neuve Chapelle was awarded to another man from the Garhwal Bde, Pte William Buckingham, 2nd Bn, Leicester Regt, who received his award for saving lives during the battle. Early on 10 March his battalion, deployed in its assembly positions, suffered a number of casualties when German artillery opened fire on the Port Arthur defences. The leading companies of the battalion advanced and with relative ease crossed the German front line, which was defended by *10th Coy, 16th Infantry Regt*, and occupied a line of trenches near the River Layes (see map on page 25).

On the battalion's right was a section of German front line, about 200 yards long, which was not attacked in the initial assault. This stretch of trench was assigned to 1/39th Garhwal Rifles. It was not an easy task, for not only had the trench escaped much of the artillery bombardment as shells fell behind the German front line, but the Garhwalis had veered off in an easterly direction instead of following their intended north-east line of advance as they left their assembly positions at Port Arthur. As a result, the Germans in the trench had escaped virtually unscathed and were 'full of fight'. Brave efforts were made to dislodge them but it was not until about 17.00 hours that 'A' Coy, assisted by other British units, finally forced them to surrender. The Leicesters remained in their captured trenches throughout 11 March under shell-fire. A German counter-attack was launched early on the next day but was repulsed with very heavy loss of life to the attackers. The battalion helped to halt this attack, with the enemy on its right unable to get closer than 100 yards.

The next day, 13 March, the battalion continued to hold its trenches despite sniper and artillery fire, but by midnight it had been relieved and reached its billets early on 14 March.

The four days at Neuve Chapelle had cost 250 casualties, and much praise was accorded those who assisted the wounded; the highest accolade was reserved for 6276 Pte Buckingham, who was awarded the VC. The authors of *The Indian Corps in France* described his actions:

> During the attack [of the 10th] and again on 12 March, Private William Buckingham, 2nd Leicesters, on several occasions displayed the greatest bravery and devotion in rescuing and aiding wounded men. Time after time he went out in the heaviest fire and brought in those who would certainly have perished. In the performance of this noble work, Private Buckingham was severely wounded in the chest and arm.

The *London Gazette* published his VC citation on 28 April 1915.

The eldest son of William John and Annie Susan Billington, William Henry Billington was born in the second quarter of 1886 in Bedford. His brother, Frederick Ernest, was born the following year and both boys were placed in the Countesthorpe Cottage Homes by the time William was six. This was probably due to the hardship brought on by the death early in 1888 of William John Billington when he was less than twenty years old. Annie Billington remarried in the summer of 1891, her new husband being Thomas Henry Buckingham. It would appear that when the two brothers entered the Home they were enrolled with the name of Buckingham, their mother's then married name. The colony of cottages which formed the Homes was run by a superintendent, Mr Harrison, whose wife was the matron. A local newspaper reported that Mrs Harrison described Buckingham as one of the nicest lads they had ever had. Though not an angel, he had a strong will of his own and strong-willed persons occasionally came into contact with authority.

In 1901 Buckingham, together with a number of other boys, left the Cottage Homes to join the Army and in November of that year joined the 2nd Bn, Leicester Regt. Giving his occupation as a tailor he was 15 years 9 months old, just over 5 feet 2ins tall and gave his next of kin as his brother, Frederick Buckingham. With his battalion he saw service in Guernsey, Belgium, Madras and Rhamiket, and was stationed in India when war began. The Leicesters moved to France, disembarking at Marseilles on 12 October 1914, and fought in France with the Indian Corps throughout the winter. At Givenchy, on 19 December, Buckingham's name was among those brought to the special attention of the Corps Commander, Gen. Willcocks, in his case 'for great gallantry'.

Buckingham returned to Countesthorpe when on leave, and was convalescing from his injuries received at Neuve Chapelle (a packet of postcards in his pocket deflected a bullet which might otherwise have caused serious injury.) in late April when the news of his award was published in the newspapers. He had no idea he had been recommended for the VC so was surprised when Mr Harrison arrived at his cottage with the newspaper, asking him for his regimental number (6276) so that he could confirm that the William Buckingham in the paper was the same boy he had brought up.

A modest man, Buckingham said little about his experiences and it was only during a meeting with Cpl Tarry, one of the men he rescued at Neuve Chapelle, that more details emerged. The two men met at a garden party for wounded soldiers, given by Mrs Abel Smith of Coleorton Hall. The corporal related how, after he had been wounded, Buckingham had carried him out of the firing line under heavy fire, thus saving his life. Buckingham was persuaded to recount a further story of Neuve Chapelle:

> During the battle, I came upon a badly wounded German soldier. One of his legs had been blown off. He was lying right in the fire zone. His piteous appeal for help – well, I rendered first-aid as well as I could, and just carried him to a place of safety. Of course, I did what I could for others too, but really it's not worth talking about.

Mr and Mrs Harrison accompanied Buckingham when he went to receive his award from the King on 4 June 1915, and Mrs Harrison's scrap-book contained many newspaper cuttings of him, including a photograph of Buckingham proudly showing his award to the Harrisons outside Buckingham Palace. Much was made in the Press of 'Leicester's Own VC' as he was nicknamed, and the Mayor of Leicester presented him with a 'purse of gold' and £100 of War Loan Stock donated by the Leicester Board of Guardians. Buckingham's response to this presentation was a simple salute, as he explained in a later letter of thanks:

As a soldier not used to speaking in public, I regret I could not publicly return thanks at Countesthorpe for the handsome gift you were good enough to make on behalf of the citizens of Leicester; but I can assure you that I value it most highly, and if I am spared to my native town after the war, I shall come back to it with feelings of warm affection.

He remained in England for recruiting purposes before returning to France on 13 April 1916; appointed acting corporal at the end of this month he joined the 1st Leicesters in May and reverted to the rank of private at his own request on 21 May 1916. Buckingham was killed at Thiepval on 15 September 1916, while serving as orderly to Capt. R.W. Mosse of the 1st Leicesters in the Battle of the Somme. Capt. Mosse broke the news of Buckingham's death to the Leicester Board of Guardians in a letter, in which he wrote that it would be 'impossible to replace him'. As Buckingham's body was not recovered, his name appears on the Thiepval Memorial to the Missing.

It was only after the award of his VC was announced that Buckingham's mother was discovered to be still living, and in the Register of the Thiepval Memorial to the Missing, Mrs A. Buckingham was shown as living at 35 York Street, Bedford. On the 1911 Census Annie Buckingham, 45, is described as a widow and as living with her mother and son, Frederick Billington (23) at 37 York Street, Bedford.

Amongst his army papers is Army Form 5080, a statement of living relatives of a deceased soldier and is dated May 1919.

The information supplied by the solicitors for the executors of William Buckingham is interesting because the father of the soldier is recorded as *William John Buckingham, not heard of for years*, no full blood siblings but a half blood brother as *Fred Billington, age 29, 10290 16th Lancers.*

In his memory a 'Buckingham Memorial Fund' was set up, and still exists, managed by a committee in Leicester. Buckingham Road, Countesthorpe was named after him in 1986 and a metal plaque set into a rock to mark it as a memorial. A late addition, the name of W BUCKINGHAM, was made to Countesthorpe War Memorial in 1986. His VC and other medals were in the possession of the Countesthorpe Cottage Homes until 1958 when the Homes were closed. The medals were then passed for safe-keeping to the City Children's Committee of the Child Welfare Department, Leicester, where they remained until 1966. The medals are now on loan to the Leicestershire Regimental Museum in Leicester.

J. RIVERS

Neuve Chapelle, France, 12 March

The first of three Victoria Crosses won by the 8th Division at Neuve Chapelle was another posthumous award, this time to Pte Jacob Rivers, 1st Bn Sherwood Foresters (Notts and Derby Regt), for bombing actions on 12 March.

Only two days before, the 1st Sherwood Foresters, 24th Bde, 8 Div., had been in divisional reserve. The battalion moved forward during the morning of the 11th, and after a long wait were ordered to attack at 17.30 hours in the direction of Piètre. Their advance of about 1,000 yards was halted by machine-gun fire from a group of houses north-west of Piètre, known as Nameless Cottages. This machine-gun strongpoint (*Stützpunkte*) was occupied during

the initial artillery bombardment by *12th Coy, 13th Regt.*
The Sherwood Foresters entrenched along the Mauquissart
Road, its left company in an orchard, centre companies
astride a sunken lane and the right company at the Sign Post
Lane junction.

Enemy shelling inflicted several casualties on the battalion
early on the 11th and during the morning C Coy attacked
and occupied some ruined houses on the left. At about
16.00 hours an attack was mounted by D Coy but heavy
machine-gun fire halted the assault. These machine-guns
sited in another *Stützpunkte* were positioned to defend the
bridge over the River Layes, which had been occupied and
reinforced by the Germans during the previous night.

By the night of 11 March the battalion held two wrecked
farmhouses and a connecting trench line which formed a
pronounced salient 100 yards forward of the British lines, later
named The Duck's Bill (see map on page 174). Before dawn
German artillery fire was directed onto the new British line and
the battalion was attacked by the *21st Bavarian Regt.* A trench
on the left flank was completely overwhelmed, and fierce
hand-to-hand fighting took place in the courtyard and rooms
of the left-hand farmhouse; only eight defenders escaped. In
the semi-darkness and early morning mist, the British troops
had mistaken the Bavarians for the listening patrol they were
expecting to return; this enabled the enemy to get within 50
yards. The main German attack was made on the right of the
battalion and although a machine-gun sited in the second farm
inflicted severe losses on the enemy, the battalion was forced
to retire. Pte Jacob Rivers got very close to the enemy on the
battalion's right flank and bombed them with such ferocity
that the Germans there were forced to retire. The citation
was published in the *London Gazette* of 28 April 1915 and
included the following description: 'Private Rivers performed
a second act of bravery on the same day, again causing the
enemy to retire. He was killed on this occasion.'

The second bombing action, which cost Rivers his life,
probably occurred between 06.30 and 07.00 hours when the
battalion and units on either side counter-attacked, driving
the Germans back to their trenches and leaving over 400 dead
between the battalion's front and support trenches.

The battalion was withdrawn during the evening, but not before casualties were inflicted by British artillery fire. It was a very costly battle: out of the 18 officers who went into action on the 10th, 9 were killed and 7 wounded; other ranks suffered losses of 90 killed (including Rivers), 265 wounded and 87 missing.

Rivers' VC was presented to his mother by King George V at Buckingham Palace on 29 November 1916; this was a moving ceremony, for on the same day a number of other posthumous VCs, all awarded for actions in 1915, were presented to relatives.

Rivers' grave was lost in later fighting and his name is commemorated, together with those of 237 other members of the Notts and Derby Regt, on the Le Touret Memorial to the Missing at Richebourg-l'Avoué.

Jacob Rivers was born on 17 November 1881, at Bridgegate, Derby, and had two brothers and four sisters. Little is known of his early life and schooling. He enlisted in the Royal Scots Fusiliers on 3 June 1899 and with this regiment he served in India and Burma for seven years before being discharged to the Reserve on 3 June 1907. He was a reservist for five years.

When war began Rivers was employed as a labourer on a ballast train by the Midland Railway Company at Derby, but he soon volunteered for the Army, joining the 1st Sherwood Foresters on 18 August 1914. He went to France on 11 Dec 1914 and, although he was involved with his regiment in several actions prior to Neuve Chapelle, he said little of this in his few letters home.

After his death a brass tablet in his memory was placed in St Alkmund's Mission Room at Bridge Street, Derby (this plaque was moved to the south wall of St Alkmunds Church in about 1967 when the Mission Hall was demolished), but his name does not appear on the Derby War Memorial. In 1923 the Freedom of Derby was conferred upon his mother, Mrs Adeline Rivers. She was in distinguished company as at the same time both Lord Haig and the Duke of Devonshire were similarly honoured. Mrs Rivers died in Derby on

1 March 1937, her funeral service being held at St Barnabas'
Church on 4 March followed by interment at Nottingham
Road Cemetery. In addition to the family, other mourners
included Capt. Warmer (who as a lance-corporal had served
as a stretcher-bearer at Neuve Chapelle) and Pte R. Hardy,
who was awarded the Croix de Guerre for bringing up
ammunition although wounded, also at Neuve Chapelle.

In accordance with Mrs Rivers' wishes, her son's VC was
given to his regiment and on 7 April 1937, at the regimental
depot, Rivers' sister, Mrs Elizabeth Potter, wearing her brother's
medal ribbons, made the presentation. After passing the medal
case to Maj.-Gen. Sir Frederick Maurice, Mrs Potter made a
short speech in which she expressed pleasure in carrying out
her mother's wishes, also thanking the regiment for their offer
to erect a stone to the memory of her mother and brother.
Following the ceremony the civil and military dignitaries
lunched in the Officers' Mess while Mrs Potter and her relatives
were only accorded the privilege of lunch in the Sergeants' Mess.

Jacob Rivers' medals are held by the Sherwood Foresters
Museum, Nottingham. On 7 May 2010 a splendid memorial
was dedicated to Nottinghamshire's twenty recipients of the VC.
Positioned in the grounds of Nottingham Castle, the memorial
includes amongst its list of names that of Jacob Rivers VC.

W. ANDERSON

Neuve Chapelle, France, 12 March

At about the same time as Pte Rivers
was throwing his bombs, Cpl William
Anderson, 2nd Bn, Yorkshire Regt, was
also handling these unreliable weapons
to great effect less than half a mile away.

The 2nd Yorkshire Regt (The Green
Howards), 21st Bde, 7th Division, was not
involved in the initial IV Corps attack. The
battalion moved up to the Rue de Tilleloy at

about 09.00 hours, enemy machine-gun fire inflicting a few casualties as the men crossed the open ground. A long wait then ensued, with only a small move forward, until the main advance at 18.00 hours. The light was fading, the ground was criss-crossed with ditches and trenches, many of which were half-full of water, and the whole area was congested with advancing troops; unsurprisingly, slow progress was made before the battalion was checked by fire from two strong German positions.

A new attack was ordered for 07.30 hours on the 11th but the supporting British artillery barrage was inadequate, the gunners unable to register in the morning mist. The attack did not take place and the battalion incurred losses throughout the day; eleven men were 'knocked out' by a single shell from a British 4.7 in gun. Aptly christened 'Strict Neutrality', these worn-out artillery pieces fired shells, the driving bands of which had a tendency to break, causing the projectile to tumble through the air out of control and with no preference for target.

Cpl William Anderson first came to prominence on 11 March, as described in *The Green Howards in the Great War*:

> A very brilliant attack was made on the enemy by the Battalion bombers under No. 8191 Corporal W. Anderson, who, with only nine other men, succeeded in bombing out and capturing sixty-two Germans in a trench opposite the left of the Green Howards.

At 04.30 hours on 12 March a fierce artillery bombardment heralded a German counter-attack. Fortunately, as with the British gunners earlier, the Germans were unable to register their shots, and consequently the majority of shells fell behind the new British defences. Thus, when the massed enemy attack was launched on the battalion's right-hand companies, no attackers reached the battalion's defences, even though the mist and darkness had enabled the Germans to approach to within 100 yards before they were spotted. To the battalion's left, where the Germans approached through a maze of trenches, their attack had more success, enabling them to dislodge two companies of the 2nd Wiltshires.

After daylight the battalion's bombers helped C Coy of the Wiltshires to retake much of the lost ground (see map on page 25). It was in this operation that Cpl Anderson won his VC. He led three bombers along a trench which was occupied by a large group of Germans, at whom he threw all his own bombs, followed by those of his comrades, all now wounded; he then fired at the Germans with his rifle as well as throwing back many of their own bombs; these combined efforts forced sixty of the enemy to surrender, bringing Anderson's own personal total of prisoners to over 120, a remarkable feat. He was posted as missing presumed killed on 13 March.

Maj. B.H. Leatham of the battalion wrote to Anderson's fiancée, Miss Dudley, saying:

> He was one of the bravest men I have ever seen . . . when I saw him during his act he was untouched and the Germans were driven back. I did not see him again, but from what I found out he was wounded later in the day. I fear he must have been killed as his pay book was eventually sent to us. We have tried to find out who found his body and where he was buried, but without success.

The battalion remained in its trenches throughout the day until relieved during the early hours of 13 March. Battalion casualties for Neuve Chapelle were 15 officers and 299 other ranks.

Anderson's VC was published in the *London Gazette* on 22 May 1915. Anderson's name appears on the Le Touret Memorial to the Missing at Richebourg-l'Avoué, together with the names of 234 other members of the Yorkshire Regiment who have no known grave.

The son of Alexander and Bella Anderson, William Anderson was born at Dallas, Elgin, Morayshire, on 28 December 1882. He was educated at Forres Academy and, prior to his original enlistment in the Army, worked for the Glasgow Tramways Depot and at Elder Hospital, Govan, Glasgow. In 1905 he joined the 2nd Bn, Yorkshire Regt, and served with it for seven years in India, Egypt and South Africa. He joined the Reserve in 1912.

He was called up from the Reserve at the outbreak of war. At that time he was living at Port Clarence, on the River Tees near Middlesbrough, where he was engaged to be married to Miss Dudley. Having been promoted to acting corporal, Anderson landed in France on 14 November 1914 to join the 2nd Bn who, by 8 November had been reduced to three officers and 220 other ranks. They were holding the line near Ploegsteert.

On Christmas Day the battalion arranged an armistice with the Germans opposite, which lasted over the New Year and enabled both sides to improve their trenches, bury their dead and exchange gifts. This truce could not last and the resumption of hostilities was described as 'war is again being waged and the potting at each other's heads has once more begun'. In early March the battalion moved to Estaires in preparation for the forthcoming action at Neuve Chapelle.

William Anderson's VC was due to be presented by the King to his brother in 1919, after his demobilization, but he was not well enough to attend the ceremony. On 19 May 1920, however, the VC was presented to Mr A. Anderson in the banqueting hall of Edinburgh Castle by Lt-Gen. Sir Francis Davies. General Davies had been in command of the 7th Division and was responsible for sending in the recommendation for Anderson's award.

In 1969 Mr Anderson presented his brother's VC to the regiment at a small ceremony in his home at Inverlochy, Fort William. The Green Howards' Museum at Richmond, Yorkshire, holds ten of the twelve VCs won by the regiment during the Great War.

C.C. FOSS

Neuve Chapelle, France, 12 March

The only Victoria Cross awarded to an officer at Neuve Chapelle was the second won by the 21st Bde, the recipient, Capt. C.C. Foss DSO, then serving with the 2nd Bn, Bedfordshire Regt.

With other units of the 21st Bde, 7th Div., the Bedfords moved out of their billets early on 10 March and by mid-morning had advanced to positions close to the Rue du Tilleloy, north-west of Neuve Chapelle. Casualties were caused by enemy shell-fire while the battalion waited nearly six hours before advancing through the former front lines to a position in support of the Royal Scots Fusiliers (RSF), who held a pronounced salient north-east of the village (see map on page 25).

The Bedfords remained in the same trenches throughout the 11th, under shrapnel, rifle and machine-gun fire. The salient to its front, close to High Trees Corner (a bend in the Mauquissart Road), was rushed by the Germans at dawn on 12 March and its defenders, a company of RSF, were overcome. A number of A Coy, led by two captains, charged across the 150 yards of open ground in an attempt to retake the position but every member of this party was killed or wounded. At 07.35 hours the battalion reported the situation to 21st Brig. HQ, who ordered that the captured trenches be retaken. Capt. Foss and a small party of bombers advanced up a trench in a flank attack, followed by a platoon in support, and after a few grenades had been thrown the occupying Germans surrendered. A single officer and 48 other ranks were taken prisoner, of whom 14 were wounded.

The Official History states that:

> . . . seeing this, some 100 more survivors of the 5 a.m. German attack, lying out in the shell holes and ditches in

front of their main position . . . returned to their trenches pursued by bullets. . . .

The recaptured position was consolidated by the battalion and, after dark, two machine-guns positioned there. The Battalion *War Diary* named nine men who accompanied Maj. Foss, although the VC citation says eight. The battalion was relieved and returned to billets late on 14 March. The casualties for the battle totalled 208 of all ranks.

Capt. Foss's VC was published in the *London Gazette* dated 23 May 1915:

> For most conspicuous bravery at Neuve Chapelle, on the 12 March 1915. After the enemy had captured a part of one of our trenches, and our counter-attack made with one officer and twenty men having failed (all but two of the party being killed or wounded in the attempt), Capt. Foss, on his own initiative, dashed forward with eight men, and under heavy fire attacked the enemy with bombs, and captured the position, including the fifty-two Germans occupying it. The capture of this position from the enemy was of the greatest importance, and the utmost bravery was displayed in essaying the task with so very few men.

It was not until 28 October that Capt. Foss received his VC. An inspection of units from the 2nd and 7th Divs was organized on a piece of ground north-west of the La Buissierre–Hesdigneul road, near Hesdigneul, France, under the command of Brig.-Gen. G.E. Corkran CMG. After inspecting the assembled troops the King presented Capt. Foss with his award.

Charles Calveley Foss, the eldest son of the Bishop of Osaka, the Rt Revd Hugh James Foss DD, was born at The Firs, Kobe, Japan, on 9 March 1885. His mother, Janet, the daughter of a Chester doctor, died in 1894. He attended

Marlborough College, and joined the Royal Military Academy, Sandhurst, in 1902 and was commissioned into the Bedfordshire Regiment at Colchester on 2 March 1904. Promoted to captain with the 2nd Bedfords on 20 November 1912, Capt. and Adjt. Foss was serving at Roberts Heights, South Africa, when war began. His battalion disembarked at Zeebrugge in early October 1914 and with it he served throughout the battles of First Ypres; his distinguished service was acknowledged by the announcement in the *London Gazette* on 1 January 1915 that Capt. C.C. Foss had been created a Companion of the Distinguished Service Order.

In June 1915 he married Vere Katherine, the widow of Capt. Pollard, an Indian Army officer. From August 1915 Foss served successively on the staffs of 20th Bde, 7th Div.; Second and First Canadian Divs, and Canadian Corps. He spent most of 1918 as an instructor at the Staff School, Cambridge, before returning to France as a staff officer with XXXII Corps in October, and was present at the final actions of the war. On Armistice Day 1918 Maj. Foss (he had received the Brevet of Major in 1916), was appointed GSO1 to the 57th (West Lancashire) Div. and remained in this post until he attended Staff College, Camberley, in 1919.

The Medal entitlement of Maj. and Brevet Lt-Col. Foss was the VC, CB , DSO , 1914 Star and Bar, BWM, BVM, Defence Medal (1939-45), War Medal (1939-45), King George V Silver Jubilee Medal, King George VI Coronation Medal, Order of Danilo (4th Class) (Montenegro) and was Mentioned in Despatches five times.

Foss attended the garden party for VC winners at Buckingham Palace on 26 June 1920, and was also present at the Cenotaph in Whitehall on Armistice Day the same year. He graduated from the Staff College in 1920 and served as a staff officer at the War Office between 1925 and 1929. In October 1930 he took command of the King's Liverpool Regiment, a post he held until 1933. In that year he was promoted to colonel and was appointed Commander Rangoon Brigade Area, also serving as ADC to King George V until 1937. During the Second World War he served with the Bedfordshire Home Guard, as Brigadier (Rtd), and County Commandant of the Bedfordshire Army Cadet Force.

Charles Foss died on 9 April 1953 in a London hospital. He was survived by his wife Phyllis Ruth, whom he had married in 1950 following the death of his first wife in 1947. His second wife died in a Bournemouth nursing home in 1968. His medals are held in Luton Museum, Bedfordshire.

E. BARBER AND W.D. FULLER

Neuve Chapelle, France, 12 March

Pte E. Barber

The first Victoria Cross to be awarded to the Grenadier Guards (GG) since the Crimean War was won by the 1st Bn. Two men, Pte Edward Barber and L/Cpl Wilfred Fuller, won the coveted award on the same day, both for bombing actions but in separate incidents.

The battalion, part of 20th Bde, 7th Div., moved forward early on the second day of the battle, 11 March, for an attack in the direction of Piètre but progress was halted by enfilade fire when it was about 300 yards short of the enemy main line. After withdrawing to support trenches during the night a further advance was attempted the following day when the battalion supported an attack by the 2nd Scots Guards and 2nd Border Regt. The assaulting battalions had crossed no more than 100 yards of no-man's-land when the attack was halted, having been postponed. The

L/Cpl W. Fuller

2nd Borders in particular suffered heavy losses from the Quadrilateral, a large redoubt west of Mauquissart, where several enemy machine-guns were installed. Following an accurate artillery bombardment the attack got under way at 12.30 hours with much more success. The Scots Guards and the Borders rushed the Quadrilateral and 400 German prisoners were taken. The 1st GG, however, made little progress as direction was lost in the maze of old communication trenches. On the left of the Borders a party of bombers from the 20th Bde reserve, led by Capt. W.E. Nichol, 1st GG, and supported by a company of 2nd Wilts, quickly rushed through the old enemy trenches in no-man's-land to the German front line. The defenders were taken by surprise and large numbers surrendered to the bombers as they captured about 40 yards of trench (see map on page 25).

It was here that the two VCs were won. No. 15624 L/Cpl Fuller saw a number of Germans attempting to retreat along a communication trench. He ran to the front of this party and killed the leading man with a bomb, which persuaded the remainder, about fifty men, to surrender to him as he blocked their escape route. In the same area and at about the same time, No. 15518 Pte Barber charged well ahead of his bombing section and hurled his bombs at the Germans with such effect that a 'very great number of them at once surrendered'. When the grenade party reached Barber they found him 'quite alone and unsupported with the enemy surrendering all about him'.

Both Fuller and Barber were actually in Brigade reserve when they won their awards. The system operated as follows: each battalion in a brigade provided thirty trained bombers, of whom twenty usually remained with the battalion while the remainder – the brigade reserve – were used by the brigade as and when needed.

The battalion moved during the night of 12/13 March to new positions on the left of 8th Div., and became very scattered as the move was not completed until daylight and parties had to dig in wherever they could to avoid enemy fire. Shelling from both sides troubled the battalion throughout the day before it was relieved during the night. Losses by the GG at Neuve Chapelle amounted to 14 officers, including the commanding officer, and 325 men.

There was some confusion as to Barber's fate. Initially he was reported to have died on 12 March, but other reports stated he was killed on 19 March. The register for the Le Touret Memorial to the Missing, on which his name is commemorated, states: 'Presumed to have died on or since 12 March 1915.'

Both citations appeared in the *London Gazette* on 19 April 1915 and Fuller was invested with his VC by the King at Buckingham Palace on 4 June 1915.

Edward Barber was born on 10 June 1893 at 40 King Street, Tring, Hertfordshire, the third of four sons of William Barber, a blacksmith, and Sarah Ann, his wife. Educated at the National Schools, Tring, Barber worked as a bricklayer's labourer before joining the Grenadier Guards in October 1911.

Barber's last leave was in July 1914, when he was considering joining the Buckinghamshire Constabulary after his three-year term of service was completed later that year. Instead he was posted to France with 1st Bn Grenadier Guards. The last communication received by his parents was in early March 1915 when he wrote that he was helping to instruct Canadian troops, whom he described as 'very nice fellows indeed'.

The news of Barber's award, and of his death, was sent in a letter from Cpl Fuller to Barber's cousin, Miss Sanders, at Slough. He wrote:

> As I was a great friend of Cousin Ted, and also the NCO which he was under, I think it my duty to write and let you know what has happened to him. He was a great favourite in the Grenadiers Coy, from our Officer to the ranks and was highly respected. He had won the highest Honour that could be won, The Victoria Cross, and by doing his duty he was picked off by a German Sniper, and a bullet penetrated through his brain, death being instantaneous. Your cousin feared nothing, and he was the finest man in wit and courage, The Grenade Company send their deepest sympathy.

The family received official information from the War Office that he had been killed two days after he had captured 'a very great number of Germans'. Talking to a reporter Mrs Barber said, 'Of course we are very proud, but I can't bear to lose my boy. What is the Victoria Cross to the loss of my son?' Mrs Barber went to Windsor Castle on 16 November 1916 to receive her son's VC from the King. Barber's three brothers were all serving in the armed forces at the time of his death; Alfred, aged 32, with the RAMC, William Charles, aged 29, with the 1st Herts, and the youngest, Ernest, aged 18, in training with the 2nd Herts. Sadly 266355 Private Ernest Barber, 1st Herts, died of wounds on 18 September 1920 and is buried in Tring Cemetery, plot F.90.

Wilfred Dolby Fuller was born at East Kirkby, Nottinghamshire (now part of Kirkby-in-Ashfield), on 28 July 1893 and by 1907 the family were living at 9 Skerry Hill, Mansfield, having resided at Shirebrook and Warsop Vale in the intervening years. Fuller was a member of Warsop Vale Choir and also played the bugle in a local band. It was at Warsop Vale that he started work at the main colliery as a pony driver; his father, Walter, was also a colliery worker, and, when living at Mansfield, both were employed at Mansfield Colliery, Walter as night deputy and Wilfred as pony driver.

He had ambitions to be a soldier and on 30 December 1911 he enlisted in the Grenadier Guards without informing his parents. He was stationed at Wellington Barracks, London, as a garrison policeman when war began and was posted overseas with the 1st Bn, and promoted to lance-corporal in December 1914.

Prior to the announcement of his award, Fuller wrote home 'Look out for good news,' and in a subsequent letter, 'Barber and I have been recommended for the VC. Don't you think it an honour.' He returned to Mansfield in April and on the 20th was given a public reception in the town. It was reported in the *Nottingham Guardian* of 24 April that

Sir Arthur Markham gave the Mayor of Mansfield £100 'for a permanent record of Fuller's bravery'.

Fuller came back to Mansfield on leave immediately before his VC presentation and on 3 June was presented with an address and a gold watch by the Mayor. Most of his leave was spent addressing recruiting meetings in the mining district around Mansfield. On 29 September 1915, during a visit to the Base Hospital, the King awarded Fuller the Order of St George, 3rd Class (Russia). In the *Daily Telegraph*'s report of the event the following day, the newspaper had promoted Fuller to colonel!

Fuller's future wife, Helena Wheeler, resorted to unusual tactics to get his attention; the use of a hat-pin, deftly applied from behind while Fuller was sitting in the Victoria Palace music hall in London achieved the desired result – he certainly noticed her – and they were eventually married on 13 March 1916.

Discharged from the Army as medically unfit on 31 October 1916 with the rank of corporal, Fuller joined the Somerset Police in 1919. An odd incident occurred some ten years later when his pay was reduced by 2 shillings a week for two years, following 'discreditable conduct in that he opened a desk drawer in the police station with a key'. He served as a constable in various police stations in Somerset but after a prolonged period of poor health, when he was on sick leave for months at a time, he retired on 2 July 1940.

Fuller died at his home, Far End, The Styles, Frome, Somerset, on 22 November 1947 and was buried at Christ Church, Frome, on 26 November. The funeral was very well attended and included a hundred Guardsmen and sixty members of the local constabulary.

Fuller's medals, including the VC, were sold privately by his widow in 1974, the proceeds to benefit her children and grandchildren as her husband would have wished, and are now held by the Grenadier Guards Museum. In 1987 a new housing development in Mansfield was named Fuller Close in memory of the town's VC, seventy-two years after the council's promise to commemorate his gallant deeds.

H. DANIELS AND C.R. NOBLE
Neuve Chapelle, France, 12 March

CSM H. Daniels

The last two of nine Victoria Crosses awarded at Neuve Chapelle were gained in a joint action by two men of the 2nd Bn, Rifle Brigade, 25th Bde, 8 Div. A/Cpl Noble and CSM Daniels were good friends so it was hardly surprising they would act together on this occasion.

The battalion was on the right of 25th Bde when the attack began on 10 March and they advanced as planned through the ruins of the village with the advanced platoons as far as the old Smith-Dorrien Trench (fought over in the 1914 actions), east of Neuve Chapelle. Several prisoners were captured in this advance and the battalion entrenched at its objective, some 200 yards behind the Smith-Dorrien trench.

A/Cpl C.R. Noble

Lt-Col. Stephens, the battalion's CO, advised Bde HQ of his position and requested permission to advance further with suitable support, but was told that the left of the attack had been held up and that he must therefore keep the battalion where it was. A and C Coys were withdrawn from their covering positions in front of the main line because of losses being inflicted by British artillery.

The next day, 11 March, was spent in the same trenches and although orders were issued for the relief of the battalion this did not take place. Stephens again requested permission to advance but again he was refused. At 01.00 hours he finally received orders for an attack at 07.30 hours on 12 March. A German counter-attack began at 04.45 hours but this was easily halted by the battalion with very heavy losses being inflicted on the enemy. The proposed British attack was delayed twice, and was rescheduled for 12.30 hours, after a 30 minute artillery bombardment.

When the orders for the attack were first received Stephens requested that his battalion amend the direction of attack, with the battalion's left flank anchored on a water-filled ditch which ran along the garden of a château and advanced at right angles to the River Layes but parallel to the many drainage ditches on Stephens' front (see map on page 25). This request was refused, and consequently the attack was made diagonally over the drainage ditches and the troops were subjected to enfilade fire. A second enemy attack at 09.00 hours, much weaker than the previous one, was also stopped with little difficulty.

At 12.30 hours A and B Coys left their trenches for the assault on the enemy's line, 400 to 500 yards away; they were met by a hail of fire from both field and machine-guns; many men fell and only a handful reached the protection of the Smith-Dorrien trench, 200 yards away. In the face of such fire Stephens stopped the attack. At 16.00 hours he was sent for by Brigade and ordered to make a second attack at 17.15 hours which was 'to be pressed home at any cost'. He arrived back at the battalion minutes before the attack was due, just as a 'small and inadequate' British artillery bombardment was under way. C and D Coys were now ordered forward. C Coy, on the left, under Capt. Bridgeman charged, but under intense machine-gun fire only Capt. Bridgeman and four other ranks reached the Smith-Dorrien trench – these men were the only survivors of 11 and 12 Platoons who had led the attack.

D Coy, on the right, had an even more difficult task, as their front was blocked by uncut wire. (*The History of the Rifle Brigade* states it was their own wire but this seems very unlikely.) The wire had to be cut and instead of picking a number of men for the 'suicidal task', No. 9665 CSM Harry Daniels asked his friend, No. 3697 A/Cpl Reginald 'Tom' Noble, to accompany him as he had on many dangerous night patrols in the past. The two friends, now armed with wirecutters, shook hands before setting out; they managed to cover the few yards to the wire unhurt and, lying on their backs, began to cut the lower strands; this done they raised themselves to sever the higher wires and finally to a kneeling position to reach the highest of the wire. It was then that Daniels was hit in the left thigh and dropped to the ground; after a few minutes he heard Noble gasp. Daniels asked, 'What's up, Tom?' to which Noble replied, 'I am hit in the chest, old man'. Daniels managed to roll into a shell hole and apply rudimentary first-aid to his wound; he remained there for four hours before trying to return to the battalion's trenches after dark when he was seen and picked up by his comrades. The attack, meanwhile, had been stopped by Stephens after a number of men had been shot down.

Noble died from his wounds the following day and is buried at Longuenesse Souvenir Cemetery, St Omer, Plot I, Row A, Grave 57. The battalion lost 12 officers and 365 other ranks at Neuve Chapelle.

The citation for both men was published in the *London Gazette* on 28 April 1915, and Daniels was presented with his VC by the King at Buckingham Palace on 15 May. Talking to a reporter after the investiture, Daniels, the only VC of that day, said that the King had questioned him about the action and also whether his wound had healed. He continued: 'I shall not forget how the King looked at me when he spoke of poor old Noble. He looked most sympathetic. I could see he felt it.' When he left the Palace Daniels motored to the Wood Green Empire where he was presented to Lady French at a special charity matinee.

Daniels' tribute to Noble was, 'The best chum I've ever had, the bravest man I've ever known.'

The thirteenth of sixteen children, Harry Daniels was born in Wymondham, Norfolk, on 13 December 1885. His parents William and Elizabeth had previously run a bakery and confectionery business in St John's, Timberhill, Norwich, where most of their children were born, and after spending six years at Wymondham they returned to Norwich, where they lived in Eagle Walk, Newmarket Road.

Daniels's mother died when he was four years old and shortly after his father also died, leaving six children under the age of fourteen. Harry and one of his brothers were placed in the care of the Norwich Board of Guardians and put in the Boys' Home, St Faith's Lane, Norwich. Harry was soon nicknamed 'Spitfire'. He twice ran away from the Home, living on turnips for two days on the first occasion and being absent for two months on the second when he served as a cabin boy on a fishing smack. Daniels attended Thorpe Hamlet boys' school before being apprenticed as a carpenter and joiner to Mr Hawes at Duke's Palace Steam Joinery Works in Norwich.

While still an apprentice, Daniels heard that his eldest brother, William, who had enlisted in 1889, had been killed at Magersfontein, South Africa, while serving with the 2nd Coldstream Guards. This prompted Harry, a few months later, when he turned eighteen, to enlist in the Army. Telling no one, Daniels joined the Rifle Brigade on 31 January 1903 and after training at Gosport and Chatham went to India with the 2nd Bn in 1905. After a period in the band Harry took a gymnastics course at Lucknow. Promoted to corporal on 19 July 1909 and to sergeant on 21 December 1910, Daniels met his future wife, Kathleen Mary Perry, the daughter of a warrant officer in the Manchester Regt, at the 1912 Christmas dance at Calcutta. They were married at Calcutta on 21 January 1914. While in India Daniels won the regimental light-weight and welterweight boxing tournaments and was a prominent member of the battalion's dramatic club. Further promotion followed on 10 October 1914 when Daniels was made CQMS and, while he was serving in France, he was promoted to CSM on 12 December of the same year.

Daniels read the news of his VC in a newspaper when he was recovering from his wounds at Hammersmith Infirmary. Daniels and his wife returned to his home city of Norwich on 10 June 1915. It was his first visit to the city for eleven years, and they were met at Thorpe station by the Lord Mayor, and driven to the Guildhall in a state coach. During his stay he attended various functions, including a reception at his old school. Before leaving to resume his military duties he was presented with a purse of gold by the Sheriff, Mr Frances Horner. Men of the Royal Engineers pulled the carriage in which Daniels and his wife travelled to the railway station on their departure.

He received his commission in July 1915, remained with his battalion and was awarded the Military Cross for services on 30 March 1916, almost exactly a year after winning the VC. The citation for his MC read:

Harry Daniels, Lieutenant, Temporary Captain Rifle Brigade; When a man of his patrol was wounded on the edge of the enemy's wire, he carried him in some 300 yards under very heavy fire. On another occasion, when two successive patrols had failed to find a wounded corporal, Second Lieutenant Daniels volunteered to take out a third patrol, and brought in the corporal's body.

In September 1915 the Lord Mayor of Norwich received a telegram saying that Lt Daniels had been killed in action. Regulation field postcards received by Daniels' relatives in Norwich disproved this information and on 1 October 1915 a contradiction of his reported death was issued by the Press Association.

Promotion to lieutenant followed on 23 August 1916 and after further service with his battalion as Physical and Bayonet Training Supervision Officer he returned to England during 1917.

During the latter half of 1918 Daniels was a member of the British Military Mission to the USA. He attended the garden party for VC winners at Buckingham Palace on 26 June 1920 and was present at the Cenotaph in Whitehall on 11 November the same year. Also in 1920 he represented his country as a boxer at the Olympic Games at Antwerp. On 9 April 1921 Daniels was appointed a captain in the Loyal North Lancs Regt, and on 28 September became Assistant Provost Marshal at Aldershot. In October 1925 he was Administration Officer to Beachley Boys Army Technical School, Chepstow, where he stayed until December 1929, achieving the rank of Brevet-Major on 1 July 1929. He retired from the Army on 26 April 1930 and became the manager of hotels in Woodbridge, Dovercourt, Abergavenny and Chester before rejoining the Army as a recruiting officer at Newcastle in December 1933. A year later he was given the rank of lieutenant-colonel. Daniels left the

Army for good in 1942, taking up the post of resident manager of the Leeds Grand Theatre where he proved to be popular with artistes, staff and public alike.

In 1949 Mrs Daniels became terminally ill and as a last resort Daniels turned to an American evangelist, the nine-year-old Renée Martz, 'The Wonder Child Preacher'. The administrations of this child were sadly unsuccessful and Kathleen Daniels died at her home in West Park, Leeds, shortly afterwards. It was reported that Renée's father declared, 'We do not look upon this as one of our failures'.

Invited to attend the coronation of Queen Elizabeth, Harry Daniels suffered a heart attack in London shortly before the event and was taken back to hospital in Leeds. In what was possibly his last letter, in October 1953, he wrote to Lt-Col. Victor Turner VC, of Ditchingham, Norfolk, telling him about his heart attack and that he was also suffering from pneumonia, and was therefore unable to attend a forthcoming reunion of the 2nd Battalion Rifle Brigade.

Lt-Col. Daniels died on his 69th birthday, 13 December 1953, at the Ida and Robert Arthington Hospital, Leeds. His medals and sword lay on the Union Jack-draped coffin during the funeral service at St Simon's Church, Burley. The mourners included members of the management and staff of the Grand Theatre as well as military representatives, including Mr W.H. Butler VC and ex-Sgt R.W. Stone MM, who served with Daniels in the war. Cremation took place at Lawnswood Crematorium, Leeds and Lt-Col Daniels' ashes were later scattered at Aldershot Officers' Cricket Ground.

Daniels' medals and decorations were exhibited at Leeds City Museum for a short period and were then passed to the Regimental Museum at Winchester. They comprised the Victoria Cross, Military Cross, 1914 Star, British War Medal, Victory Medal with Palm, and Coronation Medals for King George V, King Edward VIII, King George VI and Queen Elizabeth II. A cartoon of Daniels by Bruce Bairnsfather accompanied his medals.

A bronze plaque on a Portland Stone plinth was unveiled in November 1992 to all Victoria Cross holders born in Leeds and also those buried in Leeds. Harry Daniels is listed amongst the 11 names of First World War VCs and in total 17 men from The

Indian Mutiny to The Second World War are commemorated. The plaque is located on the NW corner of The Headrow and Cookridge Street junction, very near the Leeds War Memorial now situated in Victoria Gardens after a move from the City Square in 1937 made necessary by a new traffic scheme.

A small commemorative plaque to his memory was placed in The Grand Theatre, Leeds, although the author can find no record of this today. A road in Wymondham, Norfolk, Harry Daniels Close, was named in his memory.

Cecil Reginald Noble was born in Bournemouth on 4 June 1891, the son of Frederick Leopold Noble, a decorator, and Hannah Noble. From early childhood he lived at Capstone Road, Bournemouth, and received his education at St Clement's School in the town. Noble disliked his Christian name of Cecil and was known in his family as 'Tommy'. When he enlisted in the Army in 1910 he used the name of Reginald Noble. He went to France with the 2nd Bn, Rifle Brigade, in November 1914 and in early 1915 the battalion was in the waterlogged trenches of the Laventie sector.

Mrs Noble was presented with her son's VC by the King at Buckingham Palace on 29 November 1916. A memorial bronze plaque depicting Noble's VC and the Rifle Brigade badge was placed in St Clement's School in memory of Bournemouth's first VC winner, the pupils having collected money for this.

On 18 October 1980 a housing development at 66 Surrey Road, Bournemouth, was officially named Reginald Noble Court. The block of 28 flats, run by the Royal British Legion Housing Association, offered sheltered housing accommodation for retired ex-servicemen and women, a fitting tribute to a brave man. Another road in Bournemouth, Noble Close, was named after him in March 1975. On 2 October 1995 Bournemouth Borough Council unveiled a blue plaque at 175 Capstone Road honouring Noble. A similar plaque was erected near the site of 39 Capstone Road honouring Frederick Charles Riggs VC MM, who was awarded a posthumous VC in 1918, making this road almost unique in that it was home to more than one VC winner; Valour Road, Winnipeg, Canada being the other. (See page 97). In 2000 a sculpture by Jonathan Sells was unveiled at Bournemouth International Centre including a scroll on which are the names of the three Bournemouth-born VC winners; Cpl C R Noble and Sgt F C Riggs of WWI and Lt Col D A Seagrim of WWII. In 1980 Noble's VC was in the hands of his niece, Mrs Lloyd, of Esher, Surrey.

C.G. MARTIN
Spanbroek Molen, Belgium, 12 March

During the battle of Neuve Chapelle British GHQ ordered the Second Army to make an attack as soon as possible to prevent the withdrawal of more German troops from the Ypres area to bolster the enemy defence of Neuve Chapelle. They were mistaken in their belief that German prisoners taken in the Neuve Chapelle fighting had been suddenly transferred from Ypres, nevertheless the requested attack was delivered at 14.30 hours on 12 March by the 7th Bde, 3rd Division, around the German position at Spanbroek Molen, some 2,000 yards north of Wulverghem.

Lt. C.G. Martin 56th Field Company Royal Engineers volunteered to lead a small party of six bombers against a section of the enemy's trenches which was holding up the advance. Before the raid began he was wounded by a bullet which penetrated the flesh near the hip; however, he made light of the wound and led the bombers towards the enemy trench. Here they delivered their ordnance with such speed and accuracy that the Germans were quickly driven out; Lt Martin and his men then occupied the trench and set about transferring the parapet and improving the position with sandbags, in readiness for the inevitable counter-attack.

The Germans attacked within a short while, but the six bombers, inspired by the example of Lt Martin, drove the enemy back and continued to do so in subsequent attacks despite the overwhelming numbers of the enemy. The bombers held the trench for two and a half hours before orders arrived for them to abandon the captured post and join the general withdrawal. Their bombing had held up German reinforcements who were unable to advance until this section of trench was retaken. For this action Lt C.G. Martin was awarded the VC, and each of his six bombers received a DCM. Martin was twice Mentioned in Despatches during the First World War.

Cyril Gordon Martin was born at Foochow, China, on 19 December 1891, his father, the Revd John Martin, Vicar of Grandborough near Rugby, being then principal of the Church Missionary Society College in Foochow. His mother was the daughter of Judge Goldie of the Indian Civil Service. His mother died when he was still in his early childhood and he was sent to Bath, where he was brought up by his two aunts, the Misses Goldie, who resided at 12 Somerset Place. Martin went to Hamilton House School, Bath, later attending Bath College and Clifton College. He joined the Army on 23 December 1911, continuing his education at the Royal Military College, Woolwich, and becoming a lieutenant on 15 July 1914. Lt Martin landed in France with 56 Field Coy RE on 16 August 1914 and just ten days later his gallantry earned him a DSO, his award being among the first list of decorations gazetted in the war. On 26 August at Le Cateau, in the face of heavy fire, Lt Martin and his section had held an enemy post from which the British infantry had been driven out, until they could be relieved by more infantry. His citation appeared in the *London Gazette* on Monday 9 November 1914 (page 9108). He was wounded twice before winning the VC, being shot through the shoulder and bayoneted through the hand in the above action before the relief arrived. He was invalided home and only returned to the front a few days before the fight at Spanbroek Molen on 12 March 1915. His hip wound necessitated a return to England and later in October, during a recruiting march and demonstration in Bath, he was presented with a sword of honour by his fellow citizens.

From 27 October 1915 to 19 May 1916 he was (Temporary) Assistant Instructor at the School of Military Engineering. He never fully recovered from his wounds and was sent to Egypt, being attached to the Egyptian Army from 10 July 1916. He was promoted to captain on 26 June 1917 and on 20 August that year married Mabel, the only daughter of the late Major Edward Hingston RE at Chatham parish church; she later bore him two sons and a daughter. At this time he gained the uncommon Sudan Medal with two bars, for actions in the spring and autumn of 1917. The following year he was with the Egyptian Expeditionary Force in Palestine but attached to the Egyptian Army Public Works Dept, remaining attached to the Egyptian Army after the Armistice. He returned to England to attend the VC garden party at Buckingham Palace on 26 June 1920. From 15 July 1925 until 1928 he was based at the School of Military Engineering, Chatham, being promoted to major on 10 August 1928. The years 1929 to 1938 saw him serving on the north-west frontier of India, being Mentioned in Despatches twice, first in 1930 and again on 30 October 1931. On 6 May 1932 he rose to the rank of brevet lieutenant-colonel, later becoming Staff Officer RE 2nd Grade, Northern Command, in 1933. He was created CBE in 1938 while serving as CRE Wazirforce, and from 1938 to 1941 he was Deputy Chief Engineer Northern Command India, before going to Iraq to join what later became known as Paiforce. After a short tour in the UK as Commandant RE OCTU at Newark, he returned to India in 1943, to become Commandant, School of Military Engineering at Roorkee, finally being appointed Chief Engineer, Northern Army, India, in 1945; later that year he became ADC to King George VI.

Martin retired in 1947 and took up an appointment with the Forestry Commission. He attended the VC Review on 26 June 1956 and was present at the VC garden party given at

Buckingham Palace on 17 July 1962 and at the banquet which followed, given by the Lord Mayor of London at Mansion House. The following day he joined the Third Reunion Dinner of the VC and GC Association at the Café Royal.

Cyril Martin died on 14 August 1980, aged 88, at the Royal Herbert Hospital, Woolwich, and was cremated at Eltham Crematorium. In 1980 Brigadier Martin was the second oldest holder of the VC as well as being the first individual to win both the DSO and VC in the war, and on 2 December that year his son and daughter, Sqn Ldr R.F.H. Martin and Miss M. Martin, presented their father's medals to Maj.-Gen. G.S. Sinclair, Engineer in Chief, for the RE Museum. Cyril Martin was one of five Old Cliftonians to win the VC in the First World War. Martin's VC and other medals are on display at the museum, as is the torn, muddy and bloodstained tunic worn by Lt Martin on the day he won his VC; his son had found the tunic stored with the medals in the bank.

R. MORROW

Near Messines, Belgium, 12 April

In early April the 1st Bn, Royal Irish Fusiliers (RIF) known as the Faugh-a-Ballaghs (which is Gaelic for 'Clear the Way'), part of the 10th Bde, 4th Division, was in the River Douvre sector near Messines. The ground there was waterlogged, making it virtually impassable, and the German artillery dominated the area owing to the excellent observation afforded them from Messines. The battalion had moved back to the sector on 17 March, relieving the 1st Suffolks (84th Bde, 28th Div.) who were in support, and on 25 March it took over from the Seaforth Highlanders 200 yards of front-line trench north of the River Douvre. Communication was established by a temporary bridge. On 11 April orders arrived for the relief of the whole brigade, and on the following day, advance parties of the 5th Bn Royal Warwickshire Regt (143rd Bde, 48th Div.), joined the 1/RIF in the trenches to familiarize themselves with the area. The enemy artillery was very active, shelling the area during the day.

The 1/RIF's last day in the Douvre area was eventful. The enemy artillery remained very active, bombarding the area, and at about 1700 hours, the German gunners began using heavier guns than had yet been used on this sector. They proceeded to shell the area north-west of Dead Cow Farm, a well-known target, then shortened the range until the shells reached the trench immediately south of the Douvre; this trench was systematically destroyed, and some men were simply blown to pieces while others were buried alive by falling debris. Survivors of D Coy 1/RIF took shelter in the support trench to the rear and it was from here that No. 10531 Pte Robert Morrow went forward to the fire-trench, and regardless of the shells still falling around, dug out one of his comrades and dragged him back to the relative safety of the support trench.

Morrow returned several times to the shattered front line, each time rescuing a man. Incredibly, he survived unwounded and the citation for the VC which was gazetted on 22 May ended: 'Private Morrow carried out this gallant work on his own initiative, and under very heavy fire from the enemy.' Sadly, he did not live to receive his award, being badly wounded on 25 April, when again carrying wounded soldiers to safety while under heavy fire, during the battalion's attack on St Julien during the Second Battle of Ypres. He died of his wounds the next day at St Jean, near Ypres. His company officer, Capt. Jeudwine, recommended that Pte Morrow be awarded a clasp to the VC, but this was rejected. Morrow's was the regiment's first VC of the war.

Robert Morrow was born at Sessia, New Mills, near Dungannon, County Tyrone, Ireland, on 7 September 1891, the son of Hugh and Margaret Jane Morrow. When his father died, he was taken into the care of the Presbyterian

Orphan Society. His widowed mother lived on a small farm at this time. Morrow was educated at the Carland and the Gortnaglush Nationalist Schools. He was of a quiet disposition, and after leaving school he helped to run the family farm until 1912, when he enlisted in the British Army, joining the 1st Bn Royal Irish Fusiliers as a private. Morrow went overseas on the outbreak of war and was involved in many of the early battles. After his death his VC was sent to his mother, together with a letter from the King which read:

> It is a matter of sincere regret to me that the death of Private Robert Morrow deprived me of the pride of personally conferring upon him the Victoria Cross, the greatest of all distinctions.

Morrow's CO, Lt-Col. D.W. Churcher, also wrote a letter of sympathy to his mother in which he described Robert as 'a man absolutely devoid of fear'. In recognition of his courage, Morrow was also awarded the Russian Order of St George 3rd Class on 25 August 1915.

Mrs Morrow travelled to London where King George V re-presented the medal to her at an Investiture at Buckingham Palace on 29 November 1916. Although quite poor, Mrs Morrow refused an offer for her son's decoration, declaring that only the Royal Irish Fusiliers should have it, and offering it to the regiment in 1919. A subscription was initiated among the regimental officers, and in August 1919 a ceremonial parade was held at the Depot in Armagh, at which Mrs Morrow formally donated the Victoria Cross to the regiment; in turn, she was presented with the title deeds of a piece of land she was anxious to add to her farm. Her elder son Richard served in the 12th Royal Inniskilling Fusiliers and survived the war.

Robert Morrow's citation is on display in Carland Presbyterian Church, County Tyrone, Ireland. The *Ulster Courier and News* of 9 November 1988 reported that the prominent obelisk memorial erected by subscription by the villagers of New Mills to the memory of Ulster's first VC, Pte Robert Morrow, was accidentally smashed by a petrol tanker trying to negotiate a bend in the centre of the village. The Burmah Oil Company who owned the oil tanker undertook to restore what was known locally as the 'VC Memorial'. It was the third time the memorial had been knocked down. In 1921 a mural tablet inscribed with the names of sixteen men from the parish of Newmills, including that of Private Robert Morrow VC, who made the supreme sacrifice in the Great War was unveiled in Newmills Parish Church. The tablet also records the names of a further 64 men of the parish who served. The public house in Newmills, the *V.C. Inn*, is named in memory of Robert Morrow.

Morrow is also included in a large commemorative painting which was commissioned for the French Government by M. Cairier-Bellew. Pte Morrow is buried in White House Cemetery, Plot IV, Row A, Grave 44; the cemetery is near St Jean, north of Ypres, Belgium.

HILL 60, BELGIUM

East of Verbranden Molen, the railway line between Ypres and Comines was set in a deep cutting, which crossed the ridge of high ground that runs in a south-westerly direction from Mount Sorrel to the Bluff. On the northern edge of this railway cutting stood Hill 60, described in the *History of East Surrey Regiment* as: 'a pimple near the western crest of the ridge'. The 60 metre hill was a fine artillery observation post for the Germans, who were entrenched on the summit and upper slopes. From here they overlooked the lower ground to the west and north-west of Ypres, some two miles distant from the German positions and about 120 feet below them. Before any British advance could be made this 'pimple' would have to be captured. The action at Hill 60 became a prelude to the Second Battle of Ypres.

Unbeknown to the Germans, RE sappers had driven mines under their fire-trenches. In April the British front followed the line of the road from Zwarteleen, ran around the northern base of Hill 60, and then crossed the railway by means of the road bridge. Hill 60 was, in fact, the largest of three man-made 'spoil' heaps from the railway cutting, the others being the 'Caterpillar' and the 'Dump'. At 19.05 hours on 17 April the Royal Engineers blew the mines, creating five huge craters that occupied virtually the whole area. The mine explosions signalled an Allied artillery bombardment on all the German approaches to the hill. As the last mine exploded, C Coy Royal West Kents and sappers of the 1/2nd Home Counties Field Company RE (13th Bde) left their trenches and stormed the German positions.

They reached the top of the slope in two minutes and occupied the craters and the shattered remnants of the German trenches to the south-east. The survivors of the luckless German garrison, a company of the *172nd Regiment (XV Corps)* were overwhelmed. British casualties were a mere seven men, one of whom was a victim of falling debris from the last mine explosion. Within fifteen minutes of the initial storming party reaching the crest, the supporting company of the Royal West Kents and two companies of the King's Own Scottish Borderers, together with the machine-gun section of the Queen Victoria's Rifles, were consolidating their position.

The left hand or easternmost crater formed a figure of eight because it overlapped with the middle crater. This first crater was approximately 30 yards in diameter and about 20 feet deep. The adjoining crater was slightly larger. The crater on the right was much smaller and was separated by a few yards from the middle one. Two other, smaller, craters lay to the rear, near the northern crest-line.

Two lines of trenches started from a point near the railway bridge. The forward line of trenches ran from the bridge up the slope of the hill towards the right-hand crater. At this point there was a gap, beyond which were old German support trenches, now manned as part of the British front line, which extended to the forward lip of the left crater (see map on page 64). Two German communication trenches, which crossed no-man's-land from the German front line, led into these old German support trenches; one continued through the extreme left of the British front line past the left crater and into the middle one. A spur ran from this trench straight to the left-hand crater. Both these old German communication trenches were blocked out in no-man's-land, at some distance from the British front line. The two branches of the continuation of the left-hand trench mentioned above were blocked again between the craters and the advance line. This meant that the left flank of the British advanced line was left 'in the air', the danger being increased by the German sap XZ. Such were the defences after the initial attack and consolidation. The troops on the hill had three hours to consolidate and prepare their position.

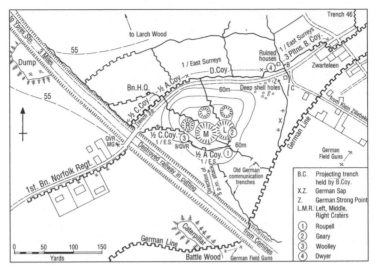

Defence of Hill 60, 19–21 April 1915

After the storming of Hill 60, German artillery fire was rather wild initially and there were reports that the Germans were using lachrymatory shells. In fact the gas that the British could smell was escaping from ruptured cylinders that the Germans had dug in on the hill ready for attack. In the early hours of 18 April desperate German attacks were launched against the troops on the hill, and heavy shelling and fighting continued throughout the day. The German troops made some progress, but at 18.00 hours the Duke of Wellington's, supported by the KOYLI as second wave, counter-attacked, regaining possession of the whole hill again for 13th Brigade.

There was a lull in the fighting during the night of 18/19 April, and during the next day the enemy contented themselves with shelling the hill. Furious fighting was renewed by the Germans on the 20th, which mainly consisted of bombing attacks, and the brutal struggle for the hill continued through the night and into the next morning. Any semblance of trench lines had been obliterated by this time. The Official History states:

The surface of Hill 60 was a medley of confluent mine and shell craters, strewn with broken timber and wire: and in this rubbish heap it was impossible to dig without disturbing the body of some British or German soldier.

Operations continued on the 21st, following two night attacks, but on 22 April attention was diverted from the hill by the German gas attack near Ypres, which heralded the Second Battle of Ypres. Hill 60 was finally lost by the British on 5 May, partly as a result of repeated gas attacks.

If you walk the ground in the sunlight today, the hill does not appear particularly high or steep. Trees on the lower slopes shade the uneven ground, and worn pathways take the visitor past small sections of damaged pill-boxes that peep out of the surrounding ground, to the Queen Victoria's Rifles Memorial on the summit. Despite the grassy surface, it is clear that the ground is heavily cratered; some of the craters are surprisingly deep, even eighty years on. Nature has softened the contours but it is still obvious that this was a place of terrible violence. The struggle for the hill cost the British over 100 officers and 3,000 men. The area of Hill 60 is not extensive; you can walk across it in just a few minutes; the intensity of the fighting is all too clearly illustrated by the fact that so small an area still contains the remains of several thousand unaccounted-for soldiers from both sides. It was perhaps this, together with its role in the defence of Ypres, that caused such outcry in October 1920 when it was announced that Hill 60 had been sold to the brewers Messrs Samuel Allsop Ltd from Burton-on-Trent. The company issued a vigorous denial that they were considering building an hotel on the site. They declared their purchase was necessary in order 'to secure it for a war memorial to regiments which suffered there'. It seems unlikely that the cratered area could revert to its pre-war popularity as a place for lovers to meet (in those days it was known as 'Côte des Amants' – Lovers' Hill). A small museum relating to the bloody action here stood on the opposite side of the road until its closure in 2006.

G.R.P. ROUPELL
Hill 60, Belgium, 20 April

The 14th Bde was ordered to send a battalion to reinforce 13th Bde at Hill 60. Two companies (A and B) and Battalion HQ of the 1/East Surreys (14th Bde, 5th Div.) moved off at 16.00 hours on 18 April to a position one mile short of the hill. Two hours later the remainder of the battalion joined them and awaited orders. During this time they suffered their first experience of gas, which was drifting across from the cylinders buried in the German lines in preparation for the attack which was launched on 22 April, which became known as the Second Battle of Ypres. The desperate ferocity of the German efforts to regain control of the heights may perhaps be explained by a desire to keep the existence of these cylinders a secret; they also faced the prospect of losing an excellent observation platform.

The battalion took over a portion of the front line on Hill 60 at 05.00 hours on 19 April. Initially Lt G.R.P. Roupell, commanding A Coy, relieved the right hand trenches as far as the communication trench which ran up to the left hand crater. Deep shell holes pitted the area near the base of Hill 60 where D and B Coys met. A mere 20 yards from B Coy's right was a German strongpoint (marked Z on the map on page 40). Further to the left, and at right angles to the original British line, was a short trench (marked BC) that projected out into no-man's-land and was also under B Coy's control. Two ruined houses stood alongside this short 'extension' and obscured the view towards the shell-holed area at the north-north-east base of the hill. Lt Darwell's machine-gun section, comprising five guns, was divided up; four machine-guns were allocated to B and D Coys, to sweep the eastern slopes of the hill, and the other went to C Coy, near the bridge. The Bedfordshire Regt was in support, some 500 yards behind the hill, based in trenches with dug-outs around Larch Wood. The troops spent 19 April clearing the dead and wounded out of the front line and improving the defences despite continuous shelling by the Germans which was directed primarily on the support and communication trenches at the rear of the hill. The enemy bombardment increased at 17.00 hours, with all trenches being pounded by trench mortars and heavy howitzers. The British batteries replied and the German shelling stopped after half an hour, but damage to the trenches was extensive and when the enemy bombardment lifted the battalion immediately began to repair the smashed defences.

At 22.00 hours half of A Coy under Lt Roupell relieved the two C Coy platoons which had originally held the old German support trenches on the forward slope of the hill. Repair work continued through the night despite enemy shelling and bombing. Dawn on 20 April heralded a hot, fine day and the day was relatively quiet for those in the advanced line, although at about 15.00 hours B Coy successfully defended trench BC from enemy bombers. A heavy bombardment opened up on the British positions about 11.00 hours, lasting until midday when shelling became sporadic, allowing some repair work to be done on the defences. Shortly after 16.00 hours the Germans began a concerted effort to retake their lost positions, beginning with an intense bombardment of all British-held areas on and around Hill 60. Roupell's half of A Coy in the advanced line was accurately shelled by field batteries near Zwarteleen and the Caterpillar, choking the trenches with dead, wounded and debris. All telephone lines were cut by shellfire, stopping all communications, not only between units, but also with sector headquarters and the artillery batteries. In Roupell's section of the line, 2/Lt Davis was in command of the platoon on the left, in front of the left crater, while Lt G.L. Watson's platoon was holding the right trench, which bent back to join C Coy's trench. Lt Watson's platoon was badly hit by German field batteries, and Watson and twenty men were soon killed. Lt Roupell sent back orders to Lt Abercrombie to bring up his platoon as reinforcements. When they arrived they found all of Lt Watson's platoon buried by explosions but struggled to hold the trench, despite mounting losses; their efforts offered an escape route for Lt Davis's platoon on the left, who had no other exit from their trench. As the *History of the East Surrey Regiment* notes of this bombardment: 'The little hill was covered with flame, smoke and dust, and it was impossible to see more than ten yards in any direction'. Shortly after 17.00 hours the enemy bombardment lifted from the front line trenches, instead concentrating on the support and communication trenches to prevent reinforcements moving up to the front. Soon after the 'lift', a large party of German infantry advanced across the open towards the right-hand crater, having deployed from the railway cutting near the Caterpillar. This attack was quickly stopped by concentrated fire from British artillery supported by the machine-guns of the 1/Norfolks, who were positioned on the right of the 1/East Surreys on the far side of the railway cutting, and the single machine-gun manned by Cpl F.W. Adams in the advanced trench held by C Coy 1/East Surreys.

Two other German attacks developed simultaneously with this one. One was launched against Roupell's A Coy in the advanced line and the other against B and C Coys on the left of the hill. Roupell's half company was attacked by groups of enemy bombers who crawled along the old German communication trench, supported by parties of infantry who every so often attempted short rushes forward across the open ground. A Coy, though suffering heavy losses from grenade and rifle fire, fought on, picking up German grenades and hurling them back before they exploded, and stopping infantry rushes with rapid rifle fire. The East Surrey men found their own long-handled bombs impossible to use in the narrow confines of their trench. Lt Roupell, under severe pressure owing to heavy casualties, called for reinforcements for A Coy in the advanced line. Maj. W. Allason of the 1/Bedfords had received pleas for men from sector HQ, where Lt Darwell of the 1/East Surreys had got a message through appealing for desperately needed replacements. Maj. Allason sent a party of 1/Bedfords forward and somehow they found their way to the left-hand crater which they occupied. Roupell's message for help had also reached Lt Geary, then attached to C Coy 1/East Surreys, who collected his platoon and led them forward. Lt Geary was unable to reach the advanced line through the right communication trench, but spying the Bedford men made a rush across the open to join them in the left crater.

Despite severe losses Roupell's band of A Coy men held on against several enemy attacks which all developed in the same way: a shower of grenades hurled from the two old communication trenches, followed by an infantry charge across the open. Each attack was stopped by rapid rifle fire from Lt Roupell's dwindling number of survivors. Though wounded eight times during the intensive bombardment which preceded the final German attack, Roupell remained at his post, leading his men in repelling the enemy.

As darkness fell, a little after 19.00 hours, Lt Roupell, realizing the untenability of his position without reinforcements, decided to make his way back to HQ to explain the situation. The German bombardment had been maintained, with varying intensity, all day, but Roupell, despite feeling faint from blood-loss, made his way across the shell-swept open to the reserve trenches. He reported to the sector commander, Lt-Col. Griffiths of the Bedford Regt, at sector headquarters at about 19.30 hours, outlined the situation and was promised reinforcements for the front line. After having his wounds properly dressed, he returned to the advanced lines to resume command of his men, despite the surgeon's advice that he should report to a casualty clearing station.

By this time (about 20.00 hours) A Coy's position was delicate. Some Germans had managed to crawl along the left communication trench, penetrating the extreme left of A Coy's trench. 2/Lt Davis's platoon opened fire along this virtually straight trench, thus preventing a lodgement by the Germans, but in turn A Coy was held back by enemy bombers, thereby making this section untenable to both sides. Soon after 23.00 hours Roupell again went back to collect reinforcements and brought a party of 1/Bedfords forward. The 1/East Surreys were relieved by the Devons at 02.00 hours on the 21st.

Roupell was awarded the VC for 'most conspicuous gallantry and devotion to duty' which was gazetted on 23 June 1915; he received the award from the King himself, being decorated at Buckingham Palace on 12 July the same year.

George Rowland Patrick Roupell was born in Tipperary on 7 April 1892, the son of Col. F.F. Roupell, CO of the 1/East Surrey Regiment and Mrs E.M. Roupell (née Bryden). He was educated at Rosall and the Royal Military College, Sandhurst, before being gazetted to the East Surrey Regt as 2/Lt on 2 March 1912, becoming a lieutenant on 29 April 1914. He went to France with the BEF and saw action at Mons, Le Cateau, The Retreat, the Marne, the Aisne, and the First Battle of Ypres. He commanded a platoon until the fighting on the Aisne, where he gained command of a company, which he kept until his VC action on 20 April 1915 when he was wounded. He was also awarded the Russian Order of St George 4th Class for this same action. After recovering from the wounds he suffered at Hill 60, he was promoted to captain on 21 April 1916 and was appointed Adjutant of the 1/East Surreys; later he was General Staff Officer Grade 3 to the 17th Army Corps, becoming GSO 3 to 3rd Army in September 1916. He was awarded the French Croix de Guerre and was Mentioned in Despatches three times and wounded twice during the war. Following the Armistice he served as A/Lt-Col. from 13 December 1918 in the North Russia campaign against the Bolshevists during 1919. He was captured in that year and in an undated newspaper article made it clear that the treatment of British officers who fell into Bolshevist hands was grim:

> Capt. G. Roupell VC of the East Surrey Regt, states that at Plesetskaya on the Archangel front and again at Moscow all the British officers were informed that they would be regarded as brigands. At both places their treatment was of the most brutal nature.

Roupell relinquished his A/Lt-Col. rank in 1920 after repatriation from Russia. He attended the garden party given for VCs at Buckingham Palace on 26 June 1920. In 1921 he married Miss Doris Phoebe Sant, twin daughter of

Capt. Mowbray Sant, Chief Constable of Surrey, at Christ Church, Lancastergate; the same year he entered the Staff College, Camberley. They were later to have two children, a son and a daughter. He was restored to the establishment of officers on 21 January 1923 as a captain in the East Surrey Regiment. From May 1924 until 1928 he served as a staff captain in Northern Command, being promoted to major on 18 November that year and becoming GSO 2, Royal Military College, Kingston, Canada, from 16 March 1929 to April 1931; in July he assumed command of the East Surrey Regimental Depot, Kingston-on-Thames. In 1934/5 he was GSO 2 China Command, and from 1935 to 1939 commanded the 1/East Surrey Regt as a lieutenant-colonel. He served in the Second World War as a brigadier, commanding the 36th and 105th Infantry Brigades. On 19/20 May 1940 Brigadier Roupell's 36th Bde was severely attacked by German armoured columns supported by Stukas. At 04.00 hours on the 21st, with German units all around him, he ordered his men to split into small parties and make their escape independently. This was duly done and many were successful, though Roupell's three commanding officers were captured, a fate Roupell did not share, hiding himself in a farm where he stayed for two years before making his escape through Spain. He later took command of 105th Infantry Brigade.

He attended the victory parade in Whitehall on 8 June 1946 and the dinner at the Dorchester Hotel given afterwards. He was made Deputy Lieutenant of Surrey in 1953 and from August 1955 to April 1956 made a 'good-will' tour with his wife, visiting several military bases in Canada, Hong Kong and Australia that had links with the Queen's Royal Surrey Regiment. While in Canada he stayed for a fortnight with Maj. Handley Geary, an old friend who had also won a VC with the 1/East Surreys on Hill 60 on the same day as Roupell. Upon his return he attended the parade at the VC Centenary Review in Hyde Park, London, on 26 June 1956, the same year that he was appointed a Companion of the Order of the Bath. His wife Doris died in 1958; a year later he married again, this time to Mrs Rachel Kennedy, daughter of the late R.A. Bruce of Yeovil, Somerset; the same year he was given a full colonelcy, making him the last Colonel of The East

Surrey Regiment, holding office in 1959 when amalgamation with The Queen's Royal Regiment took place to form The Queen's Royal Surrey Regiment. He continued to take an interest in the Surrey Regt and the VC Association, attending the majority of VC celebrations up till 1973.

In 1973 Brig. C.R.P. Roupell became President of the Old Contemptibles' Association. A year later, on 4 March 1974, he died peacefully at his home at Little Chartham, Shalford, Surrey, aged 81 years and 11 months. A private cremation was held at Guildford Crematorium, followed on Friday 15 March by a Thanksgiving Service at the Church of St Mary the Virgin at Shalford, presided over by the Revd K.J. Morgan.

B.H. GEARY

Hill 60, Belgium, 20/21 April

While Lt Roupell's men held the advanced line on Hill 60, 2/Lt Geary and his platoon of C Coy men were engaged throughout 19 April in extending their trench in the advanced line up the slope to the right crater. On Tuesday 20 April the German bombardment found the range and battered the East Surreys' trenches, blowing in a parapet over 2/Lt Geary and some of his men. He managed to get free fairly easily but his men required help to get out; incredibly, only one man was wounded. Geary and his men then began trying to fill in the gaps blown by enemy shellfire, despite being shot at from the front through the gaps, and from the rear on the left, where the German trenches curved round behind them. Geary went to reconnoitre the best way up to A Coy in the advanced line and discuss with the officers what action to take in an emergency. Having returned to his section of line just before the intensification of the enemy bombardment, 2/Lt Geary then received news from a messenger (sent by Roupell) that reinforcements were urgently needed on the Hill. He quickly gathered his platoon together and led them forward, but because of the battered condition of the right communication trench, was unable to reach the advanced line by this route. Looking through a gap he saw several men of the Bedfords holding the left crater, although no trench was dug there. He rushed across the open, his men following, to join the Bedfords, who greeted their arrival with loud cheers. Geary placed his men around the inside of the rim of the crater and they held on grimly for several hours. The left crater was evidently one of the Germans' objectives, for intensive shelling around the crater began, though it seems no shells fell directly into the crater itself. The enemy's trenches were not far away and a steady fusilade of grenades was kept up against the British in the crater; the Germans also had a machine-gun trained on the only approach British reinforcements could use. The crater fast filled with dead and wounded and officers bringing up new men from both the Bedfords and the Surreys were becoming casualties at an alarming rate. The middle crater was held by neither side and had been subjected to steady shelling and bombing throughout the day. Geary himself recounted: 'I discovered I was the only officer untouched on that part of the Hill, and was the only one who lasted the whole time from 5 p.m. till nearly dawn.' It seemed to Geary that they must eventually be completely cut off.

In the meantime the Germans had begun moving up their old communication trenches, one of which led up to the left crater. Geary took a number of rifles, and with the assistance of Pte White of C Coy, who reloaded the rifles as fast as he could, fired into the enemy who were barely 10 yards away and could only advance up the communication trench in single file. Eventually, the Germans abandoned this attempt, though others had approached along another communication trench which led to the right of the middle crater, thus enabling the enemy to fire into the backs of some of Geary's men on the left. 2/Lt Geary organized his men to counter this attack, shooting the Germans down at close range and causing them to retire back to the point where the communication trench joined the advanced line. Having repelled this attack, Geary was anxious to know the situation on his flanks. He sent a corporal and two men to Lt Clarke, commanding D Coy, and he himself made his way across the summit to the advanced line. His messengers never reached D Coy, though Geary was relieved to find 2/Lt Davis of the 1st East Surreys and an officer of the Bedford Regiment with men of both regiments in A Coy's trench. The three officers conferred and decided that they could not sacrifice the Hill until they were sure there was no one behind to support them. Geary set off to make further investigation of the situation and on his way met Maj. P.T. Lees, who was bringing forward his battalion of the Queen Victoria's Rifles (QVR) with orders to recapture the portion of the advanced line reportedly occupied by the Germans. Geary gave a full report of the situation as he saw it and Maj. Lees arranged for a joint attack by Geary's men and the QVR to drive the enemy from the left of the forward line. On the signal of two or three flare lights, Geary's group was to rush across the middle crater while the QVR charged on the right. Geary then returned to his men and directed them to dig a trench to the rear of, and commanding, the middle crater. This work was in progress, despite their exposed position, when a German flare light went up, revealing the Germans at the left extremity of the advanced line. As before, Geary ordered a private to load for him while he fired on them, forcing them well back into their old communication trench, from which they continued to hurl grenades into the left of the British advanced line. Having left men to cover the position, 2/Lt Geary made his way back to the left crater, encountering on the way a party of QVR with ammunition, which he directed to the men in the crater, who were in sore need of it, their bandoliers being almost empty. He had been expecting the signal from Maj. Lee and as this had not been forthcoming set off to find him. Maj. Lee explained that an attack was now unnecessary because at about midnight the Germans had evacuated the advanced trench they had previously occupied, but they were still close to it in their communication trench and were keeping up a furious hail of grenades, making it difficult for the British to hold the areas of trench so recently regained. Geary again returned to his men in the left crater, but felt that without strong and swift reinforcement they would be compelled to retreat and dig themselves in at the rear of the left crater, as he had done with other men behind the middle crater. He set off once again to find Maj. Lee and inform him of the situation as dawn was beginning to break; however, he never reached him for he was severely wounded in the head by a bullet which cost him the sight of one eye. He recalls: 'at one time stopping for a moment and literally nearly weeping with pride to watch how these Englishmen were behaving. They were all simply grand.' He was awarded the VC, which was gazetted on 15 October 1915, for 'the splendid personal gallantry and example' he had shown. He was decorated by King George V at Buckingham Palace on 9 December 1915.

❖ ❖ ❖

Benjamin Handley Geary was born on 29 June 1891 in Surrey, the son of the Revd Henry and Mrs Geary (née Alport). He was educated at Dulwich College Preparatory School, St Edmund's School, Canterbury, and entered Keble College, Oxford, in 1910, graduating with a BA just as war broke out. He was in the Officer Training Corps at Oxford and was commissioned as 2/Lt at the outbreak of war, being sent to 4th Battalion East Surrey Regiment on 15 August 1914. He went to France in September and was attached to the 1st East Surreys in October. He won the VC some six months later on 20/21 April 1915 and was severely injured, losing the sight of one eye. He was invalided home where he did ground work for the Royal Flying Corps in England. He was made a lieutenant on 1 September 1915 and returned to France in 1916. After a spell engaged in instruction work he rejoined his battalion in 1917 and after three months' active service in Italy again returned to France. He was promoted to captain on 29 April 1918, a rank he held until 28 May 1919. During the opening days of the advance to victory, on 21 August 1918 the 1st East Surreys were in action near the Arras–Albert railway north of Irles, with Capt. B.H. Geary commanding D Coy.

It was here that Geary was wounded; a letter from his elder brother, Mr H.M. Geary, written on 18 January 1956, relates his VC brother's return to action after the head wound received on Hill 60: '. . . after his recovery [he] wormed his way back into his regiment and received his Captaincy, and received a triple wound when leading his men on the Somme under General Byng. He was carried back by German prisoners and a transfusion of blood saved his life.'

Capt. Geary was just recovering when the Armistice was signed. He received an MA from Oxford the same year, and studied at Wycliffe Hall which specialized in theological training; shortly after Geary entered the Church. He attended the garden party at Buckingham Palace on 26 June 1920 and later that year was present at the Cenotaph on 11 November. In 1921 he became curate of West Ham and on 10 June 1922, at Holy Trinity Church, Marylebone, London, he married Ruth Christiana Woakes, who later bore him two sons. In April 1923 he attended with other members of the British Legion the unveiling by HRH the Prince of Wales of the tomb of the Belgian Unknown Warrior at Brussels. On 5 October 1923 Geary was appointed Temporary Chaplain to the Forces, serving first at Portsmouth then at Aldershot, having become Chaplain to the Forces in 1926, a post which he held until 1927. On 23 August that year the Revd B.H. Geary VC, Church of England Chaplain to the troops at Ewshott Camp, Aldershot Command, was bound over at Odiham Police Court on a serious charge. The *London Gazette* stated on 30 September 1927 that Geary resigned his commission. He was granted the rank of captain and in May 1928 he left for Canada, settling in Toronto. At this time Geary became a Travelling Secretary for a peace mission, the World Alliance for International Friendship. He returned to England to attend the British Legion VCs dinner at the House of Lords on 9 November 1929, sailing back on the *Duchess of Atholl* on 22 November. In 1930 Geary began working for the Continental Life Assurance Company. His wife suddenly left him in December 1930, and he learnt in 1933 that she was living with Mr James Courtenay Sherren at Palmer's Green. By 1 August 1934 a decree nisi was granted in the divorce court. His wife did not defend the suit and costs were awarded against Mr Sherren; in 1935 the couple married.

The year 1935 was an eventful one for Geary; in January he was one of two VC holders in line for the position of Sergeant-at-Arms in the Ontario Legislature. He was given the post, becoming Sergeant-at-Arms and Historian of the Canadian Legislature. He also married again, to Constance Joan Henderson-Cleland.

The Toronto Globe reported on 19 April 1935 that Geary was on the staff of the Ontario Securities Commission and had been appointed to assist in the organization of the Toronto Better Business Bureau Incorporated. From 1937 he was on the staff of the Canadian National Institute for the Blind.

On Monday 22 May 1939 he was one of eight VCs presented to their Majesties King George VI and Queen Elizabeth at Queen's Park, Toronto.

He joined the Legion of Frontiersmen, Toronto, in 1939 and in 1940 was appointed major, second in command of Newmarket military training camp, Ontario, serving with the Canadian Army until 1945. In Toronto he was again presented to visiting royalty in October 1951, this time to the future Queen Elizabeth II and Prince Philip. His address at this time was The Cottage, Woodbridge, Ontario.

Geary returned to England to parade with the Canadian contingent at the VC Centenary Review on 26 June 1956, and attended the reception at the Mansion House, London, the following day. He represented Canada on the VC and GC Association Committee and attended the bi-annual reunions in London, being present at the association's second dinner on 7 July 1962; the following day he joined fellow members at the third dinner of the VC and GC Association at the Café Royal. His last attendance was on 15 July 1964 when he came from Canada for the Commemorative Service at St Martin-in-the-Fields and the fourth Association dinner at the Café Royal.

During his years in Canada he led an active life and was involved in a wide range of organizations, many with military links. By the end of his life he could boast of being an ex-President of the Imperial Officers' Association of Canada; a Governor in the Canadian Corps of Commissionaires; a Director of Kingsley Hall (Toronto) for Men; an Honorary

Member of the University Club of Toronto, the Empire Club, the Aitken Club, the Canadian Officers' Club and Military Institute, the Civilian Club, the Royal Canadian Military Institute, and the Royal Society of St George. He was also a Life Member of the Canadian Legion and ex-President of their Woodbridge Branch, and a member of St George's Society and, of course, of the VC and GC Association. His VC is held by the Canadian War Museum in Ottawa, Ontario, Canada. He died on 26 May 1976 in Canada, aged 84 years 11 months.

G.H. WOOLLEY

Hill 60, Belgium, 20/21 April

At 21.30 hours on 20 April A and C Coys of the 9th Bn, The London Regiment (Queen Victoria's Rifles) of 13th Bde, 5th Div., advanced from their trenches to take up positions near the top of Hill 60. They were commanded by Maj. Lees and Capt. Westby respectively. The German bombardment was so intensive at this time that it took the QVR companies two hours to traverse the 200 yards to their allocated position, digging themselves in close to the right hand crater. Towards midnight Sgt E.H. Pulleyn QVR was ordered to fill a gap in the British trench line on the very crest of the hill with a force of sixteen men; eleven made it to the position with Sgt Pulleyn but five fell wounded almost immediately; the remainder were soon forced to rejoin their comrades in their original position. By this time both Maj. Lees and Capt. Westby had been killed, and two-thirds of the 150 riflemen who had followed them had fallen. Despite constant enemy attacks throughout the night, the QVR men held on. As day began to break just thirty men were left.

At this critical moment an officer was seen making his way towards them, sometimes running, sometimes going to ground, sometimes crawling forward through the deluge of shells and bullets. Incredibly Lt Woolley slid unharmed over the parapet and joined the riflemen, immediately taking command. He saw a supply of 'jam-pot bombs' and borrowing a box of matches from 2/Lt Summerhayes to light the fuses, he proceeded to lob them over the brow of the crater, with some of the men acting as observers to direct his throws. 2/Lt Summerhayes was killed immediately after handing over his match-box (which, incidentally, is now in the Regimental Museum), leaving Lt Woolley, the only surviving officer on this part of the hill, in charge of the defence of two craters. At intervals various runners brought up boxes of Hales grenades which Woolley employed to keep the enemy back, his grenade-throwing being supplemented by rapid fire from the men around him. Two NCOs, Pulleyn and Peabody, supported Woolley's defence of the craters, despite the growing number of casualties. They each earned themselves a DCM for their bravery. An officer arrived from QVR HQ with a verbal order, and later a written order, for Woolley to bring back all the men of his regiment. He refused to comply until he was properly relieved as there were so few surviving men of other regiments left on the Hill. Woolley recounts in his autobiography, *Sometimes a Soldier*, that he was near to becoming a casualty himself when a small German egg-type hand-grenade struck him on the head; fortunately the blast went upwards and outwards, stunning him momentarily and tearing two large rents in his cap, but otherwise leaving him unscathed. The German field-guns continued to sweep away the earth rim of the craters and the men behind it, though as night fell the shelling quietened a little. Frantic requests for British artillery to reply to the German bombardment received little success owing to the fact the British batteries had suffered casualties comparable to those of the infantry.

At dawn on the 21st an officer of the Devons, who were on Woolley's left, reached him with orders to go to Trench 38 (see map on page 64) by the railway cutting to bring up a bombing section of the Northumberland Fusiliers. Woolley found there sixty 'trained bombers, with a plentiful supply of bombs', whom he led up to man the craters in support of the Devons. He then brought back the fourteen survivors of the original

150 men of A Coy who had gone into action just two days earlier. The Battalion *War Diary* is very prosaic concerning these eventful days, merely listing the number of dead, wounded and missing, though it is clear that the sacrifices of the QVR did not go unrecognized at the time, for the *War Diary* concludes its three line entry for 19-22 April with the following: 'Bn. relieved and addressed by Gen. Sir H. Smith-Dorrien in Field S. off VLAMERTINGHE road.' Lt Woolley was awarded the VC for his 'conspicuous bravery', becoming the first Territorial officer to receive the coveted Cross.

Geoffrey Harold Woolley was born at St Peter's Vicarage, Bethnal Green, London, on 14 May 1892, one of ten children of the Revd George Herbert Woolley and his wife Sarah (née Cathcart). He was educated at Parmiter's School, near Victoria Park, London, St John's School, Leatherhead, and at Queen's College, Oxford. Woolley joined the Army on 4 August 1914 as a second lieutenant in the 5th Bn, The Essex Regiment, then in training near Drayton, Norfolk. After the division of the Essex Territorial Brigade, Woolley transferred to the 9th Bn The London Regiment (Queen Victoria's Rifles), going overseas with them on 4 November 1914, and entering the trenches for the first time at the end of that month between Neuve Eglise and Wulverghem. During this period a newspaper reported (incorrectly) that he was awarded the VC for 'throwing a live bomb out of a trench and so saving men's lives'. He did throw out over the trench parapet a 'dud' mortar-bomb which had attracted the curiosity of some men after it had landed in the trench, but the award would be for his deeds at Hill 60 on 20/21 April 1915. After returning to 'rest' after the defence of Hill 60, Woolley found himself back in the area preparing to attack the Germans. On 23 April Woolley was badly affected by a fresh release of gas while preparing to move his company forward, but remained with his men, going into the line two days later. He was made a captain on 26 April. The 13th Bde was withdrawn a week later and while at rest Woolley's poor condition caused him to be sent to an officers' rest station where he learned of the award of the VC. A fortnight later he rejoined his regiment, only to be harangued by the senior MO who had ordered him to be sent to England. Woolley was sent to No. 2 Red Cross Hospital at Rouen and was eventually moved to the officers' hospital at Osborne on the Isle of Wight. Shortly afterwards he returned to his retired father's home, an Elizabethan farmhouse, Old Riffhams, Danbury, Essex, to rest his 'shattered nerves'. After weeks spent recuperating he was invited to help with the training of Cambridge University OTC and run courses for Territorial and 'New Army' officers.

In September 1915 Woolley was passed fit for active service and rejoined the QVR, now in the line at Bray, on the Somme. Being the junior company commander he was detailed in February 1916 to attend the first course of instruction organized by the Fourth Army at Flixecourt. He impressed them so much that he was told to remain as instructor at the new Third Army Infantry School at Auxi-le-Château, where he remained for five months; there he met the Revd Studdert-Kennedy, better known as 'Woodbine Willie', who joined the school as Chaplain. Woolley's organizational skills were obvious and he was appointed GSO 3 at Third Army HQ in August 1916. He was reallocated to the Infantry School in December and later he was moved to act as special staff officer to General Robertson, 17th Div., immediately after the German attack on 21 March 1918; he rejoined Third Army HQ as GSO 3 on 21 April 1918.

Woolley was granted leave in June, returning home to marry Janet Culme-Seymour, the widow of a good friend, George, the son of Admiral Sir Michael Culme-Seymour, who was present at the church at Danbury to see the couple married, the service being taken by Woolley's father.

He returned to Third Army HQ where he served until the Armistice, doing liaison work with the troops of 4th Corps, and earning himself a Mention in Despatches on 23 December 1918 and a Military Cross which was gazetted on 3 June 1919. Woolley was demobilized in March 1919, returning to Oxford University to take an MA. His wife already had a son and a daughter from her first marriage but was to bear her new husband a son in 1919 and a daughter in 1921. After gaining his Master's degree he was ordained in December

1920 in Coventry Cathedral and became an assistant master at Rugby School in 1920. Earlier that year he attended the garden party at Buckingham Palace on 26 June, and the ceremony at the Cenotaph on 11 November. He also dedicated the QVR memorial on Hill 60. From 1923 to 1926 Woolley was vicar of Monk Sherborne, near Basingstoke, prior to becoming assistant master and chaplain at Harrow School in 1927, a position he held for twelve years. He was present at the VC dinner at the House of Lords on 9 November 1929.

During the Second World War he was senior chaplain to the troops in Algiers. His son, Rollo, born in 1919, was a Spitfire pilot and was killed in a dog-fight over Tunis in early December 1942. Woolley's wife had been in poor health for some time and died of pneumonia in London in February 1943. In May he fell ill himself with pleurisy and pneumonia, contracting dysentery while in hospital. He slowly recovered and was awarded the OBE in the same year 'in recognition of gallant and distinguished services in North Africa' where he was known as the 'Woodbine Willie of Algiers'. He was vicar of Harrow from 1944 until 1952. He was married for the second time, on 12 June 1945, to Elisabeth (Betty) Nichols, daughter of Alfred Nichols of Worthing. She later bore him a son, Nicholas. In April 1952 he received a surprise visit from Queen Mary, whom he conducted on a brief tour of his church, St Mary's, Harrow. On 26 June 1956 he attended the Guildhall VC reception.

Woolley retained his military connections, being involved in various groups and attending important functions. He was President of the Harrow Branch of the British Legion, and of the Old Contemptibles' Association. As Vice-Chairman of the VC and GC Association, and later serving on its committee, he was present at the following reunions and dinners: The first dinner of the VC Association held on 24 July 1958; the second dinner on 7 July 1960; the garden party and banquet on 17 July 1962, and the third VC Association dinner held the following day; the review of the Old Contemptibles at Buckingham Palace on 26 June 1964. In 1964 he also attended the service at St Martin-in-the-Fields on 15 July, met the prime minister at No. 10 Downing Street later that day, and enjoyed the fourth Association dinner the next day.

Woolley had displayed great energy and concern for the welfare of others throughout his life, which had been recognised by the awarding of an OBE. He wrote several books, including an autobiography called *Sometimes a Soldier*, which was published in 1963. He died peacefully on 10 December 1968 at Hunter's Barn, West Chiltington, near Pulborough, Sussex. The funeral was held at noon at St Mary's Church, West Chiltington, on Saturday 14 December, and a Memorial Service was given at St Martin-in-the-Fields on 23 January 1969.

On 6 June 2007 a new memorial plaque was dedicated in St George's Church, Ypres, Belgium. After prayers and readings, the dedication was made to Second Lieutenant G. H. Woolley VC and 103 former students of Parmiter's School who gave their lives in the 1914/1918 War. The wording on the Memorial Plaque reads as follows:

PARMITER'S SCHOOL
In Honoured Memory of the 103 Old Parmiterian's
who gave their lives on Active Service during World War I
and
Second Lieutenant Geoffrey Harold Woolley VC OBE MC

E. DWYER

Hill 60, Belgium, 21 April

On 19 April Pte Edward Dwyer of B Coy 1st East Surreys was in a trench just to the north-north-east of Hill 60. Ahead and slightly to the right of the company's position was a German strongpoint (marked Z on the map on page 40), which stood at the end of a sap extending from the enemy trenches. The Germans had made several determined attacks and had heavily shelled the whole area since the 17th.

The British intention was to move B Coy forward at dusk on 20 April to relieve A Coy in the advanced line, but the change-over never took place because a concerted effort by the enemy to retake the hill developed in the afternoon, the brunt of which was borne by A Coy in the forward positions. However, at 15.00 hours, about an hour before the main German thrust began, enemy infantrymen attempted to advance from their sap near the strongpoint Z to the shell-pitted area to B Coy's right. The attacking troops were protected by their snipers in the strongpoint, and there was a real risk that the company's trench could be overrun, thereby jeopardizing the rest of B Coy's position and the trenches behind. Dwyer found himself alone in his section of trench, apart from the dead and wounded, with the Germans only 15 or 20 yards distant and throwing grenades at his trench; he swiftly gathered all the grenades he could find, 'about three hundred in all' according to his description in *The War Budget* of 8 July 1915, and because he was 'in a dead funk at the idea of being taken prisoner', he climbed on to the parapet, stood up and began throwing grenades at the Germans at a furious rate. His appearance in this exposed position brought a hail of bombs from the Germans whose aim seemed to be spoiled by their surprise at Dwyer's reaction and his accurate and effective grenade throwing. He succeeded single-handedly in keeping the Germans at bay until reinforcements arrived, and remarkably he emerged from the fray unscathed, having saved his trench. He recounted that the 'relieving party chipped me a lot and called me "The King of the Hand Grenades"'.

Earlier in the day he had shown great gallantry, leaving the safety of the trench during a heavy bombardment to bandage wounded comrades. On 27 April Dwyer was wounded in the head by 'a flying piece of shrapnel' and while he was recovering in hospital a month later, he learned of his award of the VC, which was gazetted on 22 May. He was decorated by King George V at Buckingham Palace on 28 June 1915, being accompanied by his old friend Father Browne whom he had known since the age of seven. He was promoted to lance-corporal and also received the Russian Cross of St George 4th Class.

Edward Dwyer was born in 1895 at 4 Cassidy Road, Fulham, London, the son of Mr James Dwyer, a private builder. He was baptized Edwin at St Thomas' Roman Catholic Church and attended St Thomas' Parish School. He lived with his parents at 30 Lintaine Grove, Fulham. He was apparently below average height (5ft 3½in), describing himself as 'a very little chap', and worked as a greengrocer's assistant before running away from home in the summer of 1912 aged sixteen. He had run away from home shortly after the banns were published for his father's marriage to his mother, Mary Ann. It seems he could not bear the shame of discovering his illegitimacy. Lying about his age and calling himself Edward, he enlisted in the Army at Kingston-on-Thames, entering the 1st Bn East Surrey Regiment. He was with his battalion in Dublin, recovering in hospital from VD, when war broke out, and embarked for France on 13 August 1914 as part of the BEF. Dwyer took part in all the major engagements, including the Retreat from Mons. He won his VC on 21 April at Hill 60 and, after recovering from a wound received a week later, returned to England on leave. Being modest he kept his arrival home a secret for three days before being 'discovered' and then Fulham turned out in force to welcome their hero, who was fêted enthusiastically, being celebrated, at the age of 19, as the youngest VC of the war and being dubbed in the Press as 'The Little Corporal'. He made several public appearances and attended recruiting drives, not only talking about his own war service but mentioning that of his family; his father James had enlisted in the ASC at the age of 50, and his elder brother James was in the RND in Salonika; his younger brother Andrew was in hospital having been wounded while on active service in the Dardanelles. He later died. Dwyer was engaged on a recruiting campaign for six months.

On 20 December 1915 L/Cpl Dwyer secretly married Maude Barrett-Freeman (whom he called Billie), a 21-year-old Red Cross nurse who had tended Dwyer in a French hospital when he was wounded. She was the daughter of John Barrett-Freeman, a farmer, and she lived at 5 Glenfield Road,

Balham, at the time of the marriage. The service was a quiet affair held at Dwyer's local church, which he had known all his life, the ceremony being conducted by his long-time friend Father D. Browne at St Thomas's Roman Catholic Church, Rylston Road, Fulham. Dwyer told his mother the next day.

It would seem that he had some premonition that he might not return home again. Before leaving for the Front, Dwyer left his VC with Father Brown, telling him, 'The general rule is that a VC gets knocked out the second time'. Having been promoted lance-corporal on 24 April 1915 in recognition of his feat, he then became acting corporal on 27 December. Apart from the recruiting drives he also made a recording entitled 'With our boys at the Front', which was available on record but is still extant on tape and CD entitled 'The Great War'. He rejoined his battalion on active service in France early in 1916, and his wife resumed nursing, using her maiden name. Promoted to corporal on 27 July, Dwyer was killed on 3 September 1916 while leading his men in an attack that the battalion *War Diary* says began at noon that day near Guillemont on the Somme. A solemn High Mass was celebrated at St Thomas's Roman Catholic Church on Sunday 17 September.

A mural medallion, representing the bust of the young hero in relief, was unveiled at the Fulham Central Library on Saturday 28 December 1918. The bulk of the cost was met by subscription by local schoolchildren. The proceedings began with the national anthem, followed with 'The Lord is mindful of His own' sung by Miss Christine Gordon. Sir Francis Lloyd, the former military commander of the London district, drew back the spacious flag that covered the medallion. Beneath was an inscription giving the details of Dwyer's bravery. It reads:

IN GRATEFUL MEMORY / CORPORAL EDWARD DWYER V.C. / A FULHAM LAD EAST SURREY REGIMENT / KILLED IN ACTION 3RD SEPT. 1916 AGED 20 / HE GAINED THE VICTORIA CROSS FOR / CONSPICOUS BRAVERY AND DEVOTION / TO DUTY AT HILL 60 FRANCE APRIL / 1915 IN

DISPERSING GERMANS BY HAND- / GRENADES
AND BANDAGING UNDER / SHELL-FIRE WOUNDED
COMRADES.

The memorial can still be seen in its original location. His
other medals were retained by the War Office as his legatees
could not be traced.

In 1962, after the death of Canon Brown, Dwyer's VC was
discovered among the Canon's effects by the Revd Edward J.
Hinsley, who contacted the War Office. As a result the VC
was presented to the Regimental Museum of the East Surrey
Regt at Kingston in March 1962. The youngest VC of the war
up to April 1915, Dwyer is buried in Flatiron Copse Military
Cemetery, France, in Plot III, Row J, Grave 3.

On 11 November 1996 the Public Record Office in Kew
opened an exhibition which included copies of Pte Dwyer's
Army papers and his story appeared in several newspapers at
about the same time.

THE BATTLES OF YPRES, 1915

In April 1915 the Ypres Salient was held by the British 27th and 28th Divs and 1st Canadian Div. north to the St Julien–Poelcappelle road where French troops of the 45th Algerian and 87th Territorial Divs continued the line east to the Ypres Canal.

When the Germans released poison gas on the northern sector in the early evening of 22 April the men of the two French divisions retreated in the face of this unknown weapon, and enemy infantry, following the gas cloud, advanced 2 miles southward. The gap of more than 4 miles from the original Canadian left flank to the Canal was gradually filled during the night with British and Canadian battalions, although the defensive line remained far from continuous.

Counter-attacks made against the new German line during the 23rd were unsuccessful and early on 24 April a further enemy gas attack was made, this time against the 1st Canadian Div. who, despite fighting gallantly, were forced to yield ground on Gravenstafel Ridge. A British counter-attack directed at St Julien failed in the face of enemy machine-gun fire, the troops sustaining heavy casualties.

The Lahore Div. was moved into the salient and attacked German trenches on Mauser Ridge, north of Ypres, on 26 April, in concert with French troops on its left. Shelling, machine-gun fire and gas halted the attackers before the German positions were reached; a similar fate befell an attack the next day by other battalions of the Lahore Div. In both attacks very heavy losses were incurred.

On 27 April Gen. Sir Horace Smith-Dorrien, the British Second Army Commander, advised Sir John French that a withdrawal of British and Canadian troops from the eastern part of the salient to a new line nearer Ypres was necessary so that a more defensible line could be held. French, who did not like Smith-Dorrien, took the opportunity to relieve him of command and replaced him with Gen. Sir Horace Plumer. Within days Plumer was instructed by French to carry out a withdrawal along the lines suggested by Smith-Dorrien, and by the night of 3 May the new line was established close to Ypres.

There was a lull in the fighting until 8 May when strong German attacks on the new line at Frezenberg Ridge virtually annihilated the British 84th Bde. Fierce fighting continued until 13 May, with the enemy having gained more than half a mile of ground west of Frezenberg.

British casualties for the Second Battle of Ypres approached 59,000, with the 1st Canadian Div. losing one-third of its fighting strength. German losses for the same period were fewer than 35,000.

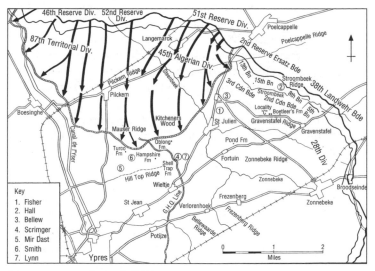

German gas attack, April 1915

F. FISHER

St Julien, Belgium, 23 April

On 22 April 1915 the 13th and 15th Bns, 3rd Canadian Infantry Brigade (CIB), were holding the front line trenches north of the River Stroombeek; on 13th Bn's left was the 45th Algerian Div. south of Poelcappelle on the Poelcappelle–St Julien Road. At 17.00 hours the Canadian sentries saw a yellow-green cloud, low to the ground, drifting towards their lines from the German trenches on a front from Steenstraat to Poelcappelle (see map on page 89). The cloud turned out to be chlorine gas, released from cylinders on the signal of three red flares dropped from a German aircraft. It took less than eight minutes for the cylinders to be emptied, by which time the gas had reached the French trenches.

Shortly after releasing the gas the Germans launched a fierce artillery bombardment; this was followed at 17.20 hours by an assault by the *51st Reserve Div.* who clambered over their parapets, many wearing gauze and cotton masks to protect them from the poisonous fumes. Some German soldiers were reluctant to keep close up to the gas cloud, and officers were seen by the French using the flats of their swords as 'encouragement'.

Resistance was very limited among the Algerians who were understandably terrified by this horrific new weapon which caused many of them to fall to the ground writhing in agony, unable to breathe. The Algerians' retreat left the 13th Bn with its left flank on the St Julien–Poelcappelle road unsupported. There was a gap of over 2,000 yards to St Julien, where its reserve company, two platoons of No. 3 Coy and Bn HQ, were situated. In the middle of this gap, in an orchard some 500 yards north of St Julien, was a battery of 18-pounders, commanded by Maj. W.B.M. King, 10th (St Catherine's) Battery CFA. King, on his own initiative (the shelling had cut telephone communication and no orders were getting through), opened fire on the German front line trenches at 17.45 hours. Although badly affected by the gas, the battery was able to keep firing while large numbers of Algerians streamed through the gun positions. At 19.00 hours a large force of Germans was spotted by a French NCO who had stopped at the battery, marching south 200 to 300 yards to the west of the road, their helmets visible over a hedge. Reversing one section of guns, Maj. King opened fire on this target, forcing the German troops to stop and dig in. Maj. King's request to the infantry for help brought a party of sixty men, drawn from 14th and 15th Bns, under Lt G.W. Stairs, together with a Colt machine-gun from the 13th Bn HQ in St Julien. No 24066 Frederick Fisher, having just recovered from a wound received a few days earlier, was in charge of this machine-gun. He made his way to a position in front of the graveyard in St Julien and then worked forward to an isolated building which commanded the ground to the north and west where the Germans were entrenching. Once in the building, he brought his gun into action, thus effectively stopping the German advance and probably saving the guns of the 10th Bty. For this he was awarded the Victoria Cross, as reported in the Supplement to the *London Gazette*, No 29202, dated 22 June 1915. The date of the action is given in the citation as 23 April, but this seems to be incorrect, although Fisher was again in action on this date.

The 10th Bty kept up an intermittent fire until nearly 22.00 hours when Maj. King was able to extricate it and by 23.00 hours all his guns had been withdrawn from their very exposed position. Meanwhile, Fisher, having lost four of his original gun-team as casualties, returned to St Julien and obtained volunteers from the 14th Bn with whom he again went forward in an attempt to reach his battalion. He reached the front line positions where the 13th Bn was holding on, with some Canadians now lining the Poelcappelle road at right angles to their original front. Fisher had become separated from his team while setting up his machine-gun when he was killed on 23 April. Fisher's military record notes that the correct date of death is 24 April 1915 so it would seem likely that Fisher was killed after midnight.

An account of Fisher's heroism, contained in a letter written by Lt Edward W. Waud Jnr, was published in the *Montreal Star* on 24 June 1915:

> Fred Fisher and many other poor chaps of our battalion are lying dead near St Julien. 'Bud' made a famous name for himself. He was in charge of a gun team in reserve in the little village of St Julien. When word of the attack on our line came back he took his team and gun and started for the front trenches. No one knew the way, but came upon some artillery trying to get some big guns out under heavy fire. He set up his machine-gun and covered their retirement. Proceeding forward again he cleared a bit of a wood of Germans, becoming separated from most of his team. He then took charge of a French machine-gun that had been abandoned, and got it working. He finally found our battalion, and reported to Lieut. J.G. Ross, the MG Officer. He was mounting the gun on the parapet when he was hit in the chest, dying instantly. Lieut. Ross and some of the other officers buried him in the trench.'

L/Cpl Fisher's body was not recovered and his name appears on the Menin Gate Memorial to the Missing at Ypres.

Frederick Fisher was born at Church Street, St Catherines, Ontario, on 3 August 1894. He had two older brothers, Don and William, and an elder sister, Alice, and in 1900 the family moved to Niagara-on-the-Lake where his father was manager of the Sovereign Bank. Frederick commenced his schooling at the Niagara Public School until the Fisher family moved again, in 1904, to Dunnville, where they stayed until about 1907 before moving to Montreal. Here Fisher attended Westmount Academy where a life-sized coloured photograph of him hangs in the rebuilt Westmount High School. In the Westmount Academy Yearbook of 1909 'Bud' Fisher was described as 'hard as nails' on the football field.

In 1912 Fisher enrolled at McGill University to study Applied Science (Engineering) and he was still a student when war broke out. He was academically capable and a keen sportsman, being a member of the 1914 championship track team as well as the Montreal Amateur Athletics Association.

On 6 August 1914 Fisher enlisted as a private in the 5th Regt (Royal Highlanders of Canada) and sailed from Valcartier, Quebec, on the *Alaunia*; she was one of the newest ships in the convoy, having been built for Cunard in 1913. Her cargo of 2,062 officers and men disembarked at Plymouth on 15 October 1914; they included the 13th Bn CEF (45 officers and 1,110 other ranks), to which unit Fisher now belonged.

During the battalion's training period on the muddy Salisbury Plain, Fisher was promoted to lance-corporal on 22 December 1914, and on 11 February 1915 he embarked with his battalion on the *Novian* at Avonmouth, arriving at St Nazaire on 16 February. After a long railway journey to Hazebrouck the battalion encamped at Flêtre on 19 February, beginning their first tour of duty in March 1915.

Fisher's VC was sent by the War Office on 5 August 1915 to his parents at 576 Lansdown Road, Westmount, Canada, and on 25 April 1916 a ceremony was held in the McGill Union when the picture of L/Cpl Frederick Fisher VC was unveiled. His parents and sister were present and his mother proudly wore her son's VC. On the same day the McGill Annual was published, and was dedicated to Fisher, the first Canadian to win the Victoria Cross in the First World War and the first of three to be awarded to the 13th Bn CEF.

A memorial tablet was unveiled at the Royal Highlanders of Canada Armouries, Bleury Street, Montreal, on 1 May 1917 and on 12 June in the same year a memorial service was held at the Church of St James the Apostle. In 1970 a plaque was unveiled at Memorial Park, St Paul Street West, St Catherines, by the Royal Canadian Legion, and a wreath was laid on behalf of the Fisher family by Kathleen E. Ball of Niagara-on-the-Lake. Fisher's VC remained with the family until the death of his mother in 1946 when his sister, Alice, presented it to The Royal Highland Regiment of Canada.

Fisher's two brothers both served with the Canadian Forces, Don with the 5th Bn's automobile section. William was awarded the Military Cross while serving with the Montreal Heavy Artillery. Both brothers died after the war from the effects of their war service. A painting of L/Cpl Fisher by George J. Coates is held by the Canadian War Museum.

F.W. HALL

Near Ypres, Belgium, 24 April

The 8th Bn CEF had moved up to the front line during the evening of 15 April 1915 and took over positions from the French. The battalion found the front to be a series of unconnected lengths of shallow (2 foot deep) trenches with inadequate 4 foot breastworks, a few strands of wire and no traversing. The Canadians spent the next few days improving their trenches and making them more habitable.

Over forty casualties were inflicted on the 8th Bn by German shelling on 22 April, the day of the first gas attack; however, no gas was released on their front and the German infantry did not attack.

The line held by the 2nd Canadian Infantry Brigade (CIB) ran from Berlin Wood across the Gravenstafel–Passchendaele road, and north-west along the valley of the River Stroombeek; it was extended by the 3rd CIB to the newly created salient astride the Keerselaere–Poelcappelle road, some 800 yards from Poelcappelle. The right of the 2nd CIB front was held by the 5th Bn almost up to the Stroombeek, and continued by the 8th Bn which joined up with the 15th Bn of the 3rd CIB.

On the night of 23 April, camp kettles full of water were set in the front line and the 8th Bn made sure that every man had a cotton bandolier to dip in the water to offer them some protection should gas be released on their sector. Three companies were in the front line, with half of C Coy in close support and the remaining two platoons, commanded by

Capt. Bertram and Lt O'Grady, further back in dug-outs 200 yards south of Bn HQ at Boetleer Farm. No 1539 CSM Frederick Hall was in Lt O'Grady's platoon (see map on page 89).

At 03.30 hours the following morning a German heavy artillery barrage was launched all along the line and at 04.00 hours sentries saw several Germans, wearing what looked like mine-rescue helmets, climb over their parapets carrying hoses. The British troops watched as what they thought was smoke drifted across no-man's-land, but it quickly changed to a green colour as it was carried towards the Canadian trenches by the light wind. The artillery bombardment continued for another ten minutes before lifting to shell the support areas, by which time the gas was rolling across the front line trenches. Lt-Col. Lipsett of the 8th Bn had telephoned an SOS to his supporting artillery as soon as the gas was reported and immediately a heavy shrapnel fire was opened on the German front where the composite brigade of the *53rd Reserve Division* was now advancing behind the gas cloud, causing heavy losses.

The improvised respirators, organized the previous evening, did provide some protection and the advancing German troops were met with a withering fire from those men remaining unaffected by gas. To add to the Canadians' problems, their notoriously unreliable Ross rifles were jamming and men wept in frustration as they used their boots and entrenching tools in order to try and loosen the bolts. The gas cloud passed over the right of the 15th Bn and the left of the 8th Bn and it was here, at the junction between the two battalions, that the *4th Reserve Ersatz Infantry Regt* broke through the stricken Canadians. Lt-Col. Lipsett ordered his reserve half company, C, to try to plug this gap of more than 100 yards. Very few of the men from C Coy reached the gap and those who did witnessed the appalling sight of the gassed survivors of A Coy, 15th Bn, vainly trying to escape the choking gas. Not a single officer survived from A Coy which was virtually wiped out; a similar fate befell C Coy on their left. Having been ordered by telephone to protect at all costs 'Locality C' (the oddly named crest of Gravenstafel Ridge, 800 yards east of Boetleer Farm), Lipsett called up his last remaining reserve, the two remaining platoons of C Coy at

Boetleer Farm, to plug the gap on his left flank. The time was now about 09.00 hours.

Under very heavy fire these platoons made their way forward, and when Lt O'Grady was killed in the advance, CSM Frederick Hall took charge of his platoon. He managed to get his men into position despite severe fire, crossing the 1,500 yards to the front line, then went back part of the way to bring in two wounded men, one after the other. Hearing the cries of a third man, Hall, together with Cpl Payne and Pte Rogerson, climbed out of their trench to attempt to rescue the wounded man, who was lying on an exposed raised bank some 15 yards behind the front line. Both Payne and Rogerson were wounded in the attempt and all three returned to their trench. After a few minutes, Hall again crawled out of the trench, this time alone, and managed to reach the injured man; still lying prone he hoisted the wounded man onto his back, and was about to return to the trench when he raised his head slightly to check his direction. A bullet hit him in the head, causing a fatal wound, and moments later the wounded man was also killed. For this act of courage Frederick Hall was awarded the Victoria Cross.

The only remaining reserve of the 2nd CIB, C Coy of 5th Bn, was rushed to the left to help, and despite considerable losses reached the front line trenches and the position was held.

The *London Gazette* of 22 June 1915 published the citation and Frederick Hall's VC was presented to Mrs M. Hall in Winnipeg, having been forwarded to Canada by the War Office on 5 August 1916. CSM Frederick Hall is commemorated on the Menin Gate Memorial to the Missing at Ypres as his body was never found.

Hall, a native of Ireland, was born in Kilkenny on 21 February 1885, the son of Bombadier F. Hall, and emigrated to Canada in about 1910, after having served for several years with the Cameronians (Scottish Rifles).

At the outbreak of war Hall was living in Winnipeg where he was employed as a clerk. He enlisted in the 106th Regt (Winnipeg Light Infantry), but later transferred to the 8th Bn

(90th Winnipeg Rifles), known as the 'Little Black Devils'. With the rest of the first Canadian contingent, the 8th Bn assembled at Valcartier Camp, Quebec, where it embarked on the *Franconia*. The convoy of thirty ships, together with escorts, sailed for England on 3 October 1914. The smooth crossing meant there was little demand for the 20,000 boxes of a secret mal-de-mer remedy in the medical stores, and the 2,310 officers and men on board (including 1,153 of the 8th Bn) disembarked at Plymouth on 15/16 October 1914. The next sixteen weeks were spent at Larkhill South Camp on Salisbury Plain, where above average rainfall and severe gales produced miserable conditions for the Canadians' stay in England. During this period of training Frederick Hall was first appointed acting sergeant on 22 October, and was promoted to colour sergeant on 1 December.

On 10 February the 8th Bn sailed on the *Archimedes* from Avonmouth, disembarking at St Nazaire on 13 February. A tedious railway journey lasting more than forty hours took the Canadians the 500 miles to Strazeele, where their induction into trench life on the Western Front began.

In 1925 Carolyn Cornell of the *Winnipeg Tribune* wrote a series of articles on Canadian Victoria Cross winners and suggested that Pine Street in Winnipeg, where Hall had been living, should be renamed. After some pressure from the Women's Canadian Club of Winnipeg, the City Council agreed and Pine Street was renamed Valour Road and commemorated with the erection of a bronze plaque on a lamp-post at Portage Avenue. This plaque commemorates three winners of the Victoria Cross in the First World War who were all living in the same block when they joined the CEF: CSM Frederick Hall VC, 8th Bn (WR), 24 April 1915, Ypres; L/Sgt Leo Clarke VC, 2nd Bn, 9 September 1916, Pozières; Capt. Robert Shankland VC, DCM, 43rd Bn (CH of C), 25 October 1917, Passchendaele.

Two of Frederick Hall's brothers also served in the First World War; Ed was a lance corporal in the 2nd Cameronians (Scottish Rifles) and Harry was a sergeant in the 10th Bn, CEF. The Menin Gate Memorial Register shows their mother, Mrs Mary Hall, living at 43 Union Street, Leytonstone, London, England. Hall's medals are in the possession of his family.

E.D. BELLEW

Near Keerselaere, Belgium, 24 April

At about the same time as CSM Hall was winning his Victoria Cross north of Boetleer Farm, Lt Bellew of the 7th Bn was fighting for his life less than a mile away at Vancouver crossroads (see map on page 89).

On 24 April 1915 the Canadians of the 8th and 15th Bns (CEF) were holding the trenches on the north-east of the River Stroombeek. To the left of the 15th Bn the line bent south-west, held by a company of 2nd East Kents, crossed the Poelcappelle road, then curved sharply southwards, running west of the villages of Keerselaere and St Julien, where the 13th Bn was positioned on the left of the East Kents; the trenches from Keerselaere to St Julien were occupied by the 7th Bn. At 04.00 hours the release of three red flares from a captive balloon near Westroosebeke signalled another gas attack by the Germans, affecting a front of over 1,000 yards.

The German artillery bombardment, begun an hour before, continued until ten minutes after the release of the gas; when the bombardment ceased German infantry advanced towards the Canadians. The enemy had a numerical superiority of about twenty-four battalions to eight, with the Canadians having the equivalent of only four companies as reserves. By 05.00 hours the 7th Bn, 2nd Canadian Infantry Bde (CIB) saw numbers of the 15th Bn (3rd CIB) streaming past their rear; infantry of the *4th Reserve Ersatz Infantry Regt* had broken through the front line where the 3rd CIB was unable to receive artillery support, its supporting batteries being out of range.

The 7th Bn had arrived at its position just over a day earlier and had dug in with their left flank on St Julien and the right near Keerselaere. In command was Maj. Victor Odlum who had taken over after Lt-Col. Hart McHaig had been fatally wounded during the night. Maj. Odlum transferred to 3rd CIB for orders at 05.15 hours but, owing to broken telephone communications, was unable to make contact. At 07.00 hours the *4th Marine Brigade* launched a renewed attack on the 13th and 7th Bns, the enemy artillery having continued their shelling throughout. The two platoons on the right of the 7th Bn were supported by two Colt machine-guns under Lt Edward Bellew, the battalion's machine-gun officer, who positioned his gun team on the high ground at Vancouver crossroads. The constant shelling caused many casualties amongst the gunners, so Lt Bellew manned one gun and Sgt H.N. Peerless the other, both firing into the Germans who were attacking the company on their right. The shell that killed Sgt Peerless also wounded Lt Bellew, but he returned to his gun and continued firing until the machine-gun failed. He then snatched up rifles dropped by his killed and wounded men and continued to fire at the enemy before being stunned by another shell, after which he was taken prisoner.

The *Canadian Eye-Witness* reported:

> Lieut E.P.D. Bellew, machine-gun officer of the 7th Battn, hoisted a loaf, stuck on the point of his bayonet, in defiance of the enemy which drew upon him a perfect fury of fire; he fought his gun until it was smashed to atoms, and then continued to use relays of loaded rifles until he was taken prisoner.

It was now about 08.30 hours and the 7th Bn *War Diary* records, rather tersely: 'right flank surrounded and wiped out'. There is no doubt that the determined action by Lt Bellew and Sgt Peerless was a deciding factor in briefly halting the German advance at this point. The 7th Bn was still in a desperate situation and, failing to receive either orders or reinforcements from 3rd CIB, by 13.00 hours Maj. Odlum ordered a withdrawal of his surviving men. At 23.15 hours Maj. Odlum reported that he had only 350 of all ranks available for duty, with casualties estimated at about 500.

After being captured, Lt Bellew, together with other prisoners, was taken to Staden where a trial was convened by the Germans. The charge against Bellew was that he had continued to fire after part of his unit had surrendered. A guilty verdict was pronounced and he was sentenced to be shot by firing squad at Staden Church. It was reported that the officer in charge of the firing squad was not convinced of Bellew's guilt and halted the execution at the last minute. A second trial was ordered, which took place at Roulers, at which Lt Bellew was acquitted. He was taken to a prison camp in Saxony and remained in various camps (six in total) until 27 December 1917 when he was moved to an internment camp in Switzerland owing to poor health, caused by the effects of gas poisoning, shell-shock and and the very inadequate diet comprising 'pig blood soup, mangold wurzels and bread of 60% sawdust.' In Switzerland he was tended by his wife Charlotte who had been allowed to join him, and on 10 December 1918 he was repatriated to England.

Details of his bravery were known during his imprisonment but it was decided not to announce the award of his Victoria Cross until after his release. The citation for his VC appeared in the *London Gazette* of 13 May 1919 and he was presented with his medal in Vancouver by Gen. Ross, Area-Commandant. Lt Bellew's VC was the first of three to be awarded to the 7th Bn.

Edward Donald Bellew was born on 28 October 1882 at Malabar Hill, Bombay. (Col. Duguid in his official *History of the Canadian Forces in the Great War* states that he was actually 'born on the High Seas'.) He was the eldest son of Maj. Patrick Bellew, Bengal Army, Assay-Master of the Bombay Mint, and Letitia Frances Bellew. He was educated in England at Blundell's School, Tiverton, Devon, and at Clifton College, Bristol, before passing out of Royal Military College, Sandhurst, in 1900 where he was prominent in boxing and rugby.

Given the family's military background it was only natural that he should enter the Army. His grandfather, Maj. Walter Henry Bellew, Assistant Quartermaster-General, Indian Army, was one of the last three men with Dr Brydon, the only survivor of the retreat from Kabul in 1842, while his great-grandfather, Maj.-Gen. Sir Patrick Bellew, was Military Governor of Quebec in 1798.

Edward Bellew was commissioned into the Royal Irish Regt as a second lieutenant in May 1901 and after serving in India and Afghanistan retired with the rank of lieutenant in August 1903. On 24 August 1901, in London, England, he married Charlotte Muriel Rees. They had no children.

Emigrating to Canada in 1907, he spent three years ranching and prospecting in Northern British Columbia, before joining the Provincial Forestry Service. At Vancouver in 1912 he was appointed Assistant to the District Engineer of Public Works employed on harbour engineering. He enlisted in the Canadian Army on 10 August 1914 and was commissioned as a lieutenant in the 11th Irish Fusiliers of Canada.

Following the creation of the Canadian Expeditionary Force at Valcartier, machine-gun officer Bellew and the rest of the men of the 7th Bn (1st British Columbia), comprising 49 officers and 1,083 other ranks, sailed on 3 October 1914 on the *Virginian*, one of the faster ships in the convoy. Disembarking at Plymouth on 16 October, Lt Bellew suffered the miseries of Salisbury Plain with the rest of the Canadian contingent until 10 February 1915 when the 7th Bn embarked on the *Cardiganshire* for France, arriving at St Nazaire on 15 February. A railway journey lasting almost two days took the battalion to Belgium where it was deployed in training prior to taking over front-line trenches.

After returning to England from Switzerland, Capt. Bellew (he was promoted on 2 January 1916) returned to Canada in April 1919, and continued his employment with the Canadian Civil Service, who had kept him on the payroll throughout the war, as Inspector of Dredging in Fraser River. After 1922 it appears that Edward Bellew went into semi-retirement on a ranch at Monte Creek, British Columbia, where he could also indulge in his hobbies of fly-fishing and gardening.

He attended the British Legion dinner in the House of Lords on 9 November 1929 and was also present in 1956 for the VC Centenary Review at Hyde Park. His last visit to England was in July 1960 for the Second Annual Dinner of the Victoria Cross and George Cross Association at the Café Royal.

Edward Bellew died at the Royal Inland Hospital, Shaughnessy, Kamloops, British Columbia, on 1 February 1961, aged 78. In June 1958 he had praised this hospital after suffering a light stroke and commented in a letter to Canon Lummis that 'the nurses are superlative'. He is buried at Hillside Cemetery, Kamloops.

After his death Bellew's VC and other medals passed to his brother-in-law, Mr S.E. Crossman, of Hendon, London, and when he died the medals were auctioned at Sotheby's of London, on 5 July 1974. They realized a then record price of £6,000 and were purchased for Stephen B. Roman, a Canadian millionaire who, in turn, presented them to the Royal Canadian Military Institute in Toronto on 29 November 1974. The VC was subsequently stolen and has not been recovered.

In October 2004 The British Columbia Regiment (Duke of Connaught's Own) Association (BCR Association) placed and dedicated a bronze plaque at the Kamloops Cenotaph in Riverside Park commemorating Captain Bellew, VC. A framed collage of Bellew's photo, citation, 1st BC Regiment cap badge and replica VC was presented to the Mayor of Kamloops for display in the City Hall. On 8 September 2008 the BCR Association dedicated a bronze plaque, commemorating Capt. Bellew's action and award, affixed to the brick wall of the café opposite the Vancouver Corner Monument in Belgium.

F.A.C. SCRIMGER

Near Ypres, Belgium, 25 April

On 22 April 1915 the Advanced Dressing Station of the 3rd Canadian Field Ambulance was situated with 3rd Canadian Infantry Brigade (CIB) HQ in a large farm to the north of Wieltje (see map on page 89). The original, rather grandiose, name of this moated farm had been Château du Nord but it had been aptly christened Shell Trap Farm by the troops (later, on Corps orders, it was renamed Mouse Trap Farm).

Capt. Francis Scrimger, MO of the 14th Bn, Royal Montreal Regt., 3rd CIB, was in charge of this ADS, having just arrived from England to replace Capt. Boyd who had been wounded.

At 17.00 hours the German gas attack, accompanied by a violent artillery bombardment, was launched along much of the front line. Eye-witnesses reported large numbers of Belgian hares running from the oncoming gas-cloud among equally dazed and bewildered French Colonial troops. Some of the gassed soldiers were treated at Scrimger's ADS while it was under shell-fire.

Reinforcements were being rapidly sent forward although German artillery cut many telephone wires and a very confused situation existed with unfounded rumours circulating between the various units, but at 19.00 hours the Canadian front line was still basically intact.

Due to confusing reports and the lack of real information, and spurred on by rifle bullets hitting the walls of the château, the Staff Captain, 3rd CIB, Capt. Harold MacDonald, organized all available HQ personnel, including cooks and batmen, for the immediate defence of Shell Trap Farm.

By 21.00 hours Brig.-Gen. Turner VC, 3rd CIB, received orders to mount a counterattack on the enemy digging in at Kitchener's Wood. He was advised that a British battalion would be coming to support the Canadians but, despite the efforts of Capt. MacDonald to find the un-named British battalion, it had already been ordered elsewhere. Turner therefore ordered the counterattack to be launched with the only battalions available, the 10th and 16th, mounting their attack at 23.30 hours.

The 10th Bn was guided to its assembly position some 500 yards north-east of Shell Trap Farm by the ubiquitous Capt. MacDonald. The 1,500 men advanced in waves, their flanks unsecured and with only three artillery batteries in support. There was one more artillery piece in support: a single gun of the 75th Battery RFA, firing from Shell Trap Farm, but with only sixty rounds available. The attack formation had emanated from 3rd CIB HQ with the orders signed by the brigade major, Lt-Col. Garnet Hughes, son of the Canadian Minister of Defence, Sir Sam Hughes. The men had covered about half the 1,000 yards to the wood when the Germans were alerted. Flares illuminated the Canadians, and two-thirds of the officers, all the company commanders and about a half of the other ranks fell.

Meanwhile, by 01.30 hours, the 3rd and 2nd Bns reported to Brig.-Gen. Turner; the 3rd took up positions along the road 300 yards south of Shell Trap Farm while the 2nd Bn was ordered to support the attack on Kitchener's Wood. News of the 16th Bn's plight was brought to Bde HQ after 02.00 hours by Maj. Godson-Godson, adjutant of the battalion, who gave his report by handwritten note because of a 'bullet-ripped gullet'. No doubt he was yet another patient for Scrimger's hard-pressed staff at the ADS.

Stretcher-bearers attempted to collect the wounded but after they incurred casualties from snipers this work was suspended until after dark. Many of the wounded were treated at Shell Trap Farm, both by Captain Scrimger and also Captain Haywood, MO of the 3rd Toronto Bn, who had set up his aid post in the stables of the farm. The wounded had to wait, many in the open courtyard, for the ambulances to come up after dark to collect them, then making their way back along the crowded roads, illuminated by the burning buildings of Ypres.

Shortly after 16.00 hours large bodies of Germans were seen moving south-eastwards from Kitchener's Wood and Oblong Farm, where they were heavily punished by guns of the 5th and 6th Batteries CFA, firing over open sights; one of the battery commanders, Maj. Harvey McLeod, was actually sitting on the roof of Shell Trap Farm directing fire. The Germans were stopped when the range was down to 900 yards. This was the last enemy attack of the day.

2/Lt Bruce Bairnsfather, 1st Royal Warwicks, took part in an abortive attack early on 25 April and carried a wounded Canadian officer, probably to Scrimger's ADS. He described the scene: 'Shells were crashing into the roof of the farm and exploding round it in great profusion.' As Scrimger recorded in his personal diary: 'April 25th. This has been a big day . . . . I got an hour's sleep this afternoon, the first for three days and nights . . . . About this time, lack of sleep and food, anxiety and the excitement of a vigorous cannonade, had worked me up to such an extent that I did not care what happened.

I caught myself once out in the open cursing the Germans and all their works. I first now felt a personal hatred towards them. I was afraid, too, to speak for fear of breaking down'.

In the late afternoon the farm was hit several times by heavy enemy artillery fire. Boxes of SAA exploded and some of the buildings caught fire; also burning was the straw in the courtyard, on which wounded men had been laid. Brig.-Gen. Turner and his staff evacuated the buildings, many of them having to wade through the moat, and the majority of the wounded were moved to relative safety. Turner's brigade captain, Capt. Harold MacDonald, was not so fortunate and in his own words, recounted by the *Montreal Star* on 16 July 1915:

> I was in the front of our Canadian headquarters staff on 25 April, which was the third day of the terrific St Julien fighting, when I was hit on the neck and shoulder. I was dragged into a building where Capt. Scrimger dressed my wounds. A few minutes later German shells found the building and set it on fire. The staff were forced to abandon the building and left me there as an apparently hopeless case. But Capt. Scrimger carried me out and down to a moat, fifty feet in front, where we lay half in the water. Capt Scrimger curled himself round my wounded head and shoulder to protect me from the heavy shell fire, at obvious peril of his own life. He stayed with me until the fire slackened, then got the stretcher-bearers and had me carried to the dressing-station. This, however, is only one of many incidents of Capt. Scrimger's heroism in those awful three days. No man ever better deserved the soldier's highest honour.

Capt. Francis Scrimger was recommended for the award of the Victoria Cross, the official announcement being published in the Supplement to the *London Gazette*, No. 29202, dated 22 June 1915. He was decorated by King George V at Windsor on 21 July 1915. As a result of Capt. McDonald's wounds he lost an arm, but this did not prevent him from reaching the rank of brigadier-general, and after the war he became Chairman of the Canadian Pension Commission in Ottawa.

Born in Montreal on 10 February 1881, Francis Alexander Caron Scrimger was the son of one of the leading Presbyterian ministers in Canada, Principal of the Presbyterian College, the Revd John Scrimger MA, DD, and Mrs Scrimger. The family resided at 83 Redpath Crescent, and while living there Scrimger attended Montreal High School before going on to McGill University Medical School, graduating as an MD in 1905. He then spent some time on post-graduate studies in Europe. Returning to Canada he was commissioned captain in the Canadian Army Medical Corps (CAMC) on 13 April 1912 and appointed medical officer of the Montreal Heavy Brigade, Canadian Artillery. When war was declared, he became MO of the 14th Bn, CEF, on 22 September 1914. Sailing from Valcartier, Quebec, on 3 October 1914, the battalion was divided between two ships, half sailing on the *Alaunia* and the rest on the *Andania*. Disembarking at Plymouth, the battalion endured a wet English winter on Salisbury Plain before sailing from Avonmouth on the *Australind* on 1 February 1915. Scrimger was not with his battalion when it disembarked at St Nazaire on 15 February as he had been detached to No. 1 General Hospital, Netheravon, Wiltshire, on 21 January.

After gaining his VC Scrimger was invalided to England following an injury and, when fit, he served in various hospitals in England, including the Canadian Hospital in Ramsgate. He was promoted to major on 5 December 1916 and returned to France, working at No. 3 Canadian Casualty Clearing Station, Boulogne.

On 5 September 1918 he married Ellen Emerson Carpenter, a Canadian nurse, at St Columba's Church, Pont Street, London. The service was performed by the Revd Archibald Fleming DD and the Revd J. Tudor Scrymgeour, Francis Scrimger's brother, who was also serving in France as a chaplain and working with the YMCA. Promoted to lieutenant-colonel on 21 April 1919, Scrimger returned to

Montreal after the war and was appointed assistant-surgeon at the Royal Victoria Hospital; he was appointed surgeon-in-chief there in 1936. A mountain near the Kootenays in the Canadian Rockies was named after him in 1918.

Francis Scrimger died suddenly on 13 February 1937 and was buried at the Mount Royal Cemetery, Montreal. On 17 October 2005 Lt-Col. Scrimger's VC and campaign medals were presented to the Canadian War Museum, Ottawa by his three daughters.

The site of Kitchener's Wood, Wijngaardstraat, Belgium is now marked by a memorial to the memory of soldiers from 10th and 16th Bns CEF killed during the night attack on 22 April. This stone, 7ft-high memorial symbolizing shattered oak trees and a gas cloud was unveiled on 22 March 1997.

MIR DAST

Near Ypres, Belgium, 26 April

The 57th (Wilde's) Rifles left its billets on 24 April to begin the trying two-day march to the Ypres sector. They reached Ouderdom on the 25th, having to bivouac in the open. The Regimental History sums up the arduous trek: 'The men were somewhat done up after two long marches following weeks of trench war, but came in very well.' An early start, at 05.30 hours on the next morning, sent the Ferozepore Brigade, of which the 57th Rifles were part, marching through Vlamertinghe and the north-west of Ypres. The battalion reached its assembly positions late in the morning, and dug in behind hedges north-west of St Jean while under heavy shell-fire. At about 12.45 hours final attack orders were received which detailed the battalions to move forward to their assembly positions, some 400 yards ahead, by 13.15 hours. French troops continued the line to the left of the Ferozepore Bde with the Jullunder Bde on its right. Hurried orders were given to company commanders and as the Regimental History comments, 'No one knew exactly what was happening. . . .' But the battalion reached its assembly positions and formed up with 2 Coy in support about 80 yards behind the centre company (see map on page 89).

A report by Lt Bainbridge, the battalion adjutant, included with the Battalion *War Diary*, gives a detailed account of the action and notes that, '. . . a very poor bombardment had been carried out at the German trenches. At 1.15 the advance started, and our guns practically ceased firing.' Casualties occurred during the initial stage of the advance, but after crossing Buffs Road, on Hill Top Ridge, the leading men 'came under a perfect hail of fire . . . men began to drop at a great rate, and we began to lose formation, owing chiefly to the men bunching together behind each scrap of cover'.

When the men were within 80 yards of the German trenches chlorine gas was released, which initially affected the French on their left, but a change of wind direction then carried the gas across the attacking battalion. The French started to turn back and:

> . . . the rest of the line, seeing them going and getting the effect of the gas at the same time, went about as well, not before several of our men had been laid out by the gas. These were left, and the remainder being unable either to combat or understand the gas, turned and went, as it was no good stopping to be mown down by MG fire and bombs.
>
> . . . the retirement having started, [it] was impossible to check, British, French and Indians being all mixed up together.

All the British officers in the front companies were killed, and two Indian officers of these companies killed and four others wounded, leaving only one British officer remaining in the actual attack, Capt. Mahon of No. 2 Coy, who, with help from the quartermaster and machine-gun officer, managed to gather some sixty men together. Meanwhile Jemadar Mir Dast, who had stayed in the British trench, collected together all the men he could, bullying and cajoling when necessary. Many of them were now recovering from the gas poisoning, and with his encouragement they managed to hold on to their position until dusk, when they received orders to retire.

During the return journey, Mir Dast picked up several men, including eight wounded British and Indian officers who would probably have died but for his efforts. He was himself wounded while helping to bring in these men and for his bravery was awarded the Victoria Cross, and on 27 April promoted to Subadar (equivalent to captain).

Numerous acts of bravery were carried out that day, including that by Havildar (sergeant) Mangal Singh, one of the men rescued by Mir Dast, who, having been brought in unconscious from the effects of gas, recovered enough to go out several times to bring in other wounded men. He was awarded the Indian Order of Merit 2nd Class. The battalion had begun the day with twenty officers (eight British and twelve Indian) and 560 other ranks; by the night of 26 April they numbered three British and three Indian officers (two of whom were slightly wounded but refused to report sick, one of them being Jemadar Mir Dast) and 216 other ranks.

The battalion was relieved and on 2 May moved into billets where a draft of two Indian officers and 151 men arrived to partially swell their depleted ranks.

Mir Dast (also known as Mir Dost) was born in Maiden, Tirah, India, on 3 December 1874, son of Mada Mir, an Afridi. Enlisting in 1/55th Coke's Rifles, Frontier Force, in December 1894, he served at Tochi Valley on the north-west frontier of India during 1897–8, receiving the Indian General Service Medal and bar. Promoted Naik (corporal) in 1901, Mir Dast again saw service on the north-west frontier during 1901–2, on this occasion receiving the Waziristan bar to add to his General Service Medal. Further promotion followed in 1904 when he was made Havilar (sergeant) and in 1908, when fighting in the Mohmand Campaign at Khan Khar Kueg, he was awarded the Indian Order of Merit 2nd Class for gallantry in action, in addition to the then new Indian

General Service Medal and bar. No Indian troops qualified for the Victoria Cross until 1911, the IOM being the highest award for bravery attainable by them.

Promoted to Jemadar (the equivalent of lieutenant) the following year, this experienced Indian officer first saw service in France on 19 January 1915, when attached to 57th Wilde's Rifles. This battalion was in reserve for the battle of Neuve Chapelle and though moving up to the front line trenches on 12 March 1915, played little part in the fighting.

Following his gallantry near Ypres, Subadar Mir Dast continued to serve with his regiment until June, when he was again wounded; his injuries, combined with the effects of his earlier gas poisoning, resulted in him being sent for treatment at the Indian Hospital, Royal Pavilion, Brighton. His Victoria Cross was announced in the *London Gazette* of 29 June 1915.

Many distinguished visitors toured the hospital and, on 4 July 1915, the Secretary of State for India, Mr Chamberlain, paid a visit. At the end of his inspection Chamberlain was introduced to all the Indian officers able to be present on the lawns of the Royal Pavilion. Still severely incapacitated from poison gas, Mir Dast, confined to his wheelchair, was presented to the Secretary of State, to the obvious approval of his fellow officers who raised a loud cheer. This was the Subadar's first trip outside the confines of his hospital room, and when Chamberlain moved on, every Indian officer present went up to the Subadar, saluted him and shook his hand. Further dignitaries continued to visit the hospital and, on 21 August 1915, Lord Kitchener was photographed shaking hands with Mir Dast, who by now was able to stand unaided, although his wheeled chair is clearly visible in the photograph.

On 25 August 1915 the King and Queen, accompanied by Princess Mary, arrived to present awards to ten wounded Indian officers and one non-commissioned officer. The day was described as 'royal weather', and the lawn was used for the investiture in front of over 1,000 wounded Indians. A contemporary booklet on the Indian Hospital describes the scene:

Their Majesties stood on a slight elevation on the Western Lawn, with their personal staff and the staff of the Indian

Hospitals behind them, while the Indians in their pictur-esque pale blue hospital uniforms formed a large half-circle in front. The recipients of the honours were brought forward by Colonel MacLeod, the Commanding Officer of the Royal Pavilion Hospital, and were individually presented to the King by Colonel Sir Walter Lawrence.

Subadar Mir Dast was the first man to be decorated and had to be pushed up to the King in a wheelchair, but he insisted on standing in front of His Majesty who addressed him thus:

It is nearly sixty years since Queen Victoria instituted this cross for conspicuous bravery in battle. At the Delhi Durbar, in 1911, I ordered that my Indian soldiers should be admit-ted to this high and coveted distinction. I have already bestowed with my own hand two VCs on Indian soldiers, and I give this third cross with infinite pleasure. I earnestly hope you will soon be completely recovered from your inju-ries and that you will live long to enjoy your honours.

Amongst the others decorated that day was Jemadar Hawinda (58th Vaughan's Rifles), Mir Dast's cousin, who received the Indian Distinguished Service Medal. It is ironic that Mir Dast's brother, Mir Mast, was awarded the Iron Cross by the Germans, following his desertion from 58th (Vaughan's) Rifles on 3 March 1915. Mir Mast was awarded the DCM (*London Gazette*, 16 February 1915) but with twenty-three other ranks, all Afridis, he deserted near Neuve Chapelle and imparted to the Germans what information they knew regarding the impending British attack. The desertions were not satisfactorily explained except that a Havildar, one of the first to desert on 2 March, was generally regarded by his officers as a troublemaker.

After presenting the other awards and visiting the patients who were too sick to be at the investiture, the royal party returned to the lawns where they spent some time talking informally with some of the assembled Indians before leaving to the sound of loud cheers. A film was made of this investiture and it is quite possible this was screened, at a later date, for the patients of The Royal Pavilion.

Stating that this was the proudest day of his life Mir Dast said, 'What did I do – nothing, only my duty; and to think that the great King-Emperor should shake me by the hand and praise me! I am his child.' In a letter to his regimental colleagues in India, the following day, he wrote, 'Service under the Government is very good. I have been given the Victoria Cross. You come, too, and you may get it.'

Unfortunately Mir Dast's health did not improve, and on 19 October 1915 he went back to India to rejoin his regiment, 55th Coke's Rifles. He was given the Order of British India, 2nd Class (Bahadur) on 3 June 1916, and the receipt of this award made him one of the most highly decorated Indian soldiers having been awarded the Russian Cross of St George, 3rd class (approved in Army Order 958 of 1915); he was the first to hold both the Victoria Cross and the IOM. He was transferred to the pension establishment on 22 September 1917. Mir Dast died on 19 January 1945 at the village of Shagi Landi Kyan, Tehsil district, Peshawar (now Pakistan), and was buried in the Warsak Road cemetery, Shagi Landi Kyan.

His name is inscribed on the inside of the pavilion roof of the Commonwealth Gates, Hyde Park Corner.

I. SMITH

(ISHROULCH SHMILOWITZ)
Near Ypres, Belgium, 26 April

The Lahore Div., Indian Corps, comprising Jullunder, Sirhind and Ferozepore brigades, was in billets in and around L'Epinette when orders were received on 23 April for it to move at short notice, destination unknown. The men left their billeting area at 13.30 hours on the 24th and after a gruelling march of 23½ miles, over wet pave roads, they arrived at Boeschepe just before midnight. They left Boeschepe at

06.00 hours the following morning and marched until 10.30 hours. The Jullunder Bde, of which the 1st Manchester Regt were part, went into camp near Vlamertinghe, after covering a distance of 12½ miles. Although orders for a forthcoming attack had been issued by Sir Horace Smith-Dorrien at Second Army HQ just after 02.00 hours on the 26th, there was a serious delay in the transmission of these orders to the brigades and subsequently to the battalions. The 1st Manchester Regt left camp at 06.30 hours, marched south of Ypres, and arrived at their forming-up position in fields to the west of Wieltje at 10.30 hours; a few minutes later several enemy shells caused about a dozen casualties. These shells turned out to contain some form of gas, which partially blinded several men for some minutes.

At 12.30 hours the Manchesters finally received their orders for an attack which placed them on the right of the Jullunder Bde, with their flank on Wieltje Farm. To their left were the 40th Pathans, and beyond them the 47th Sikhs, in touch with the Ferozepore Bde. The ground over which the attack was to be launched was very open, with minimal cover, rising slightly for the first 500 yards to the crest of Hill Top Ridge, then descending down a gentle slope for a further 500 yards before the final 500 yards up another slope to Mauser Ridge where the Germans were strongly entrenched (see map on page 89).

Thus, with very little time to study their orders, the battalion moved forward at 13.20 hours under cover of an artillery barrage, with the object of being in an assaulting position when the artillery lifted at 14.00 hours. The direction of the attack should have been due north but from the start the Jullunder Bde veered to the left, thus crowding the Ferozepore Bde. Enemy fire was heavy from the start and when the troops appeared on Hill Top Ridge, visible to the Germans, they came under what was described as 'a perfect inferno of fire of all kinds, machine-gun, rifle, and every variety of shell, many of which were filled with gas'. Despite very severe casualties parties of the Manchesters managed to reach to within 60 yards of the German trenches.

A/Cpl Issy Smith of the 1st Manchesters had a lucky escape when his platoon was hit by a shell at about 11.00 hours near Wieltje; Smith did not remain with his comrades when they ran for cover, but returned to pick up his cigarettes. His account, as reported in newspapers at the time, continued:

> Later on in the charge our commander was hit and I at once got my field dressing out and bandaged him. I carried him to the first aid post. On my way I saw Lieutenant Shipston fall. I was at this moment carrying Sergeant Rooke. I carried them both, a yard at a time, to our trenches. The bullets were flying.
>
> Then, dead exhausted, I fell down, not able to move. An officer gave me his flask and said, 'There is brandy in this; take a drop and it will revive you.' I said I would not, as I was a teetotaller, and intended to remain one – no matter what happened. But I was dreadfully weak.

The commander Smith mentions, Sgt Rooke, later gave his own account of what happened:

> During the attack I was shot through the liver and was quite helpless. Smith at once ran out to my rescue, put me on his back and carried me through a terrific hail of shrapnel, rifle and machine-gun fire into the Ypres road. I was lying only 200 yards from the German trenches and the fact that Smith escaped being hit was a sheer miracle. Just at that time the Germans turned on the poison gas . . . We were again in a most exposed position, and Lieut. W.M. Shipster who passed us, told Smith to put me down and said he would send me assistance. The officer had only gone a few yards when he was shot through the neck. Smith went to him, bandaged his wounds – all this time under heavy fire – and carried him, and afterwards me, into the trenches of the 4th Suffolks. He then helped to take me on a stretcher to the first aid post of the Suffolks and afterwards returned immediately to fight on.

Smith assisted in bringing in many more wounded men throughout the day. The attack failed. No members of the division reached the German lines, and the Manchesters were relieved in the early hours, but not before losing their CO,

Lt-Col. Hutchins, who was killed during the evening. The battalion received further drafts of men on the 27th and by the end of May their reinforcements totalled 38 officers and 1,449 other ranks.

Born of Russian Orthodox parents, on 18 September 1890, in Alexandria, Egypt, Ishroulch Shmilowitz was the son of a clerk, Moses Shmilowitz, who worked in Egypt for the French Consular Service. His father and mother, Eva, (Chudnovski) who both originated from Berditchev near Odessa were then French citizens. At the age of eleven, Ishroulch stowed away on a ship at Alexandria, and went to England, where it is believed, he lived with his brother, Maurice who later emigrated to America. He attended Berner Street School, Whitechapel and like many other children in the East End, he worked in his spare time, in his case as a fish delivery boy.

On 4 September 1904, at St George's Barracks, London, he enlisted in the British Army where his name was anglicized by the recruiting sergeant. He was then nearly 16 years old although the 'apparent age' on his attestation form is 18. His occupation is noted as plumbers mate and place of birth as St Georges in the East, London. He served with the 2nd Bn, Manchester Regt, in Aldershot and the 3rd Bn in South Africa before joining the 1st Bn at Secunderbad in India at the end of October 1906 where he won the Regimental Middleweight Boxing Championship, and in 1911 received the Delhi Durbar Medal. The physical Army regime must have suited Smith as he gained 16lbs in weight and added over an inch to his height in his first six months service. His record shows that in 1905 and 1907 he was given two periods of detention (42 and 35 days) for using insubordinate language. Discharged from the Army on 15 November 1912, Smith emigrated to Australia in early 1914 and was employed by the Metropolitan Gas Co., while living in Ascot Vale, Melbourne, where he continued his interest in boxing, fighting under the name of Jack Daniels. When war began in August 1914, he immediately enlisted in the Australian Army at St Kilda Road Barracks, Melbourne, and was with the Australian Forces in New Guinea when the

German Territories were overrun. No actual evidence has yet been found to support this although Issy was encamped at Broadmeadows camp with the Australian forces who were involved in this short campaign.

As a British Army reservist he joined the 3rd Bn, Manchester Regt, on reaching England and sailed to France where he rejoined the 1st Manchester Regt, who had disembarked from the SS *Panjola* at Marseilles on 26 September 1914. Smith was wounded at the battle of Neuve Chapelle on 11 March 1915.

Following the VC action A/Cpl Smith was gassed in May 1915, and after treatment, was sent on 8 August to the Mount Joy (Dublin University VAD Auxiliary) Hospital, Dublin, to recuperate. It was there on 24 August that he heard the news of his Victoria Cross award. The *London Gazette* had published his citation on 23 August.

An Irish newspaper report stated that: 'the hospital was besieged by Jews, who came to offer their congratulations to Cpl Issy Smith, the first Jewish NCO to win the VC'. (The first Jewish VC of the war had been won by Lt Frank de Pass on 25 November 1914, and Smith was the second of five VCs awarded to Jews.) Smith was carried shoulder-high to a restaurant in Sackville Street, where he was entertained. He later attended a reception in his honour at the Dublin Mansion House where he was presented with a purse of gold. On 25 August he was awarded the Russian Cross of St George 4th Class, and on 4 September 1915, having returned to England, Smith was presented by the Mayor of Stepney, London, with a gold watch and chain from fellow members of the Berners Old Boys Club.

King George V presented the Victoria Cross to Smith at Buckingham Palace on 3 February 1916; later, like several other VC winners, Smith embarked on a recruiting campaign in various towns and cities, particularly in the north of England. He held strong views and spoke out against conscription.

Rejoining his battalion he was promoted sergeant in March 1916 and survived the torpedoing of his ship *en route* to Mesopotamia where, at Baghdad in March 1917, he was again wounded. Smith transferred to the Royal Engineers (Inland Water Transport) on 1 April 1917 and served in Palestine during the fall of Jerusalem in December of that year.

Demobilized in 1919 he married, on 8 February, Elsie Porteous Collingwood McKechnie, who was a tailoress, at Camberwell Registry Office, London. His parents, still living in Egypt, disowned him for marrying a Gentile, even though a Jewish wedding ceremony was held on 24 March 1919 at the Hallam Street Synagogue. At this ceremony, performed by Maj. Adler DSO, Senior Jewish Chaplain, assisted by the Revd E Spero, he gave his name as Israel Shimovitz, otherwise Smith.

Living in the East End, Smith had a variety of jobs in the immediate post-war years including working as an actor, a music-hall manager and a cycle accessory salesman. In common with many other returning soldiers he found regular employment difficult to obtain.

Smith attended the garden party at Buckingham Palace on 26 June 1920 for Victoria Cross winners, and was present at the Cenotaph on 11 November of the same year. He was photographed on both occasions. On the anniversary of the Third Battle of Ypres he was among those who made the pilgrimage to Ypres on 30 July 1922. In 1924, being unable to work through illness, he pawned his medals for £20. This fact was discovered by Mrs Hertz, wife of the Chief Rabbi, who with eleven others, gave £10 each to Smith. The medals were taken out of pawn and placed in the Mocatta Library, University of London, by the Jewish Historical Society, on the understanding that Smith could acquire them at any time on payment of £20. On 8 October 1921, with Harry Kenny VC (see page 201), he unveiled the Hackney War Memorial.

Smith did redeem his medals in 1925 and, with his wife and daughter Olive, returned to Australia, where, in 1928, he was local manager for British International Pictures at Melbourne. In 1930 he was appointed Justice of the Peace, frequently sitting on the City Bench, and in 1931 unsuccessfully contested the Melbourne seat for the House of Representatives as a candidate for the United Australia Party.

A well thought of and very generous man, he was often to be found, during the Depression, helping the less well off, sometimes to the detriment of his own family. His son Maurice was born in 1932 while he was employed by the Dunlop Rubber Company as a commercial traveller. The Civil Aviation Department was his next employer, for whom he worked as a control officer at Essendon Airport, Melbourne, from 1928.

Issy Smith VC died of a coronary thrombosis at his home in Moonee Ponds on 11 September 1940 and was buried, with full military honours, in the Hebrew section of Fawkner Cemetery, Victoria. He was survived by his wife and both children.

Smith's Victoria Cross and seven other medals (1914–15 Star, BWM, BVM, Delhi Durbar 1911, Coronation 1937, Croix de Guerre with bronze palm, Russian Cross of St George, 4th class) were sold in Melbourne on 23 April 1991 for A$23,100 – approximately £10,000 – and on 10 October 1995 were again offered for sale by auction, this time in London, and were purchased by a private collector for a hammer price of £30,000, way over the expected £18,000–£22,000. His medals are not publicly held.

On 12 September 2010, at Fawkner Jewish Cemetery, Melbourne, a memorial service was held for the 70th anniversary of Issy Smith's death. More than 25 family members attended, including his son Maurice. After the ceremony and wreath laying, two trees were planted in his honour and a plaque unveiled commemorating the event, which was organized by the Victorian Association of Jewish Ex-Serviceman and Women Inc. (VAJEX) in association with the Jewish National Fund of Australia Inc. (Victorian Division).

J. LYNN

Near Ypres, Belgium, 2 May

When the German gas attack at Ypres was launched on 22 April 1915, the 2nd Lancashire Fusiliers (12th Bde, 4th Div.) were in billets at the 'Blue Factory', Armentières. The battalion was up to full strength, having received drafts totalling 38 officers and 1,440 other ranks since the beginning of the war.

Leaving Armentières on 27 April the battalion arrived at Vlamertinghe on the 29th and took over the front line from the 1st Royal Warwickshire Regt north of Wieltje. The journey was hampered by almost continuous shelling, and the battalion was impeded by numbers of French Colonial troops, many suffering from the effects of gas, moving in the opposite direction. Two of the companies lost their way during this forward move owing to lack of maps, but by 01.30 hours on 30 April the battalion was in its new position. One company was east of Shell Trap Farm, facing north, with the other three companies forming the longer arm of the L-shaped position running from the farm in a northerly direction facing east.

The battalion was equipped with four machine-guns, three of which were with B Coy. One was at the far left of the position, the second, under Pte John Lynn, was slightly west of the Wieltje–St Julien road, while the third was between Lynn's position and Shell Trap Farm (see map on page 89). The position held by B Coy was not a continuous trench, but was more like several separate banks, hedged with minimal parados, which the battalion spent time improving. The next day, 2 May, began quietly, but the peace was interrupted by British artillery shelling the enemy opposite B Coy's position, where small parties of Germans were seen behaving as if an attack was imminent. No attack materialized, but at about midday, enemy incendiary shells were directed at all the farm buildings in the area, setting them on fire and destroying a dressing station in the front line close to B Coy.

Tea had just been brought to the front line troops, shortly after 16.00 hours, when British sentries raised the alarm. Described as being 'like water out of a hose', yellow clouds of gas were shooting up in the air at about 30 yard intervals from the enemy line some 600 yards away. The gas settled down, forming waves about 3 feet high, and was carried by the light easterly wind towards the British front line. A few respirators, made of rectangular pads of compressed cotton soaked in sodium hypochloride, had been issued at Vlamertinghe – two per platoon. These pads were of little use as they did not cover the nose, so the MO improvised and arranged for containers of water and tea, with which to moisten handkerchiefs, to be placed at intervals along the trenches. Unfortunately, this liquid was spilt so he shouted for the men of B Coy nearest him to urinate on any available material, and hold it to their faces. He then proceeded to show them by example. The natural ammonia proved to be effective, neutralizing the chlorine in the gas.

The gas took two to three minutes to cross to the British trenches, during which time rapid fire was directed into it in case the Germans were following up behind. Pte Lynn opened fire with his machine-gun, but as his view was limited he lifted the gun up to the top of the bank and secured it to a tree stump. With this much wider field of fire he caused terrific casualties to the advancing enemy troops, now just visible. He continued firing although he was badly affected by the gas, and did not stop until the attackers stopped coming forward. He finally collapsed, blue in the face, and had to be lifted from the parapet and taken to a dugout. One of his comrades reports him saying, 'This is the last carry', as they lifted him from his gun. Shortly after, he was taken to hospital where he died in great agony the next day.

The *London Gazette* of 29 June 1915 announced the award of the Victoria Cross. It was through the efforts of Lynn's MO, Lt Tyrell, that Private Lynn was recommended for the award of the VC. Tyrell's methods of combatting the gas on 2 May were indeed very effective, and the only men able to carry on at the end of that fateful day were those of B Coy who had followed his example. Lt Tyrell himself won the MC on 10 December 1914 and later became Air Vice-Marshall Sir William Tyrell KBE, DSO, MC.

While the battalion's casualties on 2 May were listed as 9 men killed, 2 officers and 38 other ranks wounded, this does not give a true reflection of the state of the battalion at the end of the day. The Battalion *War Diary* reported that 18 officers and 431 other ranks were admitted to hospital suffering from the effects of gas.

On the evening of 3 May the battalion was withdrawn to reserve trenches near Vlamertinghe. Pte John Lynn VC was buried in Vlamertinghe churchyard but his grave was later destroyed by shell-fire. There is now a special memorial erected to him in Grootebeek British Cemetery, Reninghelst. Private Lynn also enjoyed the rare distinction of being named in Sir John French's Despatch.

John Lynn was born in 1887 and when only three days old was fostered by John and Elizabeth Harrison of 20 Hindsley Place, Forest Hill, London. His foster-mother worked in a laundry at Forest Hill.

Known at school as John Harrison, he was educated at Christ Church School, Forest Hill, before leaving to join the training ship *Exmouth*. In 1901 he enlisted as a band boy under his real name of John Lynn in the 4th Bn, Lancashire Fusiliers, aged 14½, and with the 2nd Bn served in Malta and India. Prior to the outbreak of war, when stationed at Wellington Barracks, Bury, Lancs., he met, and later became engaged to, Alice Mason. He left the army and worked at Armstrong-Whitworth Ltd, in Openshaw, lodging with Alice's family at 56 Queen's Road, Gorton, Manchester.

A double wedding was planned for Alice and her sister, to take place in November 1914, but Lynn's call-up as a reservist in August of that year took him with 2nd Lancs. Fusiliers to France. Alice was on holiday in Blackpool when war broke out and despite her efforts she did not see her fiancé before he left, her late arrival at his depot sadly caused by the trains being overcrowded with soldiers.

The 2nd Lancs. Fusiliers were in action from the beginning, and it was near Armentières in October that the name of Pte John Lynn first came to prominence. On 18 October orders were given for the enemy to be pushed back from the River Lys, the battalion's objective being the village of Le Touquet. Enemy shrapnel fire held up the final advance when the battalion was on the outskirts of Le Touquet, even though the Regimental History states that: 'gallant and valuable work was done by a machine-gun manned by Sergeant E.M. Parkinson and Privates H. Pulford, J. Lynn and Yates.'

On 21 October heavy shelling preceded an enemy attack in which the battalion machine-gun section played its part in holding back the attackers. One gun was positioned at the level-crossing to the north of Le Touquet but unfortunately it was alongside a white post, which provided an easy aiming mark for the enemy; this forced the team to retire quickly, but not before two men, Sgt Parkinson and Pte Pulford, were killed by two consecutive shots and one other man was slightly wounded. The gun was brought out by Ptes Lynn and Grundy. Later Lynn collected spare gun parts, together with four belt boxes and two rifles; despite being under heavy fire, his return was described as 'unperturbed and unhurried'.

Pte Lynn was awarded the Distinguished Conduct Medal for this action, which was gazetted on 17 December 1914. Some accounts attribute the award of Lynn's DCM to action in fighting on either the Marne or the Aisne, but the official name of the action was the Battle of Armentières. The 2nd Lancs. Fusiliers remained in the same sector during the winter of 1914/15, mainly being involved in static trench warfare which took its daily toll of casualties. The battalion took part in the Christmas truce, with a team from A Coy defeating a Saxon side at football 3–2.

Meanwhile the proposed wedding had been postponed, with a new date arranged for April 1915, subject to Lynn obtaining the necessary leave but his fiancée's distress on the news of his death was made worse when her bag containing his many letters from the front was lost. On 25 August 1915 Lynn was awarded the Cross of St George, 4th Class (Russia), and his VC was posted to Alice Mason by the War Office on 29 March 1916, as she was his legatee.

In 1955 Lynn's Victoria Cross and other medals were presented to the Lancashire Fusiliers Museum at the Barracks where he had been stationed over forty years earlier. John Lynn's wooden battlefield marker is in St Mary the Virgin church, Bury, Greater Manchester, and his name appears on the marble tablet inscribed with those who died in the First World War positioned, together with a stained glass window, on the right of the south entrance of Christ Church, Forest Hill. He is also commemorated on a mural to Victoria Cross Holders in Lewisham Shopping Centre, unveiled 28 May 1998.

E. WARNER

Hill 60, Belgium, 1 May

The 1st Battalion, Bedfordshire Regt (15th Bde, 5th Div.), was moved into the line to the east of Hill 60 to relieve the 1st Cheshire Regt on 25 April. The enemy had launched the main gas attack on this front on the 22nd and severe fighting had continued almost uninterrupted since. The *War Diary* notes that on 1 May the 'Enemy made sudden attack on trenches to our right with asphyxiating gas and shells, at about 6.30 p.m.' All the men were affected, being violently sick and consequently unable to fight effectively, and were forced to vacate their position, Trench 46 (see map on page 64). Private Edward Warner, No. 7602 1st Bedfords, then re-entered the trench single-handed to prevent the enemy taking possession of it. The Germans did not press home the attack, possibly, according to the *War Diary*, 'because some of the fumes blew back towards them'. Nevertheless, Warner held the trench alone against advancing enemy troops. Reinforcements were sent to Warner's aid, but they were unable to reach him because of the gas. Warner, by now becoming completely exhausted, then came back and brought up more men to hold the line. Because of his determination Trench 46 was held until the enemy's attack ceased. Warner died shortly afterwards from the effects of gas poisoning. His gallant example earned him the Victoria Cross, which was gazetted on 29 June 1915. It was presented to his mother by King George V at Buckingham Palace on 16 November 1916.

Edward Warner was born at 36 Cannon Street, St Albans, Hertfordshire, on 18 November 1883, the town where he later enlisted in the Army. Before her death his mother,

Mrs Warner, bequeathed her son's VC to Edward's niece, Mrs Dixon of Forest Gate, London. After her husband died, Mrs Dixon felt that her uncle's VC should be in safer keeping and so offered it to his regiment. On 20 June 1962 Lt-Col. Norbury, CO of the Bedfordshire Regiment, accompanied by Col. Young, the Regimental Secretary, called on Mrs Dixon at her home, 114 Earlham Grove, Forest Gate, to receive Warner's VC. Until then the medal had been kept in a recess with a framed picture showing Mrs Warner receiving the VC from the late King George V. The picture had been presented to Edward Warner's mother by the Officers of the 3rd Bn, Bedfordshire Regt. Warner's name appears on the Menin Gate, Ypres, Belgium.

THE BATTLE OF AUBERS RIDGE

9 May

Sir Douglas Haig planned to attack both north and south of Neuve Chapelle after a forty minute artillery bombardment. The southern attack was to be carried out by 1st and Meerut Divs between Chocolat Menier Corner and Port Arthur, with the Meerut Div. swinging north-east to take the *Stützpunkte* at La Cliqueterie Farm. The northern attack by the 8th Div., was to advance south-east towards Rouges Bancs and then secure a line from Rouges Bancs to Fromelles and along the Aubers Ridge where its right would join up with the Meerut Div. The attack was originally planned to begin on 8 May but was delayed to the 9th so as to act in concert with a large attack by the French in Artois.

The Germans had been quick to learn from their experiences at Neuve Chapelle in March and had strengthened their defences: front breastworks were increased in width to at least 15 feet and to a height of more than 6 feet; wire defences increased to a depth of 15 yards, some of which lay in sunken areas immediately in front of the breastworks and could not be easily seen from the British lines; sandbags of different colours disguised the position of the numerous machine-gun emplacements built into the breastworks, with guns just above ground level; and the number of German troops in both front and support lines was increased.

The British artillery bombardment began at 05.00 hours and was followed thirty minutes later by the forward companies who climbed over the British parapets and assembled 80 yards from the German line in accordance with orders. Many of these men were very quickly shot down by rifle fire and machine-gun fire as the enemy troops holding the front breastworks were, in the main, not severely affected by the artillery fire. The Germans were expecting an attack and had possibly been alerted by the destruction of a large chimney in the Rue du Bois the previous day to give British artillery an improved field of fire.

The main British assault began at 05.40 hours but few companies reached the enemy front line, except where two mines had been exploded on the left of the line in the northern sector. Because of the largely undamaged state of the enemy breastworks, further attempts during the day to cross no-man's-land resulted in severe casualties to the attacking troops. Those men who did reach the German lines were quickly attacked by the defenders. With no support able to reach them, those who remained were withdrawn after dark and further attacks were called off in the evening.

Although the British artillery bombardment on the German front defences looked effective – one eye-witness described the German lines as 'a long sheet of flame and bursting shells' – much of the wire was not cut and insufficient heavy artillery shells hit the breastworks. Some shells fell as far as 400 yards behind the German line. The British counter-battery bombardment was also not effective as the enemy was able to shell both the front and assembly positions.

Casualties on the British side totalled over 10,800, while the estimated German losses were 1,500. A special order issued by Haig on the day after the battle stated that the attack had 'proved of great assistance to our allies', which suggested the British assault had caused the Germans to move reinforcements away from the French attack near Vimy. German accounts, however, do not bear out this statement.

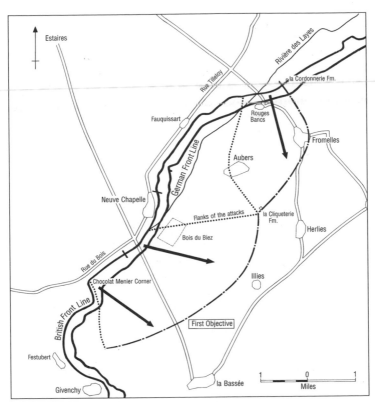

Battle of Aubers Ridge – objectives

J. UPTON

Rouges Bancs, France, 9 May

The first of four VCs won on 9 May was awarded to Cpl James Upton, 1st Sherwood Foresters (Notts & Derby Regt), 24th Bde, 8th Div., who took part in the northern section of the attack.

The Sherwood Foresters were in support of 2nd East Lancs, whose attack should have commenced from a new trench dug west of the Petillon–Rouges Bancs road in advance of the main line. This trench, however, was not completed owing to the waterlogged ground, so most of the East Lancs started forward from the main British breastworks at 05.20 hours, twenty minutes after the British artillery barrage had begun. The advance companies met with fierce machine-gun and rifle fire which inflicted heavy losses but they still attempted to cross the 150 yards of no-man's-land when the barrage lifted at 05.40 hours. Because the German trench line was at an angle to the advance the East Lancs moved to their left as they neared the enemy line and came under enfilade fire which almost annihilated the leading platoons. The attack could get no nearer than 70 yards from the German breastworks.

B and D Coys of the Sherwood Foresters were ordered up to the British defences and succeeded in moving forward from there at 06.10 hours, despite the trenches being clogged with the dead, wounded and survivors from the first advance. As the intended direction of attack was under fire from a number of enemy machine-guns and the ground covered with dead and wounded men, the companies changed direction towards the right, the advance now against the shoulder of a small salient in the German line. Some men of B and D Coys had got to within 40 yards of the enemy when they were held up by wire, through which only a single path, 4 yards wide, had been cut; close behind the wire was a ditch packed with wire that was also undamaged by the artillery fire. As the companies tried to get through the wire, the men were shot down in large numbers. At this point the order to retire was passed along part of the line and the surviving men, seeing troops to their left retiring, fell back to the British line.

A further attack by the two remaining companies of the battalion, A and C, was attempted at 07.35 hours in conjunction with the East Lancs but this advance was also halted by enemy shell and machine-gun fire before the German line was reached. Many men lay down in the open, rather than attempt the return across no-man's-land. It was here that No. 10082, Cpl James Upton won his VC. He crawled forward, near to the enemy breastwork, where a sergeant lay wounded, and bandaged the man's wound before affixing rudimentary splints, and carrying him back to safety. Discarding his heavy equipment, Upton returned to no-man's-land to rescue another man, this time with a stomach wound. The injured man was too heavy for him to carry so he dragged him to the British line on his waterproof sheet. Yet again Upton went forward, this time to rescue a soldier badly wounded in both legs; carrying the man on his back, he was within a few yards of safety when a German shell exploded close by, killing the wounded man instantly and shocking Upton badly, causing him to stop his efforts for a time to recover.

Upton remained in front of the British parapet until after 20.00 hours that night, under fire at all times but rendering first aid to seriously wounded soldiers; he also brought in ten more wounded men. For his untiring efforts throughout the day Upton was recommended for the VC. The battalion was relieved late in the evening and went back to billets; its casualties for the day totalled 359.

Upton's VC citation was published in the *London Gazette* on 29 June 1915, and when the battalion was in Brigade Reserve near Sailly, France, on 8 July, he was presented with his medal ribbon by Maj.-Gen. Sir F. Davies. On 14 July Upton returned to England and on the 24th was invested with his VC by the King at Windsor Castle.

James Upton was born in Lincoln on 3 May 1888 and was brought up by his elder sister. He enlisted in the Army at Derby on 24 July 1906 and was stationed in India when war began, arriving in France on 5 November 1914 with his battalion, the 1st Sherwood Foresters.

The battalion was in action in France throughout the winter, and was heavily involved in the battle of Neuve Chapelle. On 20 July 1915, less than a week after receiving his VC, Upton married Mary Jane Chambers at Lincoln. He returned to France and his last recorded day of service there was 9 February 1918; in total he served there for three years and ninety-six days. He was demobilized on 30 March 1919 and in the post-war years lived at Bulwell, Notts., and

Kingsbury, London. Upton and his wife had three sons, Thomas, Kenneth and George and they were survived by seven grand-children and a number of great-grandchildren. James Upton died at Uxbridge, Middlesex, on 10 August 1949, and his VC was given to the Regimental Museum in Derby by an anonymous woman donor on 26 March 1962. Upton's name appears on the Nottingham Castle Victoria Cross Memorial.

C.R. SHARPE
Rouges Bancs, France, 9 May

At the same time as the East Lancs attacked on 9 May, the assaulting companies of the three battalions on its left, 2nd Rifle Brigade, 1st Royal Irish Rifles and 1/13th London (Kensingtons), all of 25th Bde, also advanced. The Rifle Brigade and Irish Rifles, despite losses, covered the 100 yards separating the front lines and found much of the German wire cut and a 20 yard gap in the breastworks where the British artillery had been effective. Little resistance was met as the majority of the defenders, from *9 Coy, 16th Bavarian Reserve Infantry Regt,* had been killed by artillery; the battalions moved forward and took the hamlet of Rouges Bancs where the position was consolidated.

Further to the left, after a large mine was detonated under the German first and second lines, the Kensingtons charged across the 70 yards of no-man's-land to where enemy defences 80 yards wide had been destroyed by the mine. The Kensingtons occupied the mine crater, regrouped, took the *Stützpunke* at Delangre Farm (known to the Germans as *Totes Schwein* or Dead Pig Farm), advanced to the enemy third line, and formed a left-facing defensive flank. Meanwhile, the remaining companies of the Rifle Brigade, led by Lt-Col. Stephens, advanced to support the two front companies and consolidated about 250 yards of trench. Supporting troops now tried to reach the Irish Rifles but two companies of the 2nd Lincolnshire, 25th Bde, incurred such losses that they were unable to move more than a short distance across no-man's-land (see map on page 133).

The news reached 25th Bde Advanced HQ that parts of the enemy line had been taken at about 06.00 hours, whereupon the brigade commander, Brig.-Gen. A.W.G. Lowry Cole, went forward to the front breastworks. He ordered the last two companies of the Lincolns, C and D, to cross no-man's-land via a newly dug sap to the mine crater and to work along the German front line towards the Rifle Brigade. He had hardly given the order to the Lincolns when 'a number of men of the Rifle Brigade and Irish Rifles were seen streaming back over the German breastwork bringing with them the other two companies of the 2nd Lincolnshire' (*Official History*). A very confused situation existed, and German prisoners who were also running for cover in the British lines were mistaken for a counterattack; Lowry Cole mounted the British breastwork and 'by voice and gesture succeeded in arresting and turning the troops'. He was still standing on the parapet when he fell, fatally wounded and died soon afterwards. The Lincolns moved forward as ordered to the mine crater and began bombing westwards along the trenches. Leading one of the bombing parties was No. 7942, A/Cpl Charles Sharpe who cleared the enemy from a length of trench 50 yards long, and continued bombing alone as the men with him were by then all casualties. He was later joined by four other men and with them bombed his way along a further 250 yards of trench which was then held for the rest of the day. Notwithstanding Sharpe's efforts, for which he was awarded the VC, and those of his comrades, all British troops were withdrawn from the German lines after dark, their positions having become untenable.

Sharpe's VC was gazetted on 29 June and he received his award from the King at Windsor Castle on 24 July, the same day as Cpl Upton. Three of the four men who had joined Sharpe in the German lines, Ptes Bills, Donderdale and Leeman, were awarded the DCM for their gallantry on 9 May.

Charles Richard Sharpe was born at Pickworth, a small village in Lincolnshire, on 2 April 1889. His parents, Robert, a farm labourer, and Charlotte Ann, had a number of other children. After going to school at Pickworth, Sharpe worked on a farm before, at the age of 16, enlisting in the Army. With the 2nd Bn Lincolnshire Regt, he was stationed in Bermuda when war began and arrived in France at Le Havre on 6 November 1914, having travelled via Nova Scotia and England. The Lincolns were involved in various actions during the winter and early part of 1915, including that at Neuve Chapelle in March.

Sharpe returned to France after the presentation of his VC and soon afterwards was badly injured by a bomb; he was invalided out and did not serve overseas again. He left the Army in 1928 having attained the rank of Master Sgt Cook and on 9 November 1929 attended the dinner for VCs at the House of Lords.

Sharpe worked for a time as assistant garden instructor at an approved school in Bourne, Lincs., where he was regarded as a role model by the boys, and when this establishment was closed he 'went to work on the local council's ashcart', Sharpe said, 'but that was considered the wrong job for a VC, so I finished my working life as a labourer and cleaner for the British Racing Motors'.

In September 1956 the Second World War memorial at Bourne, which consisted of a miniature cenotaph with a Garden of Remembrance, was unveiled. Sharpe, or 'Shadder' as he was known to his friends and British Legion colleagues, was a daily visitor to tend the gardens.

In February 1963 Sharpe was staying in Workington with Mrs Dorothy Foster, one of his daughters, at 17 Stainbank Stairburn, when he suffered a fall on the 14th, fracturing several ribs. He died in Workington Infirmary on 17 February of cerebral thrombosis caused by the fall. The military funeral service, organized by 2nd East Anglian Regt, of which the Lincolns were then part, was held on

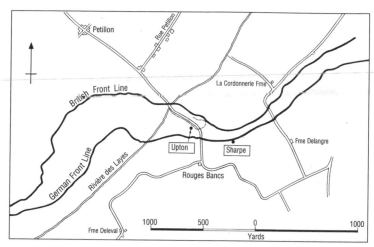

Aubers Ridge

21 February at St Nicholas Church, Lincoln, where a fullsome tribute was paid to Sharpe by the secretary of the Royal Lincolnshire Regiment Association. The well attended service was followed by interment in Newport Cemetery, Lincoln, Plot H. 354.

An obituary notice stated that Sharpe left one son, then serving in the Royal Navy, and one daughter, Mrs A. Gregory, then living in Lincoln. Presumably Sharpe had married twice, for he had been living with Mrs Cooke, another daughter (or step-daughter), before staying in Workington with Mrs Foster.

Sharpe's medals, comprising the VC, 1914 Star and Bar, BWM, BVM, 1939–45 War Medal, Coronation Medals for 1937 and 1953, and the Long Service and Good Conduct Medals, came up for auction in London on 25 July 1989 but remained unsold, the estimated selling price being £9,000–10,000. His VC is held by the Royal Lincolnshire Regiment Museum on loan from South Kesteven Council. Sharpe was the last surviving VC of his regiment.

J. RIPLEY

Rue du Bois, France, 9 May

Three battalions of the Black Watch (1st, 2nd and 1/4th), were in action in the southern section of the Battle of Aubers Ridge on 9 May and two men, from different battalions, won the VC on this day.

The initial assault south of Neuve Chapelle by battalions of the 1st and Meerut Divs fared no better than the one to the north, with only a few men reaching the German line. The losses were severe, 120 officers and nearly 3,000 men falling in less than half an hour. A further attack was attempted at 07.00 hours but the assaulting troops were mown down as soon as they came into view of the enemy. The 1st Bn, Black Watch (1st (Guards) Bde, 1st Div.), occupied support trenches vacated by 2nd Bde in the first attack, positioned with its right on the Cinder Track which ran at right angles from the Rue du Bois. Orders were received that a further attack was to be made at 12.40 hours by the 2nd and 3rd Bdes. This proposed assault was twice postponed but finally orders were received for an attack to start at 16.00 hours.

Following intense British shelling, A and D Coys left the British defences at 15.57 hours with platoons of B and C Coys following 80 yards behind. The artillery fire made a few gaps in the German defences and the Battalion *War Diary* states: 'On right in 2nd Lieut Lyle's platoon [of A Coy] Cpl J. Ripley finds gap in wire and is on parapet at 3.59 p.m. and directs men.' Thus this platoon had covered the 300 yards of no-man's-land, including the obstacles and the bodies of men killed in earlier attacks, in about two minutes. No. 2832 Cpl Ripley led his party of seven or eight men to an enemy support trench, 'where they could not fire or be fired upon', and blocked a communication trench running to the right and their own trench to the left. Meanwhile the other platoons in A Coy, together with the rest of the battalion's attacking troops, crowded through gaps in the German wire further to the left. The Germans then swept no-man's-land with artillery and machine-gun fire which prevented further support reaching the men of the Black Watch in the German line. Cpl Ripley held his position although handicapped by lack of bombs. He was attacked on three sides and eventually all his men became casualties and Ripley made his way back to the British line.

Shortly before 17.00 hours the battalion was ordered to withdraw its men to the British breastworks under cover of artillery fire and just over an hour later the surviving men were withdrawn to support trenches. Ripley's platoon commander, 2/Lt Lyle was posted as missing; he was one of 14 officer casualties, while the other ranks lost 461 men. The battalion's strength on 11 May, when it was visited by the Prince of Wales, was 8 officers and 354 other ranks.

Ripley was awarded the VC and the citation was published in the *London Gazette* on 29 June 1915. He received his medal from the King at Buckingham Palace on 12 July. Aged 48, he was one of the oldest recipients of the award.

John Ripley was born at Keith, Banffs, on 20 August 1867, but little is known of his family and early life except that he had at least two brothers. He joined the Volunteers at Montrose in 1884 and served for eighteen years with G Company, 6th Black Watch, resigning in 1912 after earlier receiving the Long Service Medal. Employed as a recruiting sergeant after war began, Ripley enlisted in the 3rd Bn Black Watch on 25 September 1914 and was given the rank of corporal. He transferred to 1st Bn Black Watch on 18 February 1915 and was promoted to acting sergeant in the 3rd Bn on 2 July.

Returning to St Andrews after receiving his Victoria Cross he was given a very enthusiastic reception and on 30 October 1915 was presented with a War Loan Scrip and a purse of sovereigns by the Provost.

Ripley transferred to the Reserve on 28 March 1919 and returned to St Andrews, taking up his pre-war trade of slater.

He attended the garden party for VC winners at Buckingham Palace on 26 June 1920 and the British Legion dinner at the House of Lords on 9 November 1929. On 14 August 1933, while carrying out roofing work for the St Leonards School in St Andrews, he fell some distance from a ladder and sustained serious spinal injuries. He was rushed to St Andrews Memorial Cottage Hospital but died shortly after admission.

After a service at the Cottage Hospital, a bearer party of sergeants from the Black Watch formed a guard of honour for the hearse on its journey to Largo churchyard where Ripley was buried. His brothers, Joseph and William, were among the chief mourners and among those present was Sgt D. Hunter, the 'Dunfermline VC'. Ripley's wife had died a few years previously and at the time of his funeral he had a son living in America. The whereabouts of his medals are not known.

D. FINLAY

Near Rue du Bois, France, 9 May

At the same time as the 1st Bn Black Watch attacked near the Cinder Track, its sister battalion, the 2nd (Bareilly Bde, Meerut Div.), was in action to the left, close to Port Arthur (see map on page 137). The 2nd Bn had relieved the 2/2nd Gurkhas (Dehra Dun Bde), who suffered many losses in early attacks on the afternoon of 9 May. Shortly before 16.00 hours, Nos 2 and 4 Coys moved forward into positions lying in front of the British parapet. As the Battalion *War Diary* states, 'The charge commenced [at 16.00 hours], but all were shot down almost immediately, few getting further than 30 yards towards the enemy.' In addition to enemy fire the battalion's advance was severely impeded by a wide water-filled ditch roughly parallel to the front line and between 10 and 30 yards in front of the battalion. This same ditch had also hindered earlier attacks and many bodies lay in the mud and water. Some bridges were placed across the ditch in the early morning but few remained by the end of the day.

One of the attackers was No. 1780, A/Cpl David Finlay, 2nd Black Watch who, having been briefly knocked unconscious by the explosion of a shell soon after crossing the British breastworks, led a bombing party of twelve men towards one of the remaining bridges. Two of his men were killed and more were hit when crossing the ditch, as the party dodged from shell-hole to shell-hole on their way towards the enemy line. When only two of his original group were left, Finlay ordered them to return. He then crawled over to a wounded man, picked him up and carried him almost 100 yards to safety. Finlay was under concerted

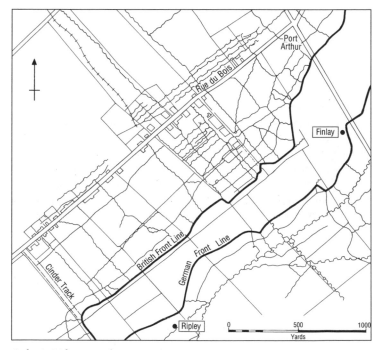

Auber's Ridge – southern sector

enemy fire during the whole of this period, and for his gallantry was awarded the VC.

The attack was halted by the CO of the battalion who realized that further efforts would only be a waste of life. Of the 450 officers and men of the battalion who actually advanced 276 became casualties.

The citation for Finlay's award was published in the *London Gazette* on 29 June and he received his medal from the King on 30 July.

David Finlay was born on 25 January 1893, the eldest of 11 children, in the parish of Guardbridge, Fife, and worked as a ploughman before enlisting in the Black Watch on 5 February 1910, shortly after his eighteenth birthday. He served with the 2nd Bn in India for almost three years and was a lance-corporal when the war began. His battalion landed at Marseilles, France, on 12 October 1914, having sailed from Karachi. The long delay in reaching France since being mobilized at Bareilly on 9 August was caused partly by the presence of the German cruisers *Emden* and *Koningsberg* in the Indian Ocean and also the very slow progress of the troop transports.

With the Bareilly Brigade the 2nd Black Watch were in action during the winter of 1914 at the Battle of La Bassée and subsequently in March at Neuve Chapelle.

Sergeant Finlay (he had been promoted to corporal on 23 May and sergeant on 27 June) returned home on leave and married, on 27 July 1915, in a civil ceremony at Cupar, Christina Cunningham of Prestonbank. After his VC presentation the local community of Glenfarg (where Finlay's family now lived) enthusiastically welcomed the newlyweds with a number of Black Watch pipers and the local laird presented him with a watch and a purse of gold. He rejoined his battalion in France after only a week's leave and was involved in various actions before being posted to Mesopotamia, arriving at Basra on the last day of 1915.

On 20 January 1916, at the Battle of Karma, Mesopotamia, the battalion dug in about 300 yards from the

Turkish line near Hannah, patrols under Sgts Mitchell and Finlay having been sent out earlier to find good positions. The next morning the battalion made a bayonet attack on the enemy line after an artillery bombardment and in this assault Sgt Finlay became one of 163 casualties. His body was not recovered and his name is commemorated on the Basra Memorial to the Missing, Iraq. Finlay's widow moved to Lanarkshire and subsequently remarried, returning his medals to George Finlay, his father. Later the medals passed into the care of Finlay's brother, David, at Cupar.

The Victoria Cross and George Cross Association were contacted by Mr George Cartwright VC of Epping, New South Wales, Australia, and advised that an officer named David Findlay VC had died in NSW on 26 July 1960. The secretary of the Association sent a letter of sympathy to the widow but asked Canon Lummis for verification. Lummis checked the available facts and discovered the man was an impostor who claimed his VC had been stolen when he was in hospital.

A family decision was made to present the medals to his regiment and on 17 March 1967 Finlay's medals, comprising the VC, 1914 Star and Bar, BWM and VM were presented at a ceremony to Brigadier Baker-Baker of the Black Watch. Finlay's brothers John, William, James and Albert made the presentation; also present were other family members including his sister Elizabeth. The medals are now held in the Regimental Museum, Edinburgh.

The name of Sgt. David Finlay VC appears on a bronze panel with other men of Leauchars Parish who fell in the Great War, set into the unusual and charming War Memorial. This Memorial stands south of the cemetery adjacent to a golf club. In the isolated churchyard at Moonzie, about three miles from Cupar, the last name on the granite War Memorial is that of David Finlay VC.

D.W. BELCHER

*South of Wieltje–St Julien Road,
Belgium, 13 May*

The next day, 13 May 1915, dawned gloomy and wet, and from 03.30 hours until early afternoon the heaviest bombardment yet seen on the Ypres Salient turned the rudimentary trenches and support areas into a muddy quagmire. The line from 600 yards east of Shell Trap Farm to Turco Farm was occupied by the 24th Bde, 4th Div., who had held this section since their withdrawal from the Gravenstafel Ridge during the night of 3 May.

The 11th Bde front, on this May morning, was held by two companies of the 1/5th (City of London) Bn, The London Regt (London Rifle Brigade), 1/East Lancs, 1/Rifle Brigade (including Shell Trap Farm), 1/Hampshire and, joining up with French troops, 1/Somerset Light Infantry. The reserves amounted to two companies of the London Rifle Brigade, plus the 2nd Essex Regt of 12th Bde.

Intense shelling flattened much of the trench line, forcing the evacuation of the 1/East Lancs and annihilating two platoons of the London Rifle Brigade who were holding Shell Trap Farm (see map on page 89). The farm certainly lived up to its fateful name, and shells were observed falling there at the rate of over a hundred per minute. One small section of trench, less than 40 yards long, just south of the Wieltje–St Julien Road, was occupied by L/Sgt Douglas Belcher and the remnants of his section, some eighteen men of the London Rifle Brigade. Gradually the incessant bombardment took its toll of Belcher's small group, who continued to pour volleys into any Germans who approached nearer than 200 yards to the battered trench. Rifles jammed with mud and became too hot to hold but still these few men held out while other troops holding another short section of trench on their right retired. Subsequently, the breastwork became almost non-existent, and Belcher decided to occupy the vacant trench to his right as it appeared to be less damaged than the position he held. His party, now reduced to only five men, quickly moved to the other position, and, within minutes the trench they had vacated was demolished by German high explosive shells. For a total of over nine hours they hung on to their trench, firing at any enemy infantry who appeared, until they were finally relieved. Belcher escaped with a graze on his chin and a shrapnel rent in his cap. For holding these short sections of the line under such trying conditions Belcher was awarded the VC.

On the same day, in an extract from Battalion Orders, as quoted in the Battalion *War Diary*, the following appeared:

> The commanding officer wishes to congratulate Sgt Belcher on the most distinguished honour he, and the Bn, have received by the honour of the Victoria Cross for his gallant conduct on May 13th.

The orders also named the eight men who were with Belcher. The *London Gazette* of 23 June 1915 published the citation:

> Douglas Walter Belcher, No. 9539, L/Sergt, 1/5th (City of London) Battn, The London Regt (London Rifle Brigade). Date of act of bravery: 13 May 1915. On the early morning of 13 May 1915, when in charge of a portion of an advanced breastwork south of the Wieltje–St Julien Road, during a very fierce and continuous bombardment by the enemy, which frequently blew in the breastwork, L/Sergt Belcher, with a mere handful of men, elected to remain and endeavour to hold his position after the troops near him had been withdrawn. By his skill and great gallantry he maintained his position during the day, opening rapid fire on the enemy, who were only 150 to 200 yards distant, whenever he saw them collecting for an attack. There is little doubt that the bold front shown by L/Sergt Belcher prevented the enemy breaking through on the Wieltje Road, and averted an attack on the flank of one of the divisions.

When a reporter from the *Daily Express* interviewed Belcher's mother, following the announcement of his award, she said:

> Douglas was home on 72 hours' leave only a very short time ago. He went to the front last November, as a private in the London Rifle Brigade, and, with the exception of the short leave I mentioned, he has been there ever since.
>
> Although we knew that he had distinguished himself, and that he had been recommended for a medal of some sort, we had no idea it was to be the VC. My son was unwilling to discuss the affair at all, saying, I remember, when someone present at his first meal home tried to get him to talk about it, 'Oh, let's get on with the tea, shall we?'

Belcher was decorated by the King at Buckingham Palace on 12 July 1915 and was pictured emerging through the Palace gates with a number of other VC winners. A few days later, his employers, Messrs Waring & Gillow, presented him with a silver rose bowl. Over 3,000 employees of the firm were present at a ceremony at the White City, London, where Waring & Gillow employed thousands on tent-making and aeroplane manufacturing, and replying to Mrs S.J. Waring's speech, Belcher replied that he often thought of his old firm when at the front, saying, 'sometimes we'd see the old vans at the front, and we'd think of home and London and all that'. Douglas Belcher was the first territorial ranker to win the VC in the First World War.

Douglas Walter Belcher was born at Surbiton, Surrey, on 15 July 1889 and went to Tiffin's School, Kingston-upon-Thames. He was very fit, regularly swimming across the River Thames and back on summer mornings. Rowing, cycling, cricket and tennis were other activities he enjoyed but his main passion was the Territorial Army. He had joined a cyclist volunteer corps in 1906 and transferred in 1908 to the Queen Victoria Rifles with whom he won a silver cup for shooting. He was employed in the antiques department of Messrs Waring & Gillow and continued with his shooting on their rifle range.

In August 1914 he joined the London Rifle Brigade, and volunteering for foreign service, went to France as a lance-sergeant in November 1914. In 1916 Belcher was commissioned as a second lieutenant in the 9th Bn, London Regt (Queen Victoria Rifles), and was promoted to lieutenant on 10 August 1917. He married in January of that year Emily Francis Luxford at St Mark's, Surbiton, where he had been a boy chorister. Serving with the Gurkha Rifles from 1918 to 1922, he was a company commander in Mesopotamia during the Arab rising of 1921 and later saw service in Burma.

Retiring from the army in 1922 with the rank of captain, Belcher suffered from bad health after the war and, as reported in the *Sunday Dispatch* of 24 May 1931 he had first obtained a job with a cigar merchant,

> . . . then had a bad breakdown and a year or so after went to work for a firm in its antique department, but I had not been in the new job long before my health went again, and the doctors told me that I had to get an open-air life or things were going to be serious.
>
> I went to Tunbridge Wells where my wife had been struggling to run our present business to help keep the home going. We hadn't any capital – my health had done away with that – but we managed to keep things going. She worked hard in the shop and I went out on the round.

He had evidently spent eighteen months going out on a pushbike getting orders and delivering vegetables.

Belcher was diagnosed as suffering from neurasthenia in 1926 and his state of health was used in evidence when he filed for divorce in February 1935. He had acquired a poultry farm in Westhorpe, Suffolk, and in the undefended divorce petition, widely reported in October 1935, Mrs Belcher admitted adultery with one 'Reg' Larkin at Westhorpe in 1931. Subsequently, it was stated, Mrs Belcher had brought the co-respondent to live in the house in Tunbridge Wells, Capt. Belcher being treated 'almost like a lodger'. Belcher, who had been in and out of hospital 'was not in a state of health to exert any authority over his wife', and 'only feebly protested'. The Tunbridge Wells shop had been sold in 1933, Mrs Belcher and Larkin going to live at Westhorpe. Belcher's health had improved by 1934 and, after the granting of a decree nisi in October 1935 he was granted custody of his two sons, then aged 17 and 9.

Belcher was active in the British Legion and Old Comrades Association, the Tunbridge Wells branch of the latter being named after him. He was working as a 'clerk-commissionaire' in a city firm of charted accountants in October 1937. In June 1938 he led the procession at a Torchlight Tattoo held at the Memorial Sports Ground, Redhill, Surrey, and on 30 October was pictured with two other winners of the Victoria Cross, Sgt Boulter and L/Cpl Wilcox, at the Ypres Memorial Service on Horse Guards Parade.

Belcher joined the London Rifle Brigade Territorials in the ranks as a rifleman before being promoted to sergeant. Following a bad fall at Woolwich Barracks he was invalided out in May 1940 and granted the rank of captain. He remarried in August 1941 at St Ethelburga's Church, Bishopsgate, London; his bride was Miss Gertrude Elizabeth Brine of Surbiton, where Belcher was now living in Villiers Avenue. A guard of honour was formed by the London Rifle Brigade and the National Defence Corps. He was present at the Victory Parade and Dinner on 9 June 1946.

Douglas Belcher VC died at Claygate, Surrey, on 3 June 1953, just over a month short of his 64th birthday, and he is buried in Holy Trinity Churchyard, Claygate, Surrey. His medals are held by the Rifle Brigade Museum, Winchester.

THE BATTLE OF FESTUBERT
15–27 May

Following the Battle of Aubers Ridge Sir John French was put under considerable pressure by the French to mount a further offensive and the action that was later to be known as the Battle of Festubert was proposed by Sir Douglas Haig on 12 May.

The broad details were not dissimilar to the attack of 9 May but on this occasion the distance between the two parts of the pincer movement were much closer. The 7th Div. would attack north of Festubert while 600 yards to the north the 2nd and Meerut Divs would attack from just north of Chocolat Menier Corner to Port Arthur. The objectives of this new attack, much curtailed from that of 9 May, were now to be an advance of some 1,000 yards along La Quinque Rue from north-west of Festubert to la Tourelle.

As the northern sector was over ground which had previously been attacked, it was proposed that this part of the action should be at night, followed by a daylight attack by the 7th Div. French attacks had achieved more success with a longer artillery bombardment so it was agreed that a 36 hour bombardment would precede the attack. The artillery began firing on the morning of 13 May and continued in a deliberate fashion with shots being observed and reported. A number of howitzer shells did not explode, possibly owing to faulty fuses. Rain fell throughout 13 May, making observation difficult, and it was considered necessary to extend the bombardment to 60 hours.

The attack of 2nd and Meerut Divs began at 23.30 hours on 15 May and the forward battalions of 6th Bde (2nd Div.) were successful in their surprise attack and occupied the German support trench. To the left 5th Bde (2nd Div.) and Garhwals Bde (Meerut Div.) were caught by rifle and machine-gun fire in no-man's-land and few men reached the German front line.

At dawn on 16 May 20th Bde of 2nd Div. advanced; 22nd Bde managed an advance of about 600 yards but 20th Bde was halted by enfilade fire from a strong enemy position to the left and only the right section of the brigade went forward past the German front line.

During the night of 16/17 May the Germans started a withdrawal of about ¾ mile to a new line from South Breastwork to Ferme du Bois, but the British were not aware of this withdrawal for a number of days.

On 17 May the gap between the 7th and 2nd Divs in the enemy front line was joined. Various attacks were made during the period 18–24 May which resulted in some small gains. On 18 May the 7th Div. was relieved by the Canadian Div., and the 2nd Div. by the 51st Div. on 19 May. On 25 May the Canadian Div., with 47 Div. on its right, attacked and gained some ground east of Festubert. The overall gains from the battle were about 600 yards on a front of 4,000 yards. British casualties exceeded 16,600, compared to about 5,000 German.

F. BARTER

Festubert, France, 16 May

Three days after L/Sgt Belcher won his VC near Ypres on 13 May, the first of the VCs awarded during the Battle of Festubert was won by CSM Barter of 1st Bn, Royal Welsh Fusiliers (RWF).

The battalion was part of 22nd Bde, 7th Div., and was in billets at Essars when news of a forthcoming attack reached it.

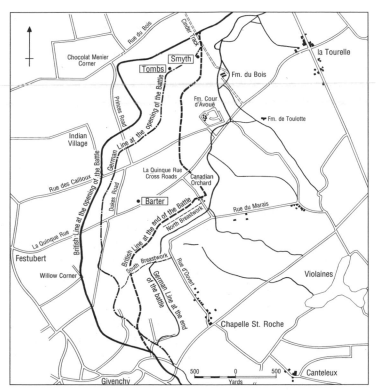

Battle of Festubert

Capt. Stockwell of A Coy, together with other officers, went to the front line on 12 May and during a night reconnaissance found a ditch, 'from five to ten feet broad and everywhere a depth of five or six feet of water'. It was arranged that the leading men in the attack would carry trench-boards to place across the ditch before the attack. The battalion's orders were to advance 450 yards behind the German lines, change direction half-right and occupy a long communication trench. A Coy, the leading company, was instructed to take an orchard, later known as Canadian Orchard, 1,200 yards from the British lines (see map above).

After sixty hours – the longest artillery bombardment of the war to date – the battalion, having moved up to its assembly positions during the night, prepared to advance. Stockwell ensured that the boards were laid across the ditch and noted in his diary that the enemy parapet was not much damaged as many of the high-explosive shells had gone over it. He also commented on the number of 'shorts' from British artillery which wounded several of his men. German artillery returned fire ten minutes before zero hour, shelling both the British front line and no-man's-land.

The first line of A Coy climbed over the British parapet at 03.16 hours (Stockwell delayed his men for one minute until the British artillery fire had lifted), followed shortly afterwards by the other half of the company. Machine-gun fire from the right, where 2nd Queen's (Royal West Surreys) were advancing and rifle fire from in front, took its toll of the RWF but, as Stockwell recorded: 'the remaining men went straight on to the enemy trenches, where half an hour's strenuous hand-to-hand fighting took place in a frightful tangled system of trenches'. It was in this fighting that No. 3902, CSM Frederick Barter, won his VC.

Having crossed the 120 yards of no-man's-land and gained entry to the German front line, Barter collected together eight men and bombed down the trench to the right forcing the surrender of the German occupants; he continued bombing until in total he cleared some 500 yards of trench. Besides being responsible for the surrender of 105 of the enemy, including three officers, Barter also discovered and cut eleven enemy mine leads. His actions considerably helped the advance of the 2nd Queen's as well as giving great assistance to the men of his own battalion. Barter was awarded the VC for his part in the attack. When interviewed later Barter praised the eight men with him in the action, in particular Pte Thomas Hardy who, when wounded in the right shoulder 10 yards from the German line, ignored Barter's order for him to retire, saying he was left-handed. After application of a field-dressing, Hardy, attached from 2nd Queen's for bomb training, ran forward, bombing nearly 30 yards of trench before being killed, shot in the head.

There was confusion in the enemy trenches, men from various battalions being mixed together. Capt. Stockwell collected a party of men from four battalions and eventually reached Canadian Orchard but his force, numbering fewer than 100 men, was not strong enough to capture this position and returned late in the day to the original British line.

The battalion was relieved on 18 May after recovering the bodies of four officers and more than 100 other ranks of the RWF from the former no-man's-land. The strength of the battalion on 16 May was 25 officers and 806 other ranks; 6 officers and 247 men came out of the battle.

Barter's VC was gazetted on 29 June and he was presented with his medal by the King at Buckingham Palace on 12 July 1915.

Frederick Barter was born at 60 Daniel Street, Cathays, Cardiff, on 17 January 1891, one of three children born to Mr and Mrs Samuel Barter. He went to school at Crwys Road Board School, Cardiff, and after working as a collier and later as a porter on the Great Western Railway, enlisted in the Royal Welsh Fusiliers (RWF) on 4 December 1908. On completion of his term of service Barter transferred to RWF Special Reserve and was working as a stove repairer for the Cardiff Gas Light & Coke Company when war broke out.

He was mobilized with 1st Bn RWF on 5 August 1914. The battalion landed at Zeebrugge on 7 October and by the 30th of the month they were reduced to 86 men and one officer after heavy fighting at Zonnebeke and Zandvoorde.

When Barter returned to his native Cardiff before his investiture, he was received at the railway station by the Lord Mayor and other dignitaries. A procession through the main streets was greeted by thousands of cheering people and later, after addressing a recruiting meeting, he was driven home in a flag-bedecked motor car. He suffered almost embarrassing attentions at subsequent recruiting meetings when the ladies of Cardiff lavished cigarettes and other gifts upon him. An impromptu collection at the Cardiff Coal Exchange raised £11 4s. to purchase War Bonds on his behalf, while his old school gave him a cheque at a enthusiastic reception by the children, and the Cardiff Gas Light & Coke Company presented him with shares in the Company and the Cardiff Coal Exchange and £50 in War Bonds.

Immediately after receiving his VC on 12 July 1915, Barter, together with three other recipients of the award (nine other VCs were awarded), Sgt Ripley (see page 134), Cpl Keyworth (see page 161) and Bandsman Rendle, hailed a taxi-cab to evade the attentions of autograph hunters and female admirers, the latter anxious to bestow kisses on the VC winners outside the Palace.

When 2/Lt Barter left Cardiff to return to the front, having been commissioned into the RWF on 26 August 1915, there were moving scenes when he bid farewell to his elderly father, sister and brother Robert.

After a further period in France, on 10 May 1916 Barter was appointed Instructor at the Western Command Bombing School, Prees Heath, Shropshire, with the rank of temporary lieutenant, a position he held until the end of that year. In February 1917, after a few more weeks in France, he was seconded for service with the Indian Army and sailed for India in March. He was stationed at Kohat, on the north-west frontier with 4/3rd Gurkha Rifles. On 30 March 1918 his battalion *War Diary* recorded that he was awarded the MC by the C-in-C EEF, Gen. Allenby. The citation for this award, published in the *London Gazette* of 26 July 1918, reads:

> For conspicuous gallantry and devotion to duty when ordered to make a flank attack [at El Kefr, Palestine]. He led his two platoons up a precipitous hill, and turned the enemy's flank. Then placing one platoon with two Lewis guns to command the enemy's lines of retreat, he gallantly led an attack with the other platoon from the rear and flank, killing and capturing practically the whole garrison.

Barter's life was saved at El Kefr on 10 April by Rfn Karanbahadur Rana who was also subsequently awarded the VC for this act.

Barter received a permanent commission in the Indian Army on 6 May 1918 and in January 1919 was invalided to England with fever. He retired from the Army with the rank of captain in 1922. During the 1920s Barter was involved in a few private enterprises and on 13 May 1925 he married Catherine Mary

Theresa Maclaren (née Wright) a divorcee and the owner of the Heathfield Hotel, Waldron, Sussex. In 1928 he began work as a labour manager with AEC at Southall, Middlesex, a position he retained until his death. As a major in the Second World War he commanded a company of 4th Middlesex Home Guard, and his wife died in 1944.

On 15 May 1953 Barter died in St Ann's Nursing Home, Canford Cliffs, Poole, Dorset, and his cremation took place at Bournemouth Crematorium, where his ashes were scattered in the Garden of Remembrance. Barter Road and Barter Court at Hightown, Wrexham, Clwyd, were named after him.

His medals were acquired by a private collector in North America at some point but reappeared early in 1992 in Kent. The RWF Regimental Museum was determined to acquire the medals but feared that the price would be forced up if it were known the Museum was actively interested. Prior to the auction, stories were circulated to the effect that the Museum could not afford the purchase. When bidding began in London on 27 March 1992, the Museum curator, Capt. Bryan Finchett Maddock, in civilian dress, kept a low profile and 'a balding man in a green duffel coat' eventually made the successful bid; as revealed later, he was acting on behalf of the Regimental Museum, acquiring the medals for them at the sale price of £18,500. The medal set comprised the VC, MC, 1914 Star and Bar, BWM, BVM(MID), Order of St George (Russia) and 1937 Coronation Medal. The Regimental Museum holds ten of the fourteen VCs won over the years by men of the RWF.

J.H. TOMBS

Near Rue du Bois, France, 16 May

A second VC was awarded on 16 May when L/Cpl Joseph Tombs, 1st Bn, King's (Liverpool) Regt (6th Bde, 2nd Div.), put the lives of wounded men before that of his own. The battalion was on the right of 6th Bde in assembly trenches a few yards north-west of Rue du Bois and 400 yards to the right of the Cinder Track which ran at right angles from the road (see map on page 147). These assembly positions were 500 yards behind the front line, which was held by 1/7th King's, one of the battalions that advanced when a surprise attack began at 23.30 hours on 15 May. There was no artillery support as the leading companies moved silently across the 300 yards of no-man's-land and on 6th Bde front the attack was successful, and most of the German front line taken. The 5th Bde on its left was less fortunate and only a small section of the allotted trench was captured.

The 1st King's moved two companies forward by 01.00 hours and prepared to advance with the remaining companies at 03.30 hours, the planned time for the next phase of the attack. The first platoon of B Coy attempted to cross no-man's-land but was mown down by enemy machine-gun fire from the right; the second platoon suffered a similar fate before it could be stopped from going forward. The remaining platoons were ordered not to advance. The enemy commenced an artillery bombardment on the British front and communication trenches which inflicted many casualties on the battalion and this bombardment continued, with varying intensity, throughout the day.

No-man's-land was littered with dead and wounded men when No. 10973 L/Cpl Tombs was given permission to leave the front line and assist the wounded. As many of the men were from his own B Coy he had an additional incentive to help them. He climbed over the battalion's parapet and ran to the nearest wounded man whom he helped back to the line, at one point carrying the man on his back. Within a few minutes Tombs repeated his journey with a second man amid heavy enemy fire, and then went back across the ground between the lines to where another injured man was calling for help. It was some time before Tombs was seen making his way back from his third rescue attempt; this man was seriously wounded and Tombs had used rifle slings around his own neck and under the man's arms to drag him back. In total he rescued four men while under fire the whole time, and was wounded himself, hit in the stomach by shrapnel.

The 1st King's were in action again on the next day when an attempted attack on a forward position resulted in heavy losses for the company involved. On the night of 19 May the battalion was relieved, by which time its casualties totalled over 650, including 14 officers.

Tombs was recommended for an award by his CO, and the *London Gazette* on 24 July published his VC citation, but incorrectly dated the action as 16 June 1915. He was later promoted to corporal and with that rank was presented with his medal by the King at Buckingham Palace on 12 August 1915. Only two other soldiers were presented with the VC this day; Private Henry May, 1st Bn The Cameronians and Private William Mariner, 3rd KRRC (see page 166).

Joseph Harcourt Tombs was born in Melbourne, Australia, on 23 March 1888, and was the son of an army officer. He was educated at the Naval College, Williamstown, before the family moved to England where he continued his education at King's School, Grantham, Lincs. (was Grantham Grammar School until 1909), from 1902 to 1906. According to a newspaper interview in 1929, Tombs stated that he ran away from home when he was 13 and sailed to Hobart on *Inverest*, a windjammer, and was employed in a variety of jobs including a short period in Peru as a mercenary before working on steamers along the west coast of South America. He made his way to Philadelphia in the United States after involvement on the Panama Canal in a dredger, before returning to England. Employed at the works of Joseph Crosfield & Son on their wharf in Warrington, he lodged at 17 Rowley Lane, off Church Street. Tombs next worked at the British Aluminium Company at Bank Quay as a sheet metal roller.

On 5 March 1912 Tombs enlisted in the King's (Liverpool) Regt when it was stationed in barracks at Warrington; when war began the battalion was stationed at Aldershot and landed in France on 13 August 1914. It is not certain that Tombs went to France with his battalion for a letter was received from him by a Warrington newspaper in January 1915 when he was part of a Mobile Field Force based on the east coast of Scotland. At about this time he spent some time in Craigleigh Military Hospital so it is possible he had been in France but had returned to England, wounded. He rejoined his battalion in February 1915 and was with it on 10 March when heavy casualties were incurred in a diversionary attack at Givenchy.

When news of Tombs's gallantry was published in Warrington newspapers, prior to the publication of his citation, doubt was raised over his identity. Mr Stewart, an official from the British Aluminium Company, corresponded with Tombs and in a letter Tombs replied:

> I am pleased to say I am the Tombs referred to in the papers. My Commanding Officer did send for me the other day and told me he'd recommended me for the VC.

It appears that Mr Stewart was not completely convinced he had the right man, for in a later letter Tombs again confirms he is the right man, and giving the names of his CSM and company commander who could be contacted for verification. In this letter Tombs also advised of his promotion to corporal.

Tombs returned to Warrington unexpectedly on 28 July and, accompanied by Mr Stewart, visited the offices of the *Warrington Guardian*, British Aluminium Company and the mayor before he was 'sent away from the town for a brief rest'. He was given a public reception in Warrington on 31 July, followed by a procession through the town where he was cheered by large crowds. Tombs was later presented with an illuminated address and after a few days embarked on a recruiting campaign in Liverpool, St Helens, and Bolton. He continued with recruiting after his investiture and on 25 August was awarded the Order of St George 4th Class (Russia).

Tombs returned to his battalion and later received a wound which necessitated the removal of a toe on his right foot. During 1916 he was transferred to 54th Anti-Aircraft Coy, RGA, and served as a gunner on the Canadian Pacific Railway Company (CPR)'s liner *Minnedosa* for a time. He was discharged from the Army in January 1920 with the rank of corporal, his last posting being with the Woolwich Ordnance School where he trained as a mechanic.

He emigrated to Canada in 1921 after working on several CPR ships, including the *Minnedosa*, and was employed in the mailing department of the Sun Life Assurance Company of Canada at Montreal, where in 1928 he was promoted to the post of special messenger.

Tombs married Minnie Sylvia Gooding in 1925 and together they attended a VC reunion in Canada organized by Lt-Col. W.H. Clark-Kennedy VC, and in November 1929 attended the VC Parade and Dinner in London. The CPR arranged free return transport to England on one of their ships, the ubiquitous *Minnedosa*, and Tombs's sister was waiting at the dock in Liverpool to welcome her brother.

Tombs was a guest at the banquet in Montreal in honour of King George VI and Queen Elizabeth in May 1939. On 4 January 1940 he enlisted in the Royal Canadian Air Force and served for five years at the Flying School, Trenton, Ontario, and was discharged with the rank of sergeant. During his service Tombs gave notice to his employers and after his return to civilian life was hospitalized several times. He never fully recovered from an operation to remove shrapnel from his stomach in 1952 and suffered a stroke in 1964, after which he was confined to bed. Tombs lodged with Mrs Frederica Johnson and her family, including Tombs' nephew William Wheaton and his daughter Sheila, on Second Avenue, Toronto, during his Air Force service and stayed on after the war.

Tombs died on 28 June 1966 and was interred in the War Veteran's Plot, Section K, 1056, Pine Hill Cemetery, Toronto, on 2 July. The funeral was organized by Major Geary VC, who also won his medal in 1915 (see page 72), in conjunction with the Royal Regt of Canada which was affiliated with the King's Regt. His six medals, comprising the VC, 1914 Star, BVM (MID), BWM, Merchant Marine Medal and Order of St George 4th Class (Russia), lay on a velvet cushion on the coffin throughout the service, and a 22 man guard of honour was provided by the Royal Regt of Canada.

After the funeral, Mrs Johnson's granddaughter, Mrs Sheila Wallace, who had grown up in the house with the quiet-spoken man known to her as 'Uncle Joe', told a reporter, 'He hardly ever talked about the war. He hated it. He lost too many of his friends who never came back.' Joseph Tombs' VC and medals were inherited by his nephew William Wheaton, and on 27 October 1966, at a ceremony in the City Hall at Toronto, the medals were presented to the Royal Regiment of Canada. It was agreed that as an affiliation existed between the Royal Regiment of Canada and the King's Regt, the medals would be shared between the two regiments and consequently have travelled between Canada and England on numerous occasions. At the time of writing it is planned that a memorial blue plaque be unveiled in honour of L/Cpl Joseph Tombs VC at The King's School, Brook Street,Granthamon 17 May 2011. A similar plaque will be unveiled at the same time to Captain Albert Ball VC DSO MC

J.G. SMYTH

Near Richebourg l'Avoué, France, 18 May

The only British officer in the Indian Army to win the VC on the Western Front in 1915 was Lt Smyth (15th Ludhiana Sikhs, Sirhind Bde, Lahore Div.) at the Battle of Festubert.

During the night of 17 May the Sirhind Bde took over part of the line held by 2nd Div.; relief was very difficult as communication trenches were knee-deep in water and blocked with wounded. One company of 15th Ludhiana Sikhs under Lt Hyde-Cates and one company of 1st Highland Light Infantry (HLI) moved forward under cover of darkness and relieved men in 200 yards of captured trench 500 yards south-east of Rue du Bois and to the right of the Cinder Track (see map on page 147). The ground between the front line and this isolated trench was near where L/Cpl Tombs had won his VC a few hours earlier, and Smyth later described this scene as 'littered with the unburied dead of many battalions, stinking to high heaven'.

Enemy attacks on the captured trench, known later as the Glory Hole, began early in the morning and efforts were made to supply the two forward companies with further ammunition and bombs. Two separate parties were sent forward by the HLI but were shot down before they covered half the distance; the same fate befell groups sent back by both of the forward companies.

Smyth watched these attempts from the front line parapet over 250 yards away and, as bombing officer, was not surprised when his CO, Lt-Col. Hill, asked if Smyth could get a party across to the beleaguered position as Bde HQ was demanding that assistance be sent. Smyth told him he did not think it was possible but would try if ordered. Hill failed to persuade Bde HQ to cancel the order, and Smyth's company commander, Maj. Hughes, a 'stickler for discipline', begged him to disobey the order but he refused.

When Smyth asked for volunteers every man stepped forward so he selected those he considered were the strongest ten men. It was then mid-afternoon and the Germans started to shell between the two lines; the smoke and debris caused by this shelling gave some cover to Smyth and his party as they climbed over the parapet. They took with them bandoliers of ammunition and two boxes, each containing forty-eight bombs, and made their way along a badly damaged trench barely 2 feet deep and full of British, Indian and German bodies, losing three men to shell-fire. Smyth's group had crawled almost one-third of the distance before they were seen by enemy machine-gunners and riflemen who occupied slightly higher ground, and who immediately opened fire on them, inflicting further losses. Further across they had to wade chest-deep along a stream until Smyth, and his one remaining man, Sepoy Lal Singh, and one box of bombs reached a shell-hole close to their objective. Under covering fire from the men in front of them Smyth and the Sepoy dashed the last few yards. Smyth reached the trench safely but Lal Singh was mortally wounded. Miraculously Smyth was unhurt, though his tunic and cap were pierced by a number of bullets.

Smyth stayed in the trench until dark while further German attacks were repelled, and then returned to the British parapet where his batman, Ishar Singh, awaited him. After a tot of rum from the CO he slept for a number of hours beneath the orderly room table. All the Sikhs in his party were killed or seriously wounded.

Smyth was recommended for the VC and the citation was published in the *London Gazette* on 29 June 1915. Early in July he was selected to receive the Order of St George 4th Class (Russia); with this award was a letter from the Tsar which entitled him, among other things, to inspect girls' schools in Russia. Nine of the men with him were awarded the Indian Distinguished Service Medal and one, Lance-Naik (lance-corporal) Mangal Singh, the IOM 2nd Class; Smyth always maintained these awards were inadequate.

Smyth was presented with his VC at Buckingham Palace on 12 July 1916, which was the largest investiture of the war to date, where he was one of the few VC recipients able to walk unaided.

John ('Jackie') George Smyth was born at Teignmouth, Devon, on 25 October 1893, the eldest of three sons of William John and Lillian May Smyth. His father worked for the Indian Civil Service in Burma.

He was educated at the Dragon Preparatory School in Oxford from 1901 and during his time there was seriously ill for two years. Although not expected to survive, he recovered and returned to the Dragon School where he obtained an exhibition scholarship to Repton at the age of 14. His ambition was for a military career and he decided to try for the Indian Army where an officer could survive on his pay. Smyth lived with his mother and brothers at 177 Banbury Road, Oxford, while he was at Repton, rarely seeing his father who was serving in Burma. He went to Sandhurst in 1911, passing out ninth of his class, and in September 1912 sailed from England to join the 1st Green Howards (Yorkshire Regt), for one year's attachment. Smyth then joined 15th Ludhiana Sikhs in Loralai, Baluchistan, and when war began left India with his battalion for France.

In the last week of October 1914 the battalion incurred nearly 400 casualties near Rue Tilleloy and spent the rest of the winter in the areas around Festubert and Givenchy.

On 28 April 1915 the 15th Sikhs were reduced to fewer than 400 of all ranks after an attack on enemy lines north-east of

Ypres was halted by machine-gun fire, which caused almost 100 casualties in ten minutes. Smyth rejoined his battalion after his VC award and with it sailed to Egypt later in the year. He fought in the Senussi Campaign in the Western Desert from November 1915 to February 1916 when his battalion was reduced even further by another 200 casualties.

The battalion returned to India to refit and with it Smyth served on the north-west frontier for nearly three years, being promoted to brigade major of 43rd Bde (16 Div.) in Lahore during 1918. In May 1919 two frontier tribes, the Wazirs and Mahsuds, rose up against the British and on 31 May Smyth won his MC when he helped to save a convoy of supplies that had been ambushed by Mahsud tribesmen. Smyth was recommended for a bar to his VC by his brigade commander, Brig.-Gen. Gwyn-Thomas. Capt. Henry Andrews of the Indian Medical Service won a posthumous VC at this action in the Tochi Valley for saving wounded men.

Smyth returned to England and on 26 June 1920 was at the first VC reunion when 324 VCs were present. He was presented with his MC by the Duke of York at Buckingham Palace on 21 July 1920, together with brother Herbert 'Bill'; all of them were so nervous that the citation did not get read. Smyth was married the next day at Brompton Oratory to Margaret Dundas.

Smyth served in Mesopotamia and was Mentioned in Despatches before joining the Staff at Indian Army HQ at Delhi for four years. He was in England for the VC dinner and procession to the Cenotaph in November 1929 and was again Mentioned in Despatches for his part in quelling a riot in Peshawar city during May 1930 after his return to India. He taught at the Staff College, Camberley, for three years and was appointed brevet lieutenant-colonel in 1933; in 1935 in India he was second in command of 45th Rattray Sikhs under Lt-Col. Hyde-Cates. Smyth returned to England on leave six weeks before the beginning of the Second World War and on 1 February 1940 was given command of 127th Infantry Bde, 42nd East Lancs Div. His first marriage was dissolved and on 12 April 1940 he married Frances Read in Southsea.

On 23 April he went to France with his brigade and was involved in the fighting prior to Dunkirk from where he sailed back to England on a destroyer on the last day of May. He was again Mentioned in Despatches.

In June 1941 he returned to India and was operated upon at Quetta hospital for an internal abcess and while recuperating had to be evacuated from the hospital becuase of a severe earthquake, which caused his operation wound to reopen. Although not completely recovered, Smyth took command of 18th Indian (Dagger) Div. in October with the rank of major-general. He was transferred to the command of 17th Indian Div. in December and in early January 1942 he arrived in Burma to command this newly formed division. Smyth's book *Before the Dawn* describes the two months after the Japanese invasion of Burma, during which period almost two brigades from 17 Div. were lost at the Sittang River. The result of these operations against the Japanese was that Smyth was deprived of his rank and retired from the service. He was not a well man and it required extensive care in England to restore his health. He became military correspondent for a number of newspapers and from 1946 was tennis correspondent for the *Sunday Times*. He entered Parliament in February 1950 as Conservative member for Norwood and was created a baronet (First Baronet, of Teignmouth) in 1955.

Smyth did much to further the cause of ex-prisoners of war in the Far East and in 1956 he was one of the co-founders of the VC and GC Association. Smyth was also a broadcaster, an author, a playwright, and a journalist. He married twice; Margaret Dundas on 22 July 1920, with whom he had three sons and a daughter before the marriage was later dissolved; then to Frances Read on 12 April 1940. One of his sons, Capt. John Lawrence Smyth, 1st Bn The Queen's Royal Regiment (West Surrey), was killed on 7 May 1944 at the Battle of Kohima. He was the author of more than thirty books, including *The Story of the Victoria Cross* and two volumes of autobiography, *The Only Enemy: An Autobiography [1959]* and a revised version, *Milestones: A Memoir [1979]*. He retired from Parliament in 1966, having been Parliamentary Secretary to the Minister of Pensions. Sir John Smyth died on 26 April 1983 at his home in Dolphin Square, London and was cremated at

Hyde Park, London, 10 July 1915

Capt. Foss and his bombers recapture a British position

Capt. Foss and his bombers recapture a British position.

Daniels and Noble attempting to break through the wire.

Nottingham Castle Victoria Cross Memorial.

Leeds plaque to VC Winners.
(*photograph by Dave Stowe*)

Headstone of Captain Campbell.

Lt Martin's bombing on Hill 60.

Lt Geary hurrying forward to the trenches on Hill 60.

L/Cpl Fuller at Mansfield with the mayor and the Duchess of Portland.

Hill 60 from The Dump, near the railway, looking south-east.

Capt. Scrimger carrying Capt. Macdonald to safety.

Headstone of Sam Harvey VC
(*photograph by Mark Brunning*)

Pte Lynn manning his machine-gun

Mir Dast with Lord Kitchener.

Cpl Upton dragging in a wounded man on a waterproof sheet.

The night of 20/21 April on Hill 60. (Woolley is throwing a bomb on the right).

VC winners leaving Buckingham Palace on 12 July 1915 (Ripley on right).

Lt Smyth and
Sepoy Lal Singh.

VCs Revd Harold Woolley (left) and Sir John Smyth (right) with Gen. Sir Lewis Hamilton.

L/Cpl Angus being helped by Lt Martin and Lord Newlands.

Moonzie War Memorial. (*photograph by Jim McGinlay*)

Piper Laidlaw and Lt Young rallying their comrades.

Loos, before and after the battle

Sgt Wells leading his men.

2/Lt Hallowes on the parapet,
encouraging his men.

Pavilion at the Commonwealth Memorial Gates, London.

Pte Dunsire rescuing a wounded comrade.

Sgt Saunders taking charge of two machine-guns. (He is erroneously pictured wearing a helmet).

Cpl Pollock bombing the enemy in 'Little Willie'.

A/Sgt Raynes putting his own smoke helmet on Sgt Ayres.

Pte Dunsire rescuing a wounded comrade.

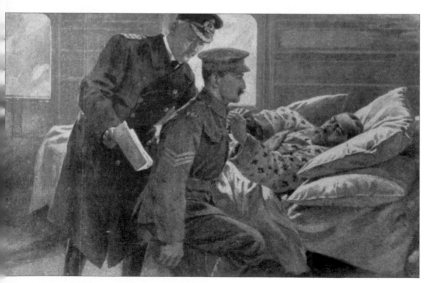

L/Sgt Brooks receiving his VC from the King.

The Hohenzollern Redoubt.

Issy Smith headstone. (*photograph by Dr. Judy Landau*)

Leuchars Parish War Memorial. (*photograph by Jim McGinlay*)

Golders Green Cemetery on 29 April. He was succeeded in his baronetcy by his grandson, Timothy John Smyth. His medals (including a replica of his VC, the original having been stolen) were bequeathed to the Imperial War Museum and are displayed in the Lord Ashcroft Gallery. The pavilion roof of the Commonwealth Memorial Gates at Hyde Park Corner bears his name along with other VC winners from the Indian Army.

L.J. KEYWORTH
Givenchy, France, 25/26 May

At 17.30 hours on 25 May, the 24th Bn, London Regt (The Queen's), 142nd Bde, 47th (London) Div., took over trenches just north of Givenchy in readiness for an attack later that evening. At 18.30 hours, after a supporting artillery bombardment, the attack began. Advancing on a stretch of the enemy line known as the 'S Bend', the leading company reached its objective, points I4 to J7, with few casualties (see map on page 164). The supporting companies followed and within thirty minutes all were in the German front line but were unable to advance further as the enemy was holding the slightly higher ground south of I4 and from there were able to inflict heavy rifle fire on the attacking troops.

The Battalion *War Diary* records: '6.45–9 p.m. Captured trench being consolidated. A severe bomb fight taking place all the time on the right flank.' L/Cpl Keyworth of No. 9 platoon was in this 'bomb fight' and as he later informed a reporter: 'I and my chums had already been "blooded" before we were engaged at Givenchy . . . for we had previously been in the neighbourhood of Festubert in a pretty tight corner.' (This was at Aubers Ridge on 9 May when the battalion had over 100 casualties). Keyworth then described how half his section were shot down by enemy machine-gun fire before reaching the German line and when bombing in the enemy lines all the bombers were killed except him. 'I had my duty to do, which was to throw bombs and do as much damage as I could', he continued. 'The bravery of my officers – poor Lt Chance died a glorious death, inspiring everybody with pluck – filled me with a "do or die feeling".' When his supply of bombs was exhausted, Keyworth was supplied with more by men behind him who continually implored him to lie down. For about two hours Keyworth remained on a parapet, throwing some 150 bombs, and although blinded with dirt on one occasion he survived unscathed, although pieces of shell brushed his ear and damaged a mirror in his pocket. The Germans for most of this time were only about 15 yards away.

The captured trench was held through the night and the whole of the next day despite being under shell and rifle fire for much of the time until the battalion was relieved by 20th Londons during the evening of 26 May. The Queen's moved into reserve dugouts at Windy Corner and then to billets in a tobacco factory at Béthune where 250 men paraded at roll call. After this action 142nd Bde was reduced in strength to 1,225 and was taken out of the line.

The Battalion *War Diary* states: '. . . the most noticeable feature of the operations was the retention of the captured trench by a few exhausted, and in many cases wounded, men after it had been subjected to a very heavy enfilade rifle fire'.

Keyworth was recommended for the DCM for his actions by his company commander, Capt. Armstrong, but was actually awarded the VC, as published in the *London Gazette* on 3 July. The first Keyworth knew of his VC was when he read a newspaper containing the citation on 4 July.

Leonard James Keyworth was born on 12 April 1893 at 22 Coningsby Street, Lincoln, one of two children born to James and Emma Keyworth. He attended Rosemary Lane Wesleyan and Municipal Technical Schools in Lincoln and after leaving school worked in the offices of Wm. Foster & Co., Engineers, and subsequently as a clerk for a firm of solicitors, Messrs Burton, Scorer & White, both of Lincoln. Keyworth was a keen sportsman and played both football and cricket, the latter for the Silver Street Cricket Club and also Rechabites Cricket Club with whom he won two medals. A member of the YMCA, he also sang in the choir at the United Methodist Church, Silver Street, Lincoln.

Shortly after the outbreak of war he attempted to volunteer for service with the Lincolnshire Regt, but was not accepted, so with a friend he travelled to London and joined the 1/24th (County of London) Bn, the London Regt (The Queen's), on 16 September 1914. The battalion was then stationed at St Albans, Herts, and when Keyworth joined it there in November he was billeted at 63 Heath Road. In late January the Queen's moved to Hatfield where the men were billeted in the banqueting hall and covered tennis courts at Hatfield House.

With 6th Bde, 2nd (London) Div., the battalion went to France on 16 March, the second complete Territorial division to arrive in France. Billeted near Béthune, the Queen's first went into the front line on 25 April in the Rue de l'Epinette sector, north of Festubert. In its first engagement at Aubers Ridge on 9 May the battalion suffered over 100 casualties; on 11 May the 2nd Div. was renumbered 47 (London) Div., and on the 14th, 6th Bde became the 142nd.

Keyworth arrived at Victoria station, London, early on the morning of 11 July, although his appointment at Buckingham Palace was the following day. He visited Lincoln on the 17th and at a ceremony that was also attended by Cpl James Upton VC, he was presented with an illuminated address and a purse of money. Both VC winners were later entertained by the Mayor at the Albion Hotel. Keyworth received a number of gifts during his stay in Lincoln from the various associations and clubs to which he belonged.

Having returned to London, Keyworth rode with the Mayor of Southwark in a procession through the main streets of the Borough on 21 July, culminating with a presentation at Manor Place Baths of another illuminated address and a pair of binoculars. He appeared at a number of recruiting

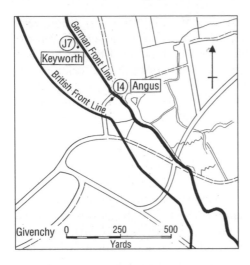

Near Givenchy, May 1915

meetings including one at the Old Vic Theatre before returning to France to join his battalion.

The Queen's went into the front line during the Battle of Loos and held trenches between Loos and Lens for three days at the end of September. In early October the battalion was in trenches near Le Rutoir and was involved in operations to capture Hulluch. On 15 October a member of 5th Field Ambulance, based at Noeux-les-Mines, recorded in his diary: ' . . . steady stream of wounded, among whom is Lance/Corporal Keyworth VC . . . hit in the head. . . .' Keyworth was moved to hospital at Abbeville and died at about 20.15 hours on 19 October without recovering consciousness. He is buried in Abbeville Communal Cemetery, Plot III, Row C, Grave 2. The *London Gazette* of 25 August announced the posthumous award of the Cross of St George 2nd Class (Russia).

Keyworth's name appears on the City of Lincoln War Memorial and also on the Great War Memorial in Silver Street Methodist Church, Lincoln. Silver Street Methodist Church was demolished in the 1960s, not having been used as a place of worship for many years, and the memorial vanished until it was discovered buried in a garden in the village of Cherry Willingham (near Lincoln). The stone tablet, bearing the names of sixteen men including Leonard Keyworth VC, was restored and on Sunday 25 November 2007 a service of re-dedication took place at All Saints Church, Lincoln. The bulk of the costs of restoration was provided by the Lincoln Branch of the Royal Lincolnshire & Royal Anglian Regimental Association. A wooden memorial, also recording his name, in St Mary's Church, Newington, was destroyed by bombing during the Second World War. The Borough of Southwark raised a fund to perpetuate Keyworth's name and in 1916 the money, £112 16s. was made over to the LCC and called 'the Keyworth VC 1915 Memorial Prize Fund'. The organizing committee rules said that the interest from this fund should provide for two school prizes each year in each of five schools in the borough. The awards of books with special book-plates and gold-blocked covers were made annually and in 1916, when the first awards were made, Keyworth's sister Lily made the presentations at three of the schools. Apart from a period during the Second World War, prizes have been given each year and on the occasion of the VC centenary in 1956, Lily Perkins (née Keyworth) presented the awards at Joseph Lancaster School. The Regimental Old Comrades' Association presented each of the five schools with a framed and inscribed photograph of Keyworth in the same year.

On 4 November 1919 Dantzig Street in London (originally Market Street) was retitled Keyworth Street; at later dates Providence Place, off Keyworth Street, was renamed Keyworth Place and an office block in Keyworth Street was named Keyworth Place. Faunce School, one of those in receipt of prizes, was renamed Keyworth School in 1951–2 after efforts by the Regimental OCA.

Lily Millie Keyworth married William Perkins in 1921 and their only son was named Leonard James Keyworth Perkins. On the death of Mrs Perkins, her son Leonard offered his uncle's medals to the Regiment and they were purchased for £460 in 1962.

W. MARINER
Near Cambrin, France, 22 May

On 22 May, less than a mile away from where the battle of Festubert was being fought, the 2nd KRRC (2nd Bde, 1st Div.) was holding the front line in the Cuinchy/ Cambrin sector, south of the La Bassée Canal, an area much fought over in the preceding months. A violent thunderstorm was in progress during the night when No. A/2452 Pte Mariner of B Coy volunteered to try to silence an enemy machine-gun which had been responsible for many casualties to working parties.

Mariner crawled through the British defences and the German wire to where the machine-gun was positioned, climbed the parapet and threw a bomb into the gun emplacement. He heard the cries of wounded men and the sound of the survivors retreating but some fifteen minutes later Germans started returning to the strongpoint, so Mariner, who had remained on the enemy parapet, climbed to the other side of the emplacement and threw another bomb into it with his left hand. Heavy enemy artillery fire was brought down near the wire protecting the German front line but Mariner lay down close to the parapet until the fire subsided. He then returned to his own trenches, and was almost killed by a sentry who thought he was a German. Mariner had been out of the British line for more than an hour and a half. An eye-witness account, written in the early 1990s by another KRRC soldier tells a slightly different story. Eighteen-year-old Jack Laister crawled out with Mariner and cut a gap in the German wire for him. Mariner had taken two bandoliers of Mills bombs with him and, after removing his tunic and shirt so as not to get snagged on the wire, commenced throwing bombs from the German parapet into the trench. Laister, who had by then managed to crawl halfway back to the British trench, described the scene:

. . . I could see him hurling bomb after bomb into the German trench. Pieces of bodies, limbs, heads were all flying out and up into the air... that's the last I'll see of him because the Germans had opened up with every gun.

Some time later, Laister, who managed to get back to the British line, says:

. . . after a while we heard people speaking German . . . . Then, pushed over the parapet, came two Germans who dropped on to the fire-step and Mariner jumped in after them, carrying part of a German machine-gun.

For this daring feat Mariner won the VC, which was published in the *London Gazette* of 23 June. He was invested with his medal at Buckingham Palace by the King on 12 August 1915.

John William Mariner was born at 12 Wellington Street, Chorley, Lancs., on 29 May 1882, one of five children born to Alice Ann Mariner. She married John Wignall towards the end of 1888 but on the 1891 census, whilst she and her husband were living with her parents at 7 Wellington Street, both her sons born before her marriage, William and Frederick, are shown as being the children of her parents. He was educated at St Laurence's Parochial School, Chorley before the family moved to 18 Fletcher Street, Lower Broughton, Salford. After leaving school he worked as a collier before enlisting in the Army where, with 2nd KRRC, he served in India. During this period he was court-martialled twice (First for striking an officer and secondly for using threatening behaviour), serving a prison sentence for each offence. He was also the regimental lightweight wrestling champion. After seven years' service he transferred to the Reserves and was working as a brick-setter when war broke out. He enlisted with his former battalion on 26 August 1914 under the name of William Mariner, having served a prison sentence for housebreaking since leaving the Army, and went to France on 29 November of that year.

He returned to Salford on leave in early August 1915 and on 12 August left his mother's house in Salford without informing her of his plans. She suspected that he was to receive his VC that day and with her daughter entrained for Windsor. At Windsor Mrs Wignall was informed that the award ceremony was at Buckingham Palace, so she joined the hundreds of people outside the Palace and was able to see her son after the investiture. The crowds were too much for Mariner and his fellow VC winners, so a taxi was called and Mariner, Pte May and Cpl Tombs (see page 151) left in it.

The Mayor and Corporation of Salford were keen to honour the VC hero and efforts were made to locate Mariner in London, but he had already returned to Salford. He was eventually tracked down and at a civic reception was presented with an illuminated address and a gold watch; he was also given a reception at Chorley.

After speaking at various recruiting rallies, mainly in the Salford district, Mariner returned to France but was wounded and sent back to England on 24 August 1915. He did not return to France until 12 October. Before this a newspaper report covered his appearance in court at Clerkenwell, London, where he had been arrested and charged as an absentee. His excuse for being two days' overdue, was 'I have been messing about with Jack Johnson and doing a bit of recruiting'.

In late June 1916 the 2nd KRRC were in the front line of an attack on the Railway Triangle, south of Loos. After the explosion of three British mines at 21.15 hours on 30 June the battalion moved forward. Mariner was in B Coy who advanced from a sap in the front line. The German line was reached but Mariner was killed in a communication trench. One of his comrades, Giles Eyre, described Mariner's death:

> And then Marriner [sic] loses his remaining senses . . . and runs down in pursuit of the retreating enemy . . . as I round a corner and glimpse Marriner in the very act of bayoneting a prone German – a whistling swish seems to fill the world – Marriner, caught full tilt by a shell, has been blown to fragments.

Eyre was covered in these 'fragments'.

The survivors of Mariner's company remained in action until 02.00 hours on 1 July and then returned to billets in Maroc. Mariner was one of 34 men of the battalion listed as missing after the action. His name is commemorated on the Thiepval Memorial to the Missing and because of the date of his death it is often assumed that he died in the first day of the Battle of the Somme. The whereabouts of Mariner's VC Medal was not known for many years but in 2006 the medal, together with the illuminated address presented to him by the mayor of Salford, was found in a tin box in a desk drawer during a house clearance in Lancashire. (Reportedly following the death of a distant relative of Mariner.) These items were sold to an unknown buyer at auction on 23 November 2006 for a hammer price of £105,000. The local museum at Astley Hall did attempt to raise the estimated price of £80,000.

On 23 November 2002, at St Laurence's Old School, Parker Street, Chorley, a slate plaque was unveiled and dedicated honouring Rifleman William Mariner VC (formerly Wignall). The erection of this plaque was arranged by Chorley Civic Society.

W. ANGUS
Givenchy, France, 12 June

Less than three weeks after Cpl Keyworth (see page 161) won his VC on 25 May a similar award was made to L/Cpl Angus of the 8th Highland Light Infantry (HLI), this time for a rescue within yards of the spot where Keyworth's action had taken place.

Angus, attached to 1/8th Royal Scots, 22nd Bde, 7th Div., who first saw action at Neuve Chapelle in March, had been wounded at the Battle of Festubert and had only just returned from hospital when his battalion took over the trenches at Givenchy. The German front line at Givenchy took advantage of an area of raised ground; an embankment along which they ran their front line with its excellent view over no-mans-land. This embankment was allocated the reference point I4. A mine was exploded under a German salient near Point I4 on 3 June and although the crater was rushed by British troops it was retaken by the enemy (see map on page 164).

A few days later twenty men of A Coy, the Royal Scots, together with fifteen bombers under Lt J. Martin, made an unsuccessful attempt to retake the now-fortified mine crater. At 21.00 hours on 10 June a similar attempt was made during which the Germans fired a mine and reduced the embankment to ground level on one edge. This explosion forced the bombing party to retreat to the British trenches where Lt Martin was later reported missing. (The embankment and the gap created is clearly visible to this day). Early in the morning his body was seen lying on loose earth close to the German parapet some 50 yards away. Initially he was thought to be dead but some time later movement was detected in one of his limbs through binoculars.

Martin had been blown several feet into the air by the mine explosion and his left arm was trapped by debris from which he slowly managed to free himself by strenuous efforts before attempting to crawl towards his own line. He was seen by the Germans who fired at him and he was soon hit twice, in his right arm and side, after which Martin stopped moving and the enemy stopped firing. Martin later crawled nearer to the German parapet where he was less likely to be seen. Meanwhile various rescue methods were discussed until a decision was made for one man, with a length of rope attached to him, to attempt the crossing to the enemy parapet.

L/Cpl Angus, whose post was some 400 yards away, had come to the point opposite where the injured man lay, and immediately volunteered for the task. With a rope fastened around him Angus slowly crawled towards Lt Martin, clearing a path through the shell-torn ground as he did so, and eventually reached the wounded officer. He produced a flask of brandy to revive Martin and it was then they were seen by the Germans, who threw a bomb, badly injuring Angus in the left eye. Nevertheless Angus tied the rope around Martin's waist, and helped him to his feet and the two men began the return journey, now under covering rifle fire from their own men. Several bombs were thrown by the Germans and although they wounded Angus they also created lots of smoke and dust which in turn gave some cover. Martin collapsed in a shell hole about 20 yards from the British line but managed to crawl the remaining distance. Angus took longer to reach the line as he went a different way to create a diversion so that Martin could crawl on unmolested; Angus was again hit by bomb fragments.

Major Sneyd MC, 8th Siege Bty, RGA, witnessed the rescue and in a letter to his sister in July, wrote, ' . . . one of the finest VC efforts I have ever heard of for it all had to be done in cold blood'. The official account of the rescue and the medal recommendation were sent in by Lt-Col. Gemmill, CO of the battalion. Doctors discovered no fewer than forty shrapnel and bullet wounds when Angus was later examined, and he lost the sight of his left eye.

The citation for the VC was published on 29 June 1915 in the *London Gazette* and Angus was decorated by the King at Buckingham Palace on 30 August 1915.

William Angus was born at Arndale, Linlithgow, Scotland, on 28 February 1888 and when he was very young his family moved to Carluke, Lanarkshire, where his father worked as a miner. On leaving the Roman Catholic School in Carluke at the age of 14, Angus also worked in a coal mine but his passion was for football and he signed as a professional with Glasgow Celtic. He had previously played for Carluke Milton Rovers as a forward, and after leaving Celtic joined Wisham Athletic as captain.

At a large recruiting meeting held at Carluke in late August 1914, Angus was one of the 29 volunteers; also included was James Martin, who was to become a lieutenant. Following training at Dunoon, Angus and Martin both volunteered to join a draft of 180 men of the 8th HLI to be despatched to France and posted to 1/8th Royal Scots. He was promoted to lance-corporal at about this time.

After his heroic feat at Givenchy Angus went first to a hospital in Boulogne, and was later moved to the Military Hospital at Chatham, Kent, where he saw again Lt Martin, who was also recuperating from his injuries.

At Buckingham Palace for his investiture, Angus was dressed in the blue uniform of a wounded soldier and needed the support of two sticks to walk. On hearing that Angus' father was outside the Palace gates the King insisted he was brought in and congratulated him on having such a brave son.

Angus, the first Scottish Territorial to win the VC, returned to Carluke from Chatham Hospital, where he received a tremendous reception. He was met at the railway station by his five younger sisters and brother. At a public reception Lord Newlands presented him with a clock and a public gift of £1,000 in War Stock, which included £100 from Glasgow Celtic. This money had been raised with the active support of a local newspaper. Lt Martin was also at the reception and presented Angus with a gold watch and chain.

Angus was invalided out of the Army later in the year with the rank of acting sergeant. He married Mary Nugent at Carluke Roman Catholic Church in January 1917 and was photographed outside the church with his new wife together with Lt Martin. Angus went to London in 1920 and was present at the garden party for VC winners in June and at the Cenotaph on 11 November.

He emigrated to Australia in November 1927, leaving his wife and five children in Carluke until he was settled, but returned to Scotland in 1928. A year later, in a newspaper interview, James Martin described his rescue, interest in the event having been rekindled by a letter to the *Daily Sketch* in which one Mr Wakefield of Mansfield wrote about a broken cross in his possession. This cross bore details of Lt Martin and had been made early on 12 June 1915, when his body was first seen, the intention being to recover the body after dark. Martin considered this to be a rather peculiar distinction. But he never forgot his saviour, and every year since 1915 on the anniversary of his rescue, Martin sent a telegram to Angus, always with the same words, 'Congratulations on the 12th'; after Martin's death in 1956, the practice was continued by his brother.

Angus worked as master of works at the Racecourse Betting Control Board and was also a JP. In September 1957 large crowds watched a parade of 500 ex-members of the HLI protesting against the amalgamation of the HLI with the Royal Scots. Two First World War VC holders led the parade, William Angus, and David Hunter of Dunfermline.

William Angus died in Law Hospital, Carluke, on 14 June 1959, almost 44 years to the day since winning his VC. The funeral service was held on 17 June at St Athenasia Roman Catholic Church, Carluke, and was conducted by Bishop Scanlon. Many people attended the service and lined the route to Wilton Cemetery as the cortege, accompanied by pipers from the HLI, passed through the town. His headstone displays a replica of the Victoria Cross. Angus was survived by his wife, three sons and a daughter. A road in Carluke is named in his honour.

Two other men from Carluke won the VC: Thomas Caldwell and Donald Cameron. The latter was awarded the VC for piloting a midget submarine in the Second World War. His Victoria Cross is displayed in the Scottish War Museum in Edinburgh Castle, where the display tells the story of the two men from Carluke. The medals of Lt Martin are displayed alongside William Angus's VC.

F.W. CAMPBELL

Givenchy, France, 15 June

The fifth and last member of the Canadian Expeditionary Force to be awarded the VC in 1915 was also the oldest; Capt. Frederick Campbell won the medal on his 48th birthday. At the end of May, a provisional date of 11 June was fixed for simultaneous attacks north and south of the La Bassée Canal, with the objective of capturing La Bassée itself; this date allowed for sufficient artillery ammunition to be obtained, but even so insufficient artillery shells reduced the attack to a narrow frontage directed towards Violaines, north-east of Givenchy.

The southern sector of the attack was allotted to 1st Can. Bn (Western Ontario Regt), 1st CIB, with battalions from the British 21st Bde, 7 Div., on its left. The Canadians' direction of attack was against the German line at H2 to H3 (see map), held by *13th Regt*. The date of the attack was postponed a number of times, but was finally fixed at 18.00 hours on 15 June.

To conserve shells the supporting 60 hour artillery bombardment was slow for the first 48 hours but early on 15 June it increased and 30 minutes before the assault began it became intense. In addition, two 18-pounder guns were moved into the front line at the Duck's Bill, a semi-circular embankment projecting forward opposite H2; a third gun was positioned behind a ruined farmhouse 300 yards from H3. The two guns opposite H2 opened fire at

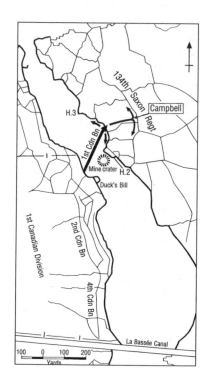

Near Givenchy, June 1915

17.45 hours and destroyed three machine-guns and part of the enemy embankment before they were put out of action by concentrated German artillery fire. The third gun did not fire as the officer in command was afraid of hitting Canadian infantry assembled in trenches in front of him; consequently the enemy redoubts at H3, containing several machine-guns, were only slightly damaged. At 17.59 hours a mine which had been laid by men of 176th Tunnelling Coy RE, was exploded in front of the enemy strongpoint at H2; it was intended to explode under the German strongpoint but the engineers had struck water in the gallery just short of their objective and the charge was therefore increased to 3,000 lbs of ammonal in the hope that it would totally destroy the strongpoint. When it was exploded the resulting crater was over 40 yards wide; the German line was little damaged but many men in the Canadian front line were killed or injured. In addition, both stores of bombs in the 1st Bn's line were either destroyed or buried.

The 1st Bn attacked at 18.01 hours and within nine minutes the leading two companies were in the German second line, and the third company, No. 2, was in the front line. Capt. Campbell, the battalion machine-gun officer, crossed no-man's-land with No. 2 Coy and took two Colt machine-guns and their crews with him to the German front line.

Although the battalion captured the front line trenches between points H2 and H3, lack of bombs meant that the strongpoint at H3 could not be taken; consequently, by 20.00 hours, machine-guns firing from H3 and I4 (450 yards north) controlled no-man's-land for a mile north from the Duck's Bill.

A German counter-attack forced many of the battalion's men back towards the mine crater and at this point Campbell took one of his guns forward to meet the attack. Only one man, Pte Howard Vincent, a lumberjack from Bracebridge, Ontario, remained from Campbell's original detachment, and he went forward with his captain. The tripod of the machine-gun was damaged by shell-fire so Campbell used Vincent's back as a support while he fired over 1,000 rounds, all the ammunition he had. He then ordered Vincent to retire, and although badly burned by the hot barrel of the gun, the private dragged it back to the Canadian line. Campbell was hit in the right thigh by a bullet and had started to crawl back when he was picked up by CSM C. Owen, in command of No. 1 Coy, who carried him back for treatment. Campbell was passed down the medical chain of command and reached No. 7 Stationary Hospital at Boulogne on 17 June. At noon on 19 June he became unconscious and died three hours later. In a letter to Mrs Campbell the doctor explained that the wound was septic, 'as all these cases are'. Campbell was buried in Boulogne Eastern Cemetery Plot II, Row A, Grave 24.

His commanding officer, Lt-Col. F.W. Hill, also wrote to Campbell's wife and told her how much he would be missed. He continued, 'I had twice before recommended him for promotion and honours, and have again done so. This time I feel his name will be found in the list.' This was the case as the *London Gazette* of 23 August 1915 published the VC citation. The medal was sent by the War Office to Canada on 28 August 1915 and subsequently given to Mrs Campbell.

Frederick William Campbell was born at Mount Forest, Oxford County, Ontario, Canada, on 15 June 1867 and later that year moved with his parents, Ephraim B. and Esther A. Campbell to a farm near Gleneden, Grey County. Educated at Mount Forest School, Campbell joined the local militia, the 30th Bn Wellington Rifles, in 1885 when he was 18.

When the Boer War began he enlisted in the South African Contingent in London, Ontario, and served with the Royal Canadian Regt. Campbell was present at the actions at Johannesburg, Drenfontein, Paardeburg and Cape Colony as part of a Maxim machine-gun crew and was Mentioned in Despatches for an incident at the Modder River. One wheel of his machine-gun was damaged by shell-fire so Campbell improvised, replacing the damaged spokes with legs from a table from a nearby house. (This wheel is held in the Citadel Museum in Quebec.) He was awarded the Queen's Medal and four clasps and returned home in 1900 with the rank of sergeant.

On 25 November 1903 he married Margaret Annie McGillivray and their three children, Arthur Clive, Jean Margaret and Freda McGillivray, were all born at the farm he had purchased near his father's home, where he bred horses. In 1911 Campbell was present in London at the Coronation of King George V. He was a public school trustee of a school at Normanby, his home town, and a director of the Mount Forest Agricultural Society. Campbell remained in the militia and when war began immediately obtained permission to recruit in his local area. On 17 August 1914 he went to Valcartier Camp with a dozen volunteers. Assigned to 1st Bn, 1st Bde, with the rank of lieutenant, Campbell sailed on 3 October with the other 1,165 members of his battalion on the *Laurentic*. They disembarked at Plymouth on 18 October and proceeded to Salisbury Plain, Wiltshire, where they encamped at Bustard.

The battalion arrived at their billets in Merris, France, on 14 February 1915 and incurred heavy losses on 23 April in a counterattack north-east of Ypres, when the machine-guns under Lt Campbell were very effective.

A plaque was unveiled to Campbell's memory at the Royal Canadian Legion Hall, Mount Forest, by his daughter, Mrs V.S. de Vore on 20 June 1965. The whereabouts of Campbell's medals is unknown.

S.C. WOODROFFE

Hooge, Belgium, 30 July

The 8th Bn, the Rifle Brigade (RB), of 41 Bde, 14 [Light] Div., entered the trenches at Hooge at about midnight on 30 July to relieve their sister battalion, the 7th RB. The relief was completed by 02.00 hours, but a group of 7th RB bombers remained in the line with the 8th RB on the express orders of the GOC, perhaps on account of their relative inexperience, as they had only arrived in France in May.

The British front line was divided by a large crater approximately 90 feet across and 40 feet deep, which proved untenable for either side due to the amount of shelling it attracted and the difficulty in defending it. A Coy, 8th RB, took up their positions in the front line; Lt Woodroffe's platoon on the left was separated from Lt Carey's men on the right by the crater. *The War Diary* lists a number of concerns regarding the weakness of this part of the line; for example, there was no barbed wire to speak of in front of their position and the front trenches themselves were deep and narrow, making communication along them very difficult; the same was true of the communication trenches. The crater was defended by bombers' posts established on each side. Worst of all, the opposing lines were very close together, in many places just 15 yards apart.

The 8th RB had been in the line for just three hours when the Germans attacked. At about 03.15 hours there was a large explosion at the stables (see map opposite) and the enemy began an intensive bombardment of the front trenches which lasted only two or three minutes. The whole front line had been 'standing-to' before the shelling began, so casualties in the tightly packed trench were high. Without warning, immediately following the shelling, sheets of flame broke out along the front with clouds of thick black smoke. This 'liquid fire' was sprayed from hoses in the German line, the flame-throwers having a range of about 20 yards or so. One eye-witness, Pte A.P. Hatton, described the phenomenon in *I Was There*:

We first heard sounds as of a splashing to our front, then there was a peculiar smoky smell just like coal-tar; next, a corporal of C Company cried out that he had been hit by a shell; yet when we went to look at him we found that a huge blister as from a burn was on his forehead, while the back of his cap was smouldering.

We had no time to notice anything else, for after that preliminary trial the Boches loosened their liquid fire upon us with a vengeance. It came in streams all over the earthworks, while shells containing star lights ignited the black fluid. Sandbags, blankets, top-coats, and anything of the sort that was handy smouldered and then flared. We were choked by the smoke and half scorched by the heat.

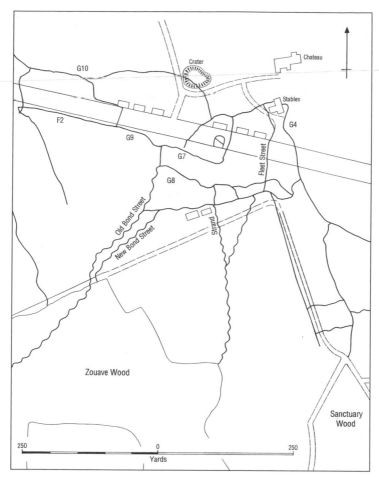

Hooge – the scene of the first flame-thrower attack

The 'liquid fire' was aimed at the trenches on either side of the crater and under cover of the flames and smoke large parties of German bombers swarmed forward through the crater and then swung left and right down the trenches; others appeared on the parapets of the trenches hit by the fire. The fighting soon became very confused and four machine-guns in the front were soon out of action. Casualties in the trenches hit by the liquid fire were almost 100 per cent, although the platoons on the extreme right under Carey, and the extreme left under Woodroffe, unaffected by the flame throwers, repulsed all efforts to bomb them out. The two forward companies, connected by telephone to Bn HQ, both signalled an SOS at about 03.30 hours. Woodroffe's platoon was heavily attacked on their right flank by enemy bombers making their way down the trench line from the crater and from the rear, the Germans having fanned out behind the British front line after breaking through the centre of the front at the crater.

B Coy, 8th Rifle Bde, was in support some 500 yards back in Zouave Wood under Capt. A.L.C. Cavendish, with D Coy under Capt. C. Sheepshanks. Cavendish was ordered to counterattack between 04.00 and 05.00 hours, but by this time the Germans had consolidated their position in the former British front line and fortified it with several machine-gun positions and rifles, and the British counterattack failed. This left Woodroffe and his remaining men in his trench position virtually surrounded, but he continued to defend his post until his supply of bombs was used up. He then very skilfully withdrew his platoon, in good order, fighting their way back, moving first west along the Menin road (just south of the Stables), and then returning to the British-held lines via a culvert further down the road. Meanwhile the enemy tried to bomb down the two communication trenches called Old Bond Street and The Strand but these were blocked about halfway up and were held throughout the day. By the end of the action C Coy had ceased to exist, having borne the brunt of the fire attack, and A and B Coys had suffered severe losses.

Reinforcements arrived from Brigade Reserve – a single company of the KRRC, which arrived at about 09.00 hours. At noon orders came from GOC to mount a counterattack at 14.45 hours, following a 45 minute artillery bombardment. The 8th RB, despite its losses, was to lead the attack, D Coy under Capt. Sheepshanks making a two platoon front, their right resting on The Strand to permit a bombing attack on that trench as they went forward; the remains of A and B Coys were told to attack Trench G9, their right resting on Old Bond Street. The Germans seemed untouched by the bombardment but at 14.45 hours the counterattack went in.

The *War Diary* noted: 'The whole ground was absolutely swept by bullets,' and the attacking troops barely got halfway towards their objectives. The German fire was so intense that the few reinforcements available to the British were unable to get any further either. 2/Lt Woodroffe, leading his men on the left of Old Bond Street, was killed in the act of cutting barbed wire to enable the attack to be continued. His CO, Lt-Col. R.C. Maclachlan, wrote to Woodroffe's father: 'Your younger boy was simply one of the bravest of the brave, and the work he did that day will stand out as a record hard to beat.' Woodroffe was just 19 years and 7 months old.

Sidney Clayton Woodroffe was born at Lewes, Sussex, on 17 December 1895 and was the fourth and youngest son of Henry Long Woodroffe, of Woodmoor, Branksome Avenue, Bournemouth, and Clara, daughter of Henry Clayton. Woodroffe was educated at Marlborough College, where he was Senior Prefect, Captain of the OTC, winner of the Curzon-Wyllie Medal, and a member of the football XV in 1912, 1913 and 1914, the hockey XI, and cricket XXII. He gained a classical scholarship at Pembroke College, Cambridge. He was gazetted second lieutenant in the 8th Bn, the Rifle Brigade, on 23 December 1914, going to France with the battalion on 25 May 1915; he was killed in action at Hooge, Belgium, on 30 July 1915. His two eldest brothers were also killed in France. Lt K.H.C. Woodroffe MC, 8th RB, was severely wounded on 30 July 1915 at Hooge, and was unable to return to his battalion until 1 June 1916, on which day he was again wounded, dying of these wounds three days later. Both had been to Marlborough College and like their younger brother were successful scholars and sportsmen.

Sidney Woodroffe's Victoria Cross was presented to his parents by King George V in the ballroom at Buckingham Palace on 29 November 1916. He was Marlborough College's third VC, the previous two being Capt. Bradbury and Capt. Foss. His rugger cap and sword were put on display in All Hallowe's Church, Bournemouth, though the sword was stolen during the Blitz. Woodroffe is commemorated with his brothers on a memorial in All Saints' Church, Branksome Park, Bournemouth; and there is a tablet to his memory outside 42 Trinity Square, Tulse Hill, London. His name appears on panels 46–58 and 50 of the Menin Gate.

G.A. BOYD-ROCHFORT
Between Cambrin and La Bassée,
France, 3 August

 On 3 August 1915 the 1st Bn Scots Guards, 4th (Guards) Bde, 2nd Div., was in trenches south of the La Bassée Canal (where it had been in action at the beginning of the year when Cpl O'Leary won his VC, see page 15). A similar award was earned on that day in August when 2/Lt G.A. Boyd-Rochfort became the first Guards officer to gain the award in the war.

Working parties were sent out every night by the battalion to improve the condition of the trenches and fortifications. 2/Lt Boyd-Rochfort was in charge of a party of about forty men working in a communication trench close to the front line. At 02.00 hours an enemy trench-mortar shell landed on the edge of the parapet beside the men. Boyd-Rochfort shouted a warning, then ran towards the missile, grabbed it and threw it over the parapet where it exploded almost immediately. Boyd-Rochfort and the men nearest him were buried by loose earth blown up by the detonation but no one was hurt. The only damage was to his cap, which was destroyed. Boyd-Rochfort later commented, 'My men were very appreciative of my action and cheered and thanked me. Afterwards they wrote and signed a statement of what I had done, which they handed to the Colonel.'

His prompt and courageous action saved the lives of the men closest to the mortar shell and Boyd-Rochfort could easily have saved himself by taking cover behind a nearby corner in the trench. Shortly after the incident a French soldier photographed 2/Lt Boyd-Rochfort with the four men whom he had saved and his company commander. The similarities between this action and that of Cpl Burt (see page 250) are remarkable, both in deed and vicinity.

The *London Gazette* of 1 September 1915 published the citation of his VC award and Boyd-Rochfort was invested by the King at Windsor Castle on 6 September 1915.

George Arthur Boyd-Rochfort, the eldest son of Major Rochfort Hamilton Boyd, was born on 1 January 1880 at Middleton Park, County Westmeath, Ireland. When he was only 11 his father died at the age of 46; in his will he decreed that his sons be named Boyd-Rochfort. Florence, Boyd-Rochfort's mother, was English and came from Bentley Manor, Worcester. They had seven children, three boys and four girls. Educated at Eton, Mr H. Morley's House, and Trinity College, Cambridge, where he was Master of Beagles, Boyd-Rochfort took up his residence at the Middleton Park family home when he was 21, having been a ward of Chancery since his father's death. A popular landlord of his estates, he spent much of his time big-game hunting, travelling, horse-race riding and playing polo; among other things he rode the winners of the Westmeath Gold Cup and the National Hunt Cup.

In 1901 he married Olivia Ellen Ussher of Eastwell, Galway, in Dublin and in 1904 was High Sheriff for County Westmeath. During the last week of August 1914, Boyd-Rochfort was badly hurt in a polo match which resulted in a hospital operation in November, followed by a lengthy stay in the hospital. He applied for an Army commission in February 1915 but was rejected because of varicose veins; he entered hospital again for an operation to cure this problem and on re-applying was commissioned into the Scots Guards in April. He went to France in June and joined the 1st Bn.

Boyd-Rochfort returned from France on leave on 2 September 1915, and was informed by his brother, who met him at a London railway station, of his VC award. He treated this information with some disbelief until reading his citation in a newspaper shortly afterwards. He was accompanied by Pte Thorowgood, his butler before the war, and a former Boer War veteran, who enlisted as a private when Boyd-Rochfort first applied for his commission. He rejoined his battalion and was later promoted to lieutenant and in an incident with two Germans in which he silenced one with a blow from his revolver butt and the other with his fist, Boyd-Rochfort was wounded. He spent his sick leave at Middleton Park.

He was promoted to captain and later became adjutant of the Guards Division. Mentioned in Despatches, he served on the Western Front for the rest of the war. Both his brothers served in the war: Harold, a major, was awarded the DSO and MC, and commanded a brigade of tanks during 1918; and Cecil, a captain, was awarded the Croix de Guerre with Palms, served with Scots Guards and was a brigade major with the RFC. Three cousins were killed; one was a colonel in the RHA; another was a colonel in the Warwickshire Yeomanry and the third was a major in the Worcestershire Yeomanry.

After the war he concentrated on his stud farm at Middleton Park where he bred the winners of the 1936 St Leger and the 1937 Ascot Gold Cup. His brother, Capt. Sir Cecil Boyd-Rochfort, was a very successful horse trainer and became trainer to the King, based at Newmarket. Boyd-Rochfort was greatly involved with horse racing and was a steward of the Irish National Hunt and the Irish Turf Club, as well as a director of Westmeath Race Company.

He died on 7 August 1940 after a serious operation in a private nursing home in Dublin. The funeral was held at Castletown-Geoghegan Church on 9 August, and he was buried in the churchyard which overlooks his home. His will was published in 1941 in which all his personal estate in England and Eire, valued at £28,287, was left to his wife. His Victoria Cross is held at the Scots Guards RHQ.

THE BATTLE OF LOOS

A visitor looking towards Loos and Hulluch from the observation point on the Loos Memorial at Dud Corner, on the N43 to Béthune, cannot help but be struck by the terrain's open flatness, which is relieved only by slag-heaps (fosses).

In 1915 the general advantage of ground and observation lay with the Germans. The main British and German front lines were about 500 yards apart; between them, jutting out in a south-western direction from the German front line, lay a maze of trenches and fortifications known as the Hohenzollern Redoubt, the perimeter of which is still visible today. This strongpoint was linked to the main German line by Dump Trench and Fosse Trench, while two other trenches, 'Big Willie' and 'Little Willie', which ran eastwards and northwards respectively, protected the flanks of the redoubt (see map on page 186).

The Battle of Loos was forced on Sir John French, the C-in-C, by pressure from Joffre (the French C-in-C) and Kitchener. Loos was the British part of a joint offensive with the French, who were to attack in the Champagne area. The British were to attack on a 6 mile front between Grenay in the south and La Bassée in the north. There were six main pit-heads or 'fosses', as well as auxiliary shafts called 'puits', in the battle area and these were of considerable tactical importance. 'Resources' for the battle were considered inadequate, and to give the attacking troops more chance of success, the decision was taken to use gas in the offensive, in addition to the usual artillery bombardment. A series of subsidiary attacks were also launched at the same time. A total of six divisions, some 75,000 men, were to take part in the opening attack.

The preliminary bombardment began on 21 September, and at 05.50 hours on the 25th gas and smoke alternately were released along the whole front for a total of forty minutes. In some areas the gas blew across no-man's-land, allowing the assaulting troops some initial success, but in other areas the gas drifted back across the British lines, gassing the waiting attackers. Where the gas failed to reach the enemy lines, the German machine-guns caused havoc among the British assaulting troops; casualties were so great that the Germans dubbed the battle the 'Field of Corpses at Loos'.

The Hohenzollern Redoubt was taken by the 9th Div. only to be lost later; a second attack using gas to recapture it was launched on 13 October, but this also ultimately failed. The battle effectively came to an end on 16 October although it was not until 4 November that Gen. Haig informed the C-in-C that he was 'compelled to abandon any hope of

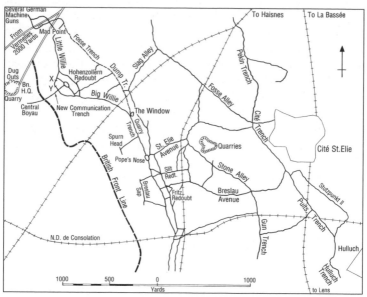

Loos, between Hulluch and Auchy

continuing the offensive'. The battle ended in stalemate, with the British having penetrated about 2 miles across 4 miles of German trenches; the British lost over 50,000 men as casualties. If the losses in the subsidiary attacks are also taken into account then the British casualties for the Battle of Loos amount to nearly 60,000. German losses were approximately half that figure.

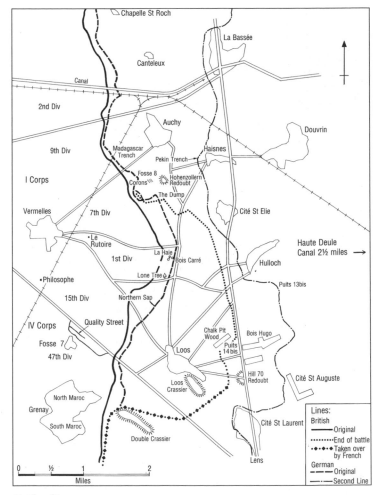

Battle of Loos

D. LAIDLAW

Near Loos and Hill 70, France, 25 September

The 7th Bn, King's Own Scottish Borderers (46 Bde, 15th Scottish Div.), was selected as an assault battalion for the coming Battle of Loos. They trained at Labeuvrière, 2 miles south-west of Béthune, for four weeks. Late on 24 September they proceeded to their assembly trenches which were roughly opposite Puits 14 behind the German lines. The two leading brigades (44th and 46th) were to capture the Lens Road and Loos Road Redoubts respectively in the initial attack and then advance eastwards down into the valley towards Loos (see map on page 187).

After the final bombardment the 7/KOSB waited for the release of gas and smoke against the German lines. However, the adverse conditions blew the gas back to the British positions, seriously affecting the troops manning the trenches. At 06.30 hours the 7/KOSB received the order to attack, but no one moved. Piper Laidlaw was standing by his company officer, 2/Lt Martin Young, who yelled to him, 'For God's sake, Laidlaw, pipe 'em together.' Disregarding the gas and enemy bombardment Laidlaw got over the parapet with 2/Lt Young and proceeded to march up and down their sector playing 'Blue Bonnets over the Border'. The KOSB reacted to the skirl of the pipes and 2/Lt Young's call and 'went over the top', led by the piper. Other troops in the brigade, the Cameronians (Scottish Rifles) and the Highland Light Infantry closely followed. The lone piper was an obvious target but incredibly was not hit while he was alone in no-man's-land. Laidlaw ran forward with his attacking comrades, playing all the time. As they approached the German lines Piper Laidlaw was hit in the left ankle and leg with shrapnel, but continued to limp along as best he could, changing the tune to 'The Standard on the Braes o' Mar' before being hit a second time in the left leg.

Laidlaw himself recounts that, 'I kept on piping and piping, and hobbling after the laddies until I could go no farther, and then, seeing that the boys had won the position, I began to get back as best I could to our own trenches.' He dragged his bagpipes back too, keeping them with him at all times. The shell that wounded Laidlaw also hit his officer, 2/Lt Young, who refused to allow stretcher-bearers to take him to the rear, insisting on walking to a dressing station. He died from blood loss the next day. Gen. Sir Philip Christianson, who was a lieutenant of the 6th Camerons on 25 September at Loos, recalls that his battalion 'was in close support of the KOSBs and heard quite clearly a piper piping them into action. It was an act of intense bravery under intensive fire. As we passed through the KOSBs I saw a badly wounded piper sitting on the ground in a severe state.'

The KOSB suffered heavily. The Battalion *War Diary* states that, 'Casualties for first 1,000 yards heavy – including all officers of the Battn. with the exception of three.' By the time 7/KOSB retired from the battle on 27 September, the *War Diary* records they had suffered 656 casualties for their three days fighting. Laidlaw's exploit won him the Victoria Cross and the French Croix de Guerre avec Palmes. No. 15851 Piper Laidlaw was promoted to corporal on the day of his gallant example, for distinguished service in the field. His VC was gazetted on 18 November 1915, and part of the citation makes it clear the enormous risk to which Laidlaw exposed himself:

> During the worst of the bombardment, Piper Laidlaw, seeing that his company was shaken from the effects of gas, with absolute coolness and disregard of danger, mounted the parapet, marched up and down and played his company out of the trench.

Daniel Logan Laidlaw was born on 26 July 1875 at Little Swinton, Berwickshire, and was the eldest surviving son of

Robert Laidlaw of Coldingham, Berwickshire. His mother, Margaret, was the daughter of Robert Logan of Jedburgh. He went to the National Schools at Berwick-upon-Tweed and Lesbury, Northumberland. Little seems to be known about his early years but he first joined the Army on 11 April 1896 and served in India in the 2nd Durham Light Infantry until June 1898. While serving with the 2nd DLI he received a certificate from the Secretary to the Governor stating that he had been 'employed on plague duty in Bombay from 22 March to 1 May 1898'. He was claimed out of the DLI by his eldest brother in 1898 and served in the KOSB as a piper until 11 April 1912. He married Georgina Mary, daughter of Robert Harive of Kilburnie, Ayrshire, on 11 April 1906 at the Baptist Church, Alnwick, Northumberland. By this time his family was living in Alnwick. Daniel and Georgina had four children before the war: Andrew Robert, born 3 February 1907; John, born 26 July 1910; Margaret, born 21 August 1911 (the year he received King George's Coronation Medal); and Georgina, born 10 December 1913.

After returning from India, Daniel Laidlaw was put on the Reserve and from 1912 to 1914 engaged in various civilian employment, including working as canteen manager at Alnwick Co-Operative Stores at Alexandria and at the horse breeding centre of D. and D.H. Porter at South Doddington. In Alnwick he spent much of his spare time acting as Assistant Scout Master of Alnwick to his brother-in-law, Scout Master Goodman. Laidlaw re-enlisted in the KOSB on 1 September 1914 and was posted to the 7th (Service) Bn, going to France in June 1915.

Following his exploits on 25 September at the Battle of Loos, Laidlaw, now a corporal, was decorated by King George V at Buckingham Palace on 4 December 1915 while still recuperating from his wounds. He later returned to his unit and was promoted to sergeant-piper on 12 October 1917. After the war Laidlaw was finally demobilized on 3 April 1919, having served with the Colours for a total of 20 years and 6 months. Like many others, after the Armistice Laidlaw found regular employment difficult to obtain, though he made great efforts, moving around Berwickshire,

Northumberland and Durham seeking work in industry or on the land. His worst period was when the post-war slump hit the Sunderland shipyards where he used to work, leaving him out of work for eight years.

He attended the VC garden party at Buckingham Palace on 26 June 1920 and the ceremony at the Cenotaph later that year on 11 November. Laidlaw, like Meekosha VC (see page 262) and others, was grateful for the railway companies' free ticket policy for VCs attending these functions. He was also present in Westminster Abbey on 11 November 1920 when the unknown warrior was laid to rest there. Indeed, Laidlaw often appeared in London as a guest at Scottish functions. His wife bore him another son in 1920, whom he named Victor Loos Laidlaw.

In 1929 he re-enacted his own legendary exploit, starring in the film 'The Guns of Loos', and later that year attended the British Legion dinner for VCs on 9 November 1929. Laidlaw took part in another film in 1934, 'Forgotten Men'. In the same year 'the piper' as he was universally known, sailed to Norway, to pipe the 'Lads and Lassies' of a Scottish dance team, a pastime that he had been involved in for some years since the war, giving concerts and providing the music for Scottish dance groups.

Laidlaw tried to set himself up in business as a chicken farmer to escape his long period of unemployment. In 1938 he became sub-postmaster at Shoresdean, a small village a few miles from Berwick-upon-Tweed. His 'office' was nothing more than a wooden shed standing in his front garden. He often played his prized 'Loos' pipes which he kept in his sitting room with his bronze medal and the other decorations he had won. He also told a reporter at this time that his once black hair had turned white within a few hours of his VC action at the Battle of Loos. When war came again his son, Victor Loos Laidlaw, joined the KOSB in 1940, aged 20. After the Second World War Piper Laidlaw was present in Whitehall on 8 June 1946 for the Victory Parade and attended the dinner that night.

Daniel Logan Laidlaw, 'the Piper of Loos', died at Shoresdean on 2 June 1950, and was buried two days later at Norham, Northumberland. Hundreds of people thronged the entrance to Norham Churchyard. Mourners came from miles away, some from Bowsden, Atterdean, Alnwick and other places where he and his family had lived. Many of the mourners had served with the KOSB, although the majority were friends. Mr A.G. Lindsay Young, whose brother Lt Young had been Piper Laidlaw's platoon commander at Loos, had read of his death in the newspaper and had come down from Cleish Castle, Kinross, to attend the funeral. Another mourner had heard about his death on the radio and travelled up from Coventry. Nearly all the menfolk of Shoresdean village were there, having been conveyed by special bus. A service was first held at 'the Piper's' home by the Revd W.A. Gainsborough of Ancroft North Moor, then Laidlaw's coffin, draped with a Union Jack, was borne slowly into Norham Church by four pallbearers, all of whom were serving soldiers from the KOSB depot at Berwick. Canon J.A. Little conducted the short service and mourners stood to attention as the body was laid to rest. Bugler Kerr sounded the Last Post and the party of KOSB, led by their CO, Maj. D.W. McConnel, stepped forward to give the salute; afterwards McConnel laid a special wreath on behalf of the regiment.

There is a plaque on the north wall of the nave in St Cuthbert's Church in Norham, Northumberland dedicated:

IN PROUD MEMORY OF / PIPER DANIEL LAIDLAW, VC. / THE PIPER OF LOOS / THE KING'S OWN SCOTTISH BORDERERS.

A ceremony also took place at St Cuthbert's Churchyard on 2 June 2002 to place a headstone over the grave of Piper Daniel Laidlaw VC – "The Piper of Loos". The project was organised by the King's Own Scottish Borderer's Museum in Berwick-on-Tweed and by members of the Laidlaw family.

His Victoria Cross group was donated to the National War Museum of Scotland on 25 September 2005.

G.S. PEACHMENT

Near Hulluch, France, 25 September

The 2nd Bn, King's Royal Rifle Corps (KRRC), was part of 2nd Bde, 1st Div., which was given the task of attacking a 600 yard frontage between Northern Sap and Lone Tree (see map on page 187). The objectives were to overrun the German front and support trenches and then cross the Loos valley in a south-easterly direction, to bring their right flank into touch with the left of the 15th Div. at Puits 14 (Pithead 14). The 2/KRRC took up their positions in the jumping off trenches with the other leading battalion, the 1/Loyal North Lancs. Just by the 2/KRRC trenches there was a slight bulge in the British front line so that the 2nd Bde front faced south-east. The British turned on the gas at 05.50 hours and smoke shells were fired from Stokes mortars. The Battalion *War Diary* noted various problems with these weapons, including premature bursting of charges and failure of weapon parts, which reduced the number of smoke shells fired on this section of front.

The problems did not end there. The wind then veered to the south and all the gas blew back, especially on to B Coy. All ranks had smoke helmets on, but although the gas was soon turned off, the old type of gas helmet proved inadequate and some 200 men from the 2/KRRC and another 200 from the 1/Loyal North Lancs were gassed badly enough to be put out of action. The second line companies were brought up to pass through those in the first line but at that point the advance was delayed because the wind had turned again, this time to the south-west, towards the German trenches, and at 06.20 hours the gas cylinders were turned on again. Most of the men, especially those in the jumping-off trenches, had retired to lie behind the parados in an attempt to avoid the fumes. All this time the German fire was intense.

The assault was finally ordered at 06.34 hours, the advancing troops moving forward into a pall of smoke and gas, quite unable to see their way and choking on the poisonous fumes. Untouched by the bombardment, two enemy machine-guns, positioned in sap-heads about 40 yards ahead of their main line, enfiladed the British line as it advanced. The *War Diary* states that, 'On reaching the [German] wire it was discovered that it was not cut, being low and wide.' During the fierce fighting the British front line 'was compelled to retire in order to reorganize' at approximately 08.00 hours. At this time, No. 11941 Pte Peachment, A Coy, 2/KRRC, noticed his company commander, Capt. G.R. Dubs, lying wounded near the barbed wire some 15 yards from the German lines. Peachment crawled over to assist him and despite intense enemy fire made no attempt to join some men sheltering in a shell-hole near by. Kneeling beside his officer in the open, he tried to bandage his wounds. While thus engaged Peachment was first wounded in the chest by a bomb. At this moment Dubs was also hit in the chest by a bullet. Despite this the wounded officer was trying to drag him to a shell-hole when Peachment received a mortal head wound from a rifle bullet. Peachment's VC citation ends: 'He was one of the youngest men in his battalion, and gave this splendid example of courage and self-sacrifice.' Rfn Peachment was just 18 years and 4 months old.

George Stanley Peachment was born at Parkhills, Fishpool, Bury, on 5 May 1897, the son of Mary and George Henry Peachment, a local barber. He went to Parkhills United Methodist Church School and when it closed he moved to St Chad's, finally attending Bury Technical School. He became an apprentice fitter's engineer at Ashworth & Parker of Elton, Bury, and afterwards worked at the nearby firm of J.H. Riley. When war began he attempted to enlist but was turned away as being too young. He managed to get accepted at Bury on 19 April 1915, joining the 2nd Bn, King's Royal Rifle Corps. His VC was awarded posthumously, and was gazetted on 18 November 1915. A memorial service was held on 17 October at Parkhills United Methodist Church to honour his memory. Including Peachment, there were eight VC recipients aged 18 in the First World War. Pte (Rfn) G.S. Peachment is commemorated on the KRRC regimental panel No. 101/102 on the Loos Memorial at Dud Corner Cemetery, France.

Peachment's VC, 1914–15 Star, BWM and VM, together with the next-of-kin bronze plaque and a selection of documents, including letters of condolence written by Capt. Dubs to Mrs Peachment, came up for sale in November 1996, with a reserve guide price of £18,000–£22,000. They were bought by a private collector for £31,050. His VC is now cited as part of the Lord Ashcroft collection.

A.M. READ

Near Hulluch, France, 25 September

The 1st Bn, Northamptonshire Regt (2nd Bde, 1st Div.) was tasked to attack the enemy trenches north of Loos. Its objectives were a chalk pit just west of the Lens–La Bassée road, the group of pithead buildings known as Puits 14 a little farther south, and the Bois Hugo, which lay farther east (see map on page 187). At 21.30 hours on 24 September the 1st Northamptonshires left the Ypres–Comines railway cutting and marched up to their battle positions in the old front and support trenches. They did not reach their positions until 02.00 hours on 25 September, the day of the battle. They were immediately behind the 1st Loyal North Lancs, and also suffered when the gas blew back over the British trenches.

The assaulting battalions (2/KRRC and 1/Loyal North Lancs) made little headway 'owing to the gas hanging in the valley between the two [opposing] lines' (1/Northants

War Diary), and after an hour or so were ordered back to the front line to reorganize.

A second assault was then attempted, involving the 2nd Royal Sussex (2nd Bde, 1st Div.) attacking on the left and the 1st Northants on the right, in the face of heavy rifle and machine-gun fire. The German wire was intact and impenetrable, so the 1st Northants were forced to lie down in the open for some hours where they suffered considerable losses from the enemy's fire. It was during this time that Capt. A.M. Read, 1st Northants, won his VC. The Battalion *War Diary* explained:

> Capt. Read had very gallantly gone out to rally a party of about 60 men of different units who were retiring disorganized owing to the gas drifting back. The men were led forward again by him and took up a position south of Lone Tree, where they maintained themselves for some hours – Capt. Read was mortally wounded during this time.

The History of the Northamptonshire Regiment 1914– 1918 cites an enemy sniper as the cause of Read's death. Capt. Read had been partially gassed prior to rounding up the party of sixty men. The citation stated that 'he led them back into the firing line, and, utterly regardless of danger, moved freely about, encouraging them under a withering fire'. The fact that he was a superbly fit athlete must have had some bearing on his ability to 'carry on' despite being gassed. His posthumous VC was gazetted on 18 November 1915.

Anketell Moutray Read, the son of Col. J. Moutray Read, was born on 27 October 1884 at Bampton, Devon, being educated at Glengarth, Cheltenham, and the United Service College, Westward Ho, where he was officer of the college cadets corps. He entered Sandhurst in 1901 and was gazetted on 21 November 1903 into the Gloucestershire Regt, serving with them for three years in India. He transferred to the 7th

Hariana Lancers, Indian Army, on 12 July 1907, moving to the Northamptonshire Regt in 1911.

He won the heavyweight boxing championship in India eight times, and the middleweight twice, winning both at the same meetings. At Aldershot and Plymouth he won the Army and Navy Heavyweight Championship three times, earning himself an unequalled record in service boxing. In 1912 he joined the Royal Flying Corps and went to France with the RFC in the original BEF on 11 August 1914, being present at both Maubeuge and Mons, and the retreat to the Marne. He was then attached to the 9th Lancers, and was severely wounded during the fighting on the Aisne in September 1914. He returned to the 1st Northants in April 1915, and was given temporary command because of casualties. Read had exhibited conspicuous bravery earlier in 1915. On the night of 29/30 July he brought a mortally wounded officer out of action 'under hot fire of rifles and grenades'. His courage was again evident during digging operations on 29, 30 and 31 August. After his death at the age of 30 years 11 months, another officer, Capt. M.H.B. Salmon DSO, later paid the following tribute to Read:

> On the 21 August 1915, my company was detailed for the hottest piece of trench warfare on the whole front. It was a section called Z2 and it lay, I fancy, between Guinchy and Vermelles. Here our front line on the left of the section was 17 yards from the Boche line and our wire practically touched. The section was well known and much talked about, and I had a few 'comforting' words with the captain I relieved – a Captain Read [A.M. Read] once of the Indian Cavalry, whom I had known well in India. One of the best, he was killed earning the VC at Loos. We relieved his company amidst a shower of bombs, our men and the Boches shouting and cursing at one another as they threw.

Capt. A.M. Read is buried at Dud Corner Military Cemetery, France, Plot VII, Row F, Grave 19. His VC is held by the Northamptonshire Regiment Museum.

A. VICKERS

Hulluch, France, 25 September

During the Battle of Loos the 7th Div.'s line faced Cité St Elie and the Hulluch Quarries some 5 miles north of Loos (see map on page 186). The 2nd Bn, Royal Warwickshire Regt, part of the 22nd Bde, was opposite Quarry Trench and the German sap called Spurn Head. The battalion went into the attack at 06.30 hours on 25 September and in the face of terrific fire reached the German front line only to find, as other units had done, the enemy wire was uncut. No. 3719 Pte Arthur Vickers, 2nd Royal Warwicks, on his own initiative, rushed forward in front of his company and, displaying immense courage, stood up in broad daylight under heavy fire and cut two gaps in the wire with bolt-cutters, thus enabling his comrades to continue their assault. His action contributed largely to the Warwickshires' successful capture of the German front and support lines before they were checked at Cité St Elie at 09.30 hours. Vickers was, as the regimental history states, 'justly rewarded with the Victoria Cross, the first that had been won by a soldier of the Royal Warwickshires'. The VC was gazetted on 18 November 1915; Vickers also received the French Médaille Militaire.

Arthur Vickers was born at 7 Court, Woodcote Street, Ashton, Birmingham, on 2 February 1882, the son of John, a tube caster, and Amy Vickers. He joined the Royal Warwickshire Regt on 29 May 1902, two days before the end of the South African War, and served with the regiment for six years. After leaving the Army he worked for GEC at Whitton. Vickers re-enlisted in his old regiment a few days after war was declared in August 1914. After winning the VC he was promoted to lance-corporal and while on leave in December visited his old school in Dartmouth Street where he received a hero's welcome from both staff and pupils. Vickers was decorated by King George V at Buckingham Palace on 5 March 1916. At the time he was living with his sister, Mrs Amy Atkins, in Park Road, Aston. During his leave in 1916 he was presented with a framed illuminated address by the then Lord Mayor of Birmingham, Alderman Neville Chamberlain. Vickers was later promoted to the rank of sergeant.

After the war Vickers attended the garden party for VC recipients at Buckingham Palace on 26 June 1920. He was married at the Church of SS Peter and Paul, Ashton, on 29 April 1922, he and his wife setting up home in Farm Street, Hockley, Birmingham, shortly afterwards. He was present at the unveiling of the War Memorial at St Mary's Church, Warwick, in September 1924, and attended the British Legion VC dinner at the House of Lords on 9 November 1929. From 1935 he was employed as a millwright's mate at Messrs Lucas Ltd. He died at the City Hospital, West Heath, on 27 July 1944 aged 62 years and 5 months. His funeral was arranged by the Birmingham Citizens' Society.

H. WELLS

Near Le Rutoire, France, 25 September

On the left of the 1st Northants, the 2nd Bn, Royal Sussex Regt, was also in support, positioned directly behind the 1st Loyal North Lancs and the 2nd KRRC who were in the advanced jumping-off trenches. They were close to Le Rutoire Farm (see map on page 187), which was used as 2nd Bde HQ during the early part of the Battle of Loos. Once the attack had started the 2/Royal Sussex were to move forward and occupy the trenches vacated by the 1st Loyal North Lancs and the 2nd KRRC, and prepare to go forward in support of the assault. The advance battalions launched their attack at 06.34 hours and the Royal Sussex duly moved forward.

The Battalion *War Diary* noted that because of the smoke and gas drifting back to the front trenches and the resulting confusion, the 'Company Commanders then on their own initiative at once advanced and pushed on the assault, the Bn thus becoming part of the Assaulting Line at a very early stage of the attack'. The battalion pushed the advance ahead, only to discover, as others had, that the German wire was uncut. The Battalion *War Diary* states that at this point 'all our officers and men who had reached or got close to the wire were either killed or wounded'.

It was at this juncture that No. 8088 Sgt H. Wells displayed great courage, taking command of his men after his platoon officer was killed, and leading them forward to within 15 yards of the enemy's wire. Nearly half of his platoon had become casualties by then and the survivors were badly shaken, but, as the citation stated, 'with the utmost coolness and bravery Sgt Wells rallied them and led them forward'. After that, only a very few men remained but Wells, standing up, urged them to attack again and was killed in the act of exhorting his men to go forward to the assault. This 'magnificent display of courage and determination', as the citation puts it, earned Sgt Wells a posthumous VC, which was gazetted on 18 November 1915. The conditions that the 2nd Royal Sussex faced was graphically illustrated by Maj. F.W.B. Willett, Royal Sussex Regt, who was present at the action and who wrote on 14 October 1919: 'Owing to the wire being entirely uncut, the assault failed, the battalion losing 19 officers and nearly 600 men in less than 15 minutes . . . Sergt Wells . . . three times rallied his men and led them against the wire under close and continuous machine-gun fire. During the third attempt Sergt. Wells and practically all the survivors of his platoon were killed.'

Harry Wells was born on 19 September 1888 at Hole Cottage, Millbank, Kent. He went to school at Loath, leaving at the age of 12 to work on a farm at Ridgeway, Herne. During this time he lost two fingers of his right hand in an accident with a haymaking machine. He later worked for Mrs Wootton at Herne Mill and lived with his widowed mother at Herne. Wells was a tall youth, over 6 feet tall at the age of 16, and joined the Army in 1904, serving for six and a half years with the Royal Sussex Regt. He left the Army in 1911 and in November of that year he became a police constable in the Ashford Division. He resigned on 31 December 1913. While in the police force he lived at the Beaver Inn, Ashford, and it seems he may have been employed there after his resignation.

When war came in August 1914 Wells was recalled to the Army, and rejoined the Royal Sussex Regt. His previous military experience helped him rise quickly to the rank of sergeant and he went to France with the BEF, seeing action early on in the war. He lost his life on Sunday 25 September 1915 in the Battle of Loos.

His VC was presented to his mother at Buckingham Palace on 27 November 1916. Wells is commemorated on the War Memorial at Herne and the Royal Sussex Regt Memorial in Chichester Cathedral. He is buried at Dud Corner Cemetery in Plot V, Row E, Grave 2. His medals are held by the Royal Sussex Regiment Museum.

H.E. KENNY

Near Loos, France, 25 September

The 1st Bn, Loyal North Lancashire Regt (2nd Bde, 1st Div.) moved into trenches opposite Hulluch in preparation for their part in the Battle of Loos, spending 24 September resting and cleaning up before taking up battle positions at 21.45 hours. The battalion advanced at zero hour, but having reached the German wire they found it uncut and fell back to their starting point. The casualties among the Loyal Lancs men was horrific, as indeed they were for most of the attacking battalions on the first day at Loos; they lost

16 officers and 489 other ranks, 55 of whom were seriously affected by their own gas drifting back to their positions. On six different occasions during the day No. 8655 Pte Henry Kenny went forward, despite being under heavy shell, rifle and machine-gun fire, and each time carried in a wounded man who had been lying out in the open. While handing the last man over the parapet Kenny himself was wounded in the neck, which caused him to be invalided home. His VC was not gazetted until 30 March 1916.

Henry Edward Kenny was born in Hackney, London, on 27 July 1888, his parents having come to England from County Limerick, Ireland. He enlisted in the Loyal North Lancs Regt in October 1906, becoming a reservist in 1911. When war broke out he was recalled to the colours, being at that time employed by Messrs Abdulla, cigarette manufacturers, in London. Kenny went overseas with the original BEF and was at Mons, the Retreat, the Marne and the Aisne, and in October 1914 took part in the defence of Ypres.

He was at Festubert in December 1914, coming out of the line to rest over Christmas before returning to the front to take part in the fighting at La Bassée, Neuve Chapelle and finally Loos, where he won his VC on the first day of the battle. The neck wound he received in performing his act of valour was severe enough to have him sent to the Duchess of Westminster's hospital at Le Touquet and afterwards to Lady Astor's hospital at Taplow. He rejoined his unit before Christmas 1915, serving throughout the rest of the campaign. He was decorated by King George V at Buckingham Palace on 20 May 1916. After being demobilized from the Army in 1919 he returned to employment, his new employer being Spencer Press Ltd, 45 Great Eastern Street, London, a subsidiary of Abdulla Ltd.

He attended the VC garden party given at Buckingham Palace by King George V on 26 June 1920, being also at the opening of the Cenotaph on 11 November that year. On 9 November 1929 he went to the British Legion Dinner for VC winners given in the Royal Gallery at the House of Lords, being flanked at table by Pte S. Harvey of the York and Lancaster Regt, and Capt. Batten Pooll, with whom he chatted about their part in the Zeebrugge raid on St George's Day 1918.

During the Second World War Kenny served in the Local Defence Volunteers, the forerunner of the Home Guard, challenging the King when he came to inspect some 2,000 LDV men at their headquarters at Woodford, Essex. Kenny was later formally introduced to the King who recalled meeting Kenny at the Hackney Empire in 1920 when, as Duke of York, he paid a visit to a special performance for a discharged soldiers' organization. After the war Henry Kenny took part in the Victory Parade and the subsequent Dinner on 8 June 1946, and returned ten years later for the VC Centenary Review on 26 June 1956 in the presence of Queen Elizabeth II. He attended only the first two VC and GC dinners, given on 24 July 1958 and 7 July 1960. He died in St Peter's Hospital, Chertsey, Surrey, on 6 May 1979, aged 90 years and 9 months, and was buried on 15 May in St John's Cemetery, Woking, Surrey. His VC is now part of the Lord Ashcroft VC Collection.

F.H. JOHNSON

Hill 70, France, 25 September

The 73rd Field Coy, Royal Engineers (RE), was based at Noeux-les-Mines throughout August but moved to Mazingarbe in September in preparation for the Battle of Loos. When the battle opened with the release of chlorine gas and smoke on 25 September, the 73rd Field Coy was attached to the 44th Bde. The RE men were there to help the infantry dig in and consolidate the positions as they were taken, though the 73rd Field Coy's *War Diary* notes that 'the Company acted as Infantry practically the whole time'. 2/Lt Johnson, with his No. 3 Section, 73 Field Coy RE were with No. 4 Section behind the 10th Gordon Highlanders, waiting to move forward shortly after the main assault once Nos 1 and 2 Sections had followed the Black Watch and Seaforth Highlanders respectively into the attack. During the wait No. 4 Section was ordered to bridge a trench over the Lens road; while this operation was being carried out their officer, Lt Nolan, and ten NCOs and men became casualties. Capt. Cardew then took command, ordering Johnson's No. 3 Section and the survivors of No. 4 Section to advance behind the 10th Gordons to a point between Loos Towers and the Windmill (see map on page 187). At Loos the officer commanding the Gordons ordered Capt. Cardew to advance to Hill 70.

The RE men reached the crest of the hill at about 09.30 hours, from where they could see the hard-pressed infantry in the Hill 70 Redoubt; the RE men joined them in an effort to hold the strongpoint but all were forced to retire because of German machine-gun fire. They went back behind the ridge to dig in but after Capt. Cardew and 2/Lt Johnson 'found' a machine-gun and moved it into position, Cardew decided to have another go at the redoubt. The officers advanced with RE men only and Capt. Cardew and Lt Johnson and about ten men got into the strongpoint but were forced out again. At this moment Capt. Cardew was seriously hurt and 2/Lt Johnson was wounded in the leg. Nevertheless, Johnson stuck to his duty, leading several efforts to retake the German redoubt and constantly rallying the men near him while under heavy fire. He remained at his post until midnight when he was finally relieved. The *War Diary* of the 73rd Field Coy makes special mention of 2/Lt Johnson 'who, although wounded, carried on until midnight, rallied his men and the parties of infantry without officers, and showed great coolness and gallantry'. He was awarded the VC for his courageous example, the award being gazetted on 18 November 1915.

Frederick Henry Johnson was born on 15 August 1890 at 13 Dedfor Row (now High Road), Streatham, London. He was the son of Samuel Roger Johnson and Emily, daughter of Henry White of Ewell. He attended Middle Whitgift School, Croydon, and St Dunstan's College, Catford, and was a day scholar at Battersea Polytechnic.

Academically he was very bright, being a Whitworth Exhibitioner and obtaining a BSc (Hons) Engineering degree at London University. Johnson joined the London University OTC in August 1914, and soon after was commissioned 2/Lt in the 73rd Field Coy RE. After winning the VC at Hill 70 he was made lieutenant and in May 1916 was given a tumultuous reception when he visited Battersea Polytechnic while on leave. He won quick promotion, becoming captain in 1916 and major a few months before he was reported killed in action on 11 December 1917, having died of wounds on 26 November in France. His name appears on the Cambrai Memorial and his VC was secured for £9,000 in March 1989 by the then Minister for Trade, MP Alan Clark.

A.F. DOUGLAS-HAMILTON

Hill 70, France, 25/26 September

The 15th Div. was to attack on a 1,500 yard frontage astride the Béthune–Lens and the Vermelles–Loos Road redoubts on 25 September. After capturing the redoubts and Loos village itself they were to carry on to Hill 70 (see map on page 187).

As the battle progressed, the fighting in Loos pulled in men of the 44th and 46th Bdes from their initial direction, and at the eastern end of Loos village a mass of intermingled Scottish units began the ascent of Hill 70 shortly after 08.00 hours on 25 September. (They were described in the Official History as having 'the appearance of a bank holiday crowd'.) The Germans could be seen running away, making the Scotsmen even more eager to pursue. About 900 Scots passed over the Hill and moved on down the bare and exposed slope, most of them moving southwards towards the houses of Cité St Laurent where the Germans were getting into position. The Scots were within 300 yards of the German second position when enfilade machine-gun fire and rifle fire from ahead brought them to a halt. Their position was utterly exposed and so, rather than lie down and be shot, they pushed forward in short rushes, only to discover uncut German wire hidden in long grass. Their situation was hopeless. The 45th Bde, 15th Div.'s reserve, had moved up to the old British front line to support the intended attack on Cité St Auguste. Soon urgent requests came in from 46th Bde for support on the brigade's left, near Puits 14, where their left flank was exposed by the failure of the 1st Div. to advance on its left. Soon 100 bombers and a platoon of the 6th Cameron Highlanders under Maj. (Temp. Lt-Col.) A.F. Douglas-Hamilton were sent forward, to be followed later by the whole battalion. They set up a defensive flank from the north-west corner of Chalet Wood to Chalk Pit Wood. On the 26th the 6th Camerons, who had been forced out of Chalet Wood by the Germans, made repeated attempts to retake the western end of the wood and desperate hand-to-hand fighting took place against detachments from the *106th Reserve, 153rd* and *178th Regts*. When the battalions on his flanks retired Douglas-Hamilton rallied his men and led them forward to the assault four times. The fourth attack, with just 50 men remaining, was a gallant but hopeless gesture. Douglas-Hamilton fell at the head of his men; the small party was annihilated and the wood lost. Douglas-Hamilton was awarded a posthumous VC, and the citation ended: 'It was mainly due to his bravery, his untiring energy, and splendid leadership that the line at this point was enabled to check the enemy's advance.' Douglas-Hamilton was one of the oldest soldiers to die at Loos, being killed at the age of 52 years and 1 month.

Angus Falconer Douglas-Hamilton was born at Brighton on 20 August 1863, the youngest son of Maj.-Gen. Octavius Douglas-Hamilton and Katherine, daughter of Capt. D. Macleod CB, RN. His education was undertaken at Foster's

Naval Preparatory School, then privately by Army tutors and finally at the Royal Military College, Sandhurst. He joined the Army on 23 August 1884, being commissioned as a lieutenant in the Queen's Own Cameron Highlanders. He served with the 1st Bn during the latter part of the Nile Expedition, receiving the Medal with Clasp and Khedive's Star, and throughout the operations of the Sudan Frontier Field Force, 1885–6, being present at Koshesh during its investment and at the engagement at Ginniss. He was promoted to captain on 7 December 1892 and from 1 February 1894 to 30 April 1899 he was adjutant of the 6th Gordon Highlanders. He married on 1 August 1894 at the Episcopalian Church, Highfield, Muir of Ord, Ross-shire, his wife being Anna Watson, the younger daughter of Capt. Alexander Watson Mackenzie, of Ord, Muir of Ord. They had one daughter, Camilla Beatrice. He vacated his position with the Gordon Highlanders and rejoined his regiment, serving with the 2nd Bn in Gibraltar, Malta, South Africa, North China and India, being promoted to major on 7 December 1901. He retired on 24 August 1912 but on the outbreak of the First World War was recalled from the Reserve and appointed as a transport officer on the Embarkation Staff at Southampton. On 1 October 1914 he was made temporary lieutenant-colonel and was given command of the 6th (Service) Bn, Cameron Highlanders. He won his VC on 25/26 September 1915, close to Hill 70 during the Battle of Loos, his award being gazetted on 18 November 1915. King George V handed the medal to Douglas-Hamilton's widow at an investiture at Buckingham Palace on 29 November 1916. Later Mrs Douglas-Hamilton was presented with a bronze statue of a Cameron Highlander by former 1914–18 prisoners of war as a token of their appreciation of her work on their behalf. Lt-Col. Douglas-Hamilton was also awarded the 1914–15 Star, and the British War and Victory medals. His widow died at Forest Hill, Muir of Ord, on 15 February 1945, willing her husband's medals to their only daughter for her lifetime. In April 1965 his VC and other medals, together with the Honour Plaque, were donated to the Regimental Museum of the Queen's Own Highlanders (Seaforth and Camerons), Fort George, Inverness-shire, Scotland. Lt-Col. A.F. Douglas-Hamilton is commemorated on the Loos Memorial in France.

R. DUNSIRE

Hill 70, France, 26 September

The 13th Bn, Royal Scots (45th Bde, 15th Div.) were brought forward as part of a brigade attack to take Hill 70. Following the wet weather on the opening day of the Battle of Loos, conditions deteriorated on 26 September: mist and low cloud and rain covered the battleground. The 45th Bde was ordered to attack from the west at 09.00 hours. However, when the orders arrived at 05.00 hours, the brigade was in position astride the track leading to the Hill 70 redoubt; in the orders this track had been designated the left boundary of the brigade line of advance. To move the whole brigade over, and reassemble both the 45th and 62nd Bdes, in accordance with the orders, was deemed too risky so the brigade commanders decided to attack from where they were. The 45th Bde was to make a frontal assault against the redoubt and the summit of the hill with three battalions: the 7th Royal Scots Fusiliers on the right would attack the south face of the redoubt; the 11th Argyll & Sutherland Highlanders would attack the centre of the strongpoint; and the 13th Royal Scots would deliver their assault against its northern face and northern flank. These units were supposed to withdraw during a short preliminary bombardment but the order to do so was not received until after the bombardment had started; although largely accurate, some shells did fall short at times, inflicting casualties in the British front lines, especially among the 13th Royal Scots. As the bombardment neared its end the mist cleared, leaving the attackers who went over the top at 09.00 hours clearly visible from the German position. Nevertheless, the assaulting battalions reached the perimeter trench and after fierce hand-to-hand fighting drove the enemy out. At 10.30 hours the Cameron Highlanders (see A.F. Douglas-Hamilton, page 205) were forced out of Chalet Wood to the east of Puits 14; this enabled the Germans to increase the weight of fire against the 13th Royal Scots on the left flank of 45th Bde. A Coy, under Capt. Penney of the 13th Royal Scots, took his platoon forward to reoccupy the Camerons' position in the wood but failed, incurring heavy losses. Pte R. Dunsire had advanced with his battalion, the 13th Royal Scots, and they now held their ground in readiness to go forward again when reinforcements should arrive. It was then that Dunsire noticed a wounded man, lying in the fire-swept area between the opposing lines, waving an arm as if signalling for assistance. Heedless of the heavy fire Dunsire crawled out to the man and brought him safely in. Shortly after returning he heard another man shouting for help; this man was considerably closer to the German lines but, disregarding the danger, Dunsire went out and brought him in as well. The author of *The Royal Scots 1914–1919* commented: 'How he [Dunsire] managed to escape without a scratch was a mystery, for the earth was madly dancing to the continuous thud of bullets.' No. 18274 Pte R. Dunsire was awarded the VC for his acts of bravery on 26 September, the award being gazetted on 18 November 1915.

Robert Dunsire was born in East Wemyss, Fifeshire, Scotland, the son of Thomas and Elizabeth Anderson Dunsire. He later resided in Kirkaldy, Fife, and was married to Catherine Pitt of 107 Denbeath, Methil, Fife. He joined up when war broke out, and after winning the VC was decorated by King George V at Buckingham Palace on 7 December 1915. By mid-January Dunsire was back with his battalion and they took over trenches to the right of Hulluch on 23 January 1916. The Battalion *War Diary*'s entry for 30 January states they were '. . . bombarded with rifle, grenades and trench mortars'. The next day's comments were brief and prosaic: 'Same trenches. Pte Dunsire VC mortally wounded yesterday by enemy trench mortar.' Philip Warner in *The Battle of Loos* quotes Joseph Wallace of the 11th Argylls in reference to Dunsire: '. . . his leg was blown off in a dug-out, and he was brought to hospital where he died. I had the honour of playing the pipes at his funeral.'

Pte Dunsire died of wounds on 30 January 1916 and is buried at Mazingarbe Communal Cemetery, Grave 18. He is also commemorated on the War Memorial in Kirkaldy. His VC is held by the Regimental Museum of the Royal Scots, Edinburgh Castle, Scotland.

A.F. SAUNDERS

Near Loos, France, 26 September

Due to a shortage of seasoned troops and the great extent of line on which British troops would be operating during the Battle of Loos, Sir John French decided to retain a strong general reserve to meet any emergency arising from the battle. The 21st and 24th (New Army) Divisions, both untried units, were put into the reserve. Unfortunately, they were kept too far back. When the situation on 25 September became apparent, HQ formed a plan for both divisions to attack between Hill 70 and the village of Hulluch (see map on page 187). The plan was not changed despite the crucial fact that the 15th Div. had failed to capture Hill 70 and Hulluch was still in German hands.

The 71st Bde, 24th Div., of which the 9th (Service) Bn, Suffolk Regt, was a part, arrived at Béthune at about 01.00 hours on 25 September. The 9th Suffolks were exhausted following a succession of night marches intended to bring the brigade (and the division as a whole) closer to Loos to support the action. They were promised 48 hours to recuperate but in the event they were ordered to be ready to move forward by 07.00 hours; in fact it was 11.30 hours before they set off for the battle line. The 24th Div. was to act as support to the 9th (Scottish) Div., the 9th Suffolks and 11th Essex forming the first line.

At about 20.00 hours the 9th Suffolks wended their way across the Loos battlefield, being held up at about midnight when they dug in with the German second (support) line behind them. At 05.00 hours on 26 September they were ordered back to the German support trenches behind them. The 21st and 24th Divs were to attack again at 11.00 hours. The 72nd Bde was to deliver the assault with the 11th Essex (on the left) and the 9th Suffolks (on the right) as brigade support, 600 yards to the rear. This order was not received until 11.25 hours and as it was passed down the line the 9th Suffolks were ordered forward immediately, moving ahead under heavy artillery fire towards the previous night's objective. The advance was maintained until about 200 yards beyond the Hulluch–Lens road where it was finally checked. At 17.00 hours the right flank began to give way but for three hours the centre held, during which time the flanks advanced and retired twice. The left flank then came under intense machine-gun fire from the direction of Hulluch, forcing it back and causing the greatest losses of the day for the 9th Suffolks. The Suffolks were relieved in the early hours of 27 September.

No. 3/10133 Sgt A.F. Saunders had distinguished himself the previous day when his officer had been wounded, and Saunders unhesitatingly took command of two machine-guns and a handful of men and, although severely wounded himself, closely followed the last four charges of another battalion (6th Cameron Highlanders) and provided every possible support. As the remnants of the battalion were forced to withdraw he continued to fire one of the guns and, as the citation said, 'continued to give clear orders, and by continuous firing did his best to cover the retirement'. Saunders himself never expanded upon the deed that earned him the VC, but many years later details emerged from memoirs written by Gen. Sir Philip Christison who had been a 2/Lt in the 6th Cameron Highlanders at the Battle of Loos and was with Saunders during his deed of gallantry. 2/Lt Christison was lying wounded in a shell-hole when the 9th Suffolks passed through his position. Things seemed to be going well at first but then, to his horror, the Suffolks and their flanking troops doubled back under fire, leaving him isolated. Christison takes up the story:

But one stout fellow, Sergeant A.F. Saunders, refused to retire. He had a Lewis Gun he had picked up with a full drum on it. He crawled over to me and said he'd stay and fight. He made to crawl over to the next shell-hole and, as he did so, a shell landed and blew part of his left leg off about the knee. I crawled over and got him into the shell-hole, putting a tourniquet on his leg and giving him my water bottle as his was empty. I crawled back to my hole and a few minutes later . . . saw a fresh wave of German troops advancing. . . . There seemed to be no point in opening fire as there were, perhaps, 150 enemy advancing rather diagonally across our front. To my amazement, I heard, short sharp bursts of Lewis Gun fire coming from the shell-hole on my right; this was Sergeant Saunders, more or less minus a leg. The Germans were taken by surprise and bunched, so I joined in and between us we took a heavy toll and the rest retired out of sight. I took down Sergeant Saunders' number, name and regiment . . . stretcher-bearer parties from the RE . . . got me and Sergeant Saunders on stretchers . . . but shells dropped close and we were abandoned. We were lucky, a stretcher-bearer party from the Scots Guards picked us up and got us to an Advanced Dressing Station, where emergency surgery was carried out.

. . . Sergeant Saunders, now without a leg, was awarded the VC, while I was given the MC. He and I correspond regularly.

Although badly wounded in the leg, Saunders did not lose the limb as Christison suggests.

Arthur Frederick Saunders was born on 23 April 1878 in St John's parish, Ipswich, Suffolk. The 1881 Census has him listed as living with his parents and seven siblings at 63 Spring Road, Ipswich and later, according to the 1891 Census they had moved to Holly Cottage, Ringham Road in the same town. His father Thomas worked for Mr Henry Finn, a harness-maker, in Ipswich for forty-five years. Arthur Saunders attended the California School and at the age of 15 years and 9 months joined the Navy at Shotley Naval Barracks. He trained for the Merchant Navy on HMS *Warspite*, the Marine Society Training Ship, from November 1883 to February 1884, but later joined the Royal Navy, becoming a 1st Class Petty Officer and serving for fifteen years. After leaving the Navy he took up engineering and was employed at Ransomes, Sims & Jeffries in Ipswich. He enlisted in the 9th (Service) Bn, Suffolk Regiment on 19 September 1914, and was promoted to the rank of sergeant within a month. His regimental number cited in the London Gazette as 3/10133 indicates that he had served pre-war with the 3rd (Special Reserve) Bn, a Territorial part of the Suffolk Regiment and so was trained prior to joining the 9th (Service) Bn. After winning the VC at Loos, the first for the Suffolk Regt in the war, he was given a public welcome home on 22 June 1916, reaching Ipswich Town Hall via 'gaily decorated streets and . . . cheering . . . and flag-waving' to be met by the Mayor and Corporation, many Suffolk Regt officers and Lt-Col. Bretell, who commanded the 9th Suffolks at Loos. The band of the 3rd Suffolks was also present. Saunders was entertained to tea in the Town Hall and was later presented with a sum of £365, which had been subscribed by the residents of Ipswich and district and the Suffolk Regt 'in recognition of his bravery'. He was then accompanied to his home in Cauldwell Hall Road, Ipswich, by the drum band of the 2/1st London Regt (Royal Fusiliers). Saunders had been in hospital at 'Beaulieu', Harrogate, on 10 May 1916, prior to returning home and he was back in hospital at Harrogate in July, apparently not having fully recovered from his wounds. It appears that at some point Saunders used his cash gift to purchase a new home, 354 Foxhall Road, Ipswich, where he and his wife Edith lived for the rest of their lives.

In April 1920 he was made an honorary Freeman of the Borough and later, on 26 June, he attended the VC garden party at Buckingham Palace. Saunders was one of the Guard of Honour for Field-Marshal Lord Allenby on 6 October the same year, when he received the Freedom of the Borough of Bury St Edmunds, Suffolk. Saunders gained further honours in January 1923, becoming a JP for Ipswich. The Prince of Wales visited HMS *Warspite* at Greenhithe in July that year, where he met Saunders who was present as an 'old boy'. He attended the British Legion dinner for VCs at the House of Lords on 9

November 1929 and was present at several reunion dinners of the 9th Suffolks which were held at Bury St Edmunds; they had been instigated in 1926 and took place every two years. When the Prince of Wales visited Ipswich for the Royal Show on 4 July 1934, Saunders was one of the Guard of Honour made up of members of the British Legion and the Old Contemptibles. From 1940 to 1944 he served as an RQMS in the Home Guard. He died on 30 July 1947, aged 69 years and 3 months, having never really recovered from his wounds received in 1915. He was cremated on 5 August 1947 and his ashes were scattered in the Garden of Rest in the Old Cemetery, Ipswich. His name appears on a panel in the Temple of Remembrance there, in Room D, Panel 64. He left a widow, a daughter and two sons, both of whom were Mentioned in Despatches during the Second World War. In 1989 his widow, Mrs Edith Saunders, who was 99 on 11 February that year, presented her late husband's VC to the Suffolk Regiment on her birthday. The ceremony took place at Howard House Retirement Home, Brig. Bill Deller receiving the medal on behalf of the Regiment in the presence of the Saunders' family and friends. On the 95th anniversary of his action, 26 September 2010, *The Ipswich society* put up a blue plaque on 180 Cauldwell Hall Road, Ipswich, to commemorate Saunders' VC, who lived at that address at the time of his award.

J.D. POLLOCK

Hohenzollern Redoubt, France, 27 September

On 27 September the 5th Bn, Queen's Own Cameron Highlanders, who had been part of the 26th Bde, 9th Div., assault against the Hohenzollern Redoubt on 25 September, prevented disaster when the 73rd Bde, which was holding the redoubt, was gradually forced to give ground in the face of repeated enemy attacks and incessant shelling. At about

10.00 hours 70 men of the Black Watch and 30 Camerons, among them No. 12087 Cpl Pollock of 'C' Coy, 5th Bn (26th Bde), were sent up to the redoubt; this party rallied the defenders and checked the German advance after several prolonged bombing fights. At about 12.00 hours a superior number of enemy bombers approached Hohenzollern Redoubt, working their way up the trench called 'Little Willie' (see map on page 186). Cpl Pollock, having sought permission from an officer, climbed out of the trench alone and walked along the enemy parapet 'with the utmost coolness and disregard of danger' to bomb the German bombing party in 'Little Willie' from above. He carried his grenades across to the trench under heavy fire and worked his way along it hurling bombs at the enemy. The Germans were taken completely by surprise and were held at bay for an hour by Pollock who, although under heavy machine-gun fire, remained unscathed until he jumped down into his own trench when he was wounded in the arm. His single-handed act of bravery earned him the VC.

James Dalgleish Pollock was born on 3 June 1890 at Tillicoultry, Clackmannanshire, Scotland, where he spent his early years before moving to Glasgow in 1910. Two years later he was living and working in Paris, attached to the Paris branch of his London firm, and was in the French capital when war was declared. He quickly returned to Britain to enlist, only to discover that his local Territorial unit, the 5th Scottish Rifles, had mobilized to its full complement. He therefore joined 'Lochiel's Battalion', as it was known in the area, of the Queen's Own Cameron Highlanders, which was raised by Lochiel in Glasgow. This 5th Bn was in the first of Kitchener's Army Divisions – the 9th (Scottish). Pollock crossed to France with his battalion in March 1915. After winning the VC on 27 September he was decorated by King George V at Buckingham Palace on 4 December 1915. Astonishingly, Cpl Pollock's cousin, Cpl Dawson (see page 233), won his VC at Hohenzollern Redoubt just sixteen days later.

In 1916, after recovering from his arm wound, Pollock attended the first officer cadet school at Gailes, Ayrshire. During this time he met his future wife. He was commissioned as a second lieutenant in the 6/Camerons on 7 July 1916 and served with them for a time on the Somme. During preparations for the Battle of Arras in 1917, the then Capt. Pollock was injured by the premature bursting of a rifle grenade which caused the loss of sight in his left eye. He was invalided out and worked for the Ministry of Munitions for a while. After the Armistice he spent some time in France working with the board responsible for the disposal of war surplus stores before returning to marry in 1919, settling in Ayr with his wife. He attended the VC garden party at Buckingham Palace on 26 June 1920 and in September paraded at Inverness when the Duke of York (later King George VI) presented Colours to the 7th and 9th Camerons at the Regimental Depot.

He moved to London in 1923, working as a director of an importing company. On 9 November 1929 he attended the VC reunion dinner held at the House of Lords. He returned to Ayr in 1940 and lived there for ten years before moving to Leicester. During the Second World War he volunteered for the Royal Observer Corps. He served as Observer Officer and full time Duty Controller in No 33 Aberdeen (Ayr) Group, before being stood down on 12 May 1945, having been the only VC holder serving in the Royal Observer Corps in its history. In 1955 he went back to Ayr. During this period he was both director and sales representative for Midland Hosiery Mills in Leicester. Pollock was on parade for the VC centenary celebrations on 26 June 1956. He had returned from a biannual business trip to Canada for the firm just three weeks before he died on 10 May 1958 at Ballochmyle Hospital, Ayrshire. He was aged 57 years and 11 months. His wife had predeceased him but his daughter, Mrs Clare Cottam, was willed his VC for her lifetime after which it was offered to the Regiment.

A.B. TURNER

Slag Alley, Fosse 8, near Vermelles, France,
28 September

Several secondary attacks were made at Loos to push the British line forward, especially where local successes had left flanks exposed. On 26 September a provisional brigade under the command of Col. Carter was created from the 1/KRRC, 1/Royal Berks, and 2/Worcs, and was attached to the 7th Div. for an attack on the quarries between Hulluch and Fosse 8 (see map on page 186). The attack was made at 02.30 hours on 28 September. The assaulting troops had to pass over 800 yards of captured German trenches, then manned by British troops, on their way to their objective, the slag heap called Fosse 8. The *War Diary* of the 1/Royal Berks stated:

> Owing to the bright moonlight the enemy saw us advancing. When we were 400 yards from our objective (FOSSE 8) they put up Very lights and kept up a continuous rifle fire on us from our right front – this grew heavier as we got nearer.

The fire was so intense that the attack was held up 70 yards from the slag heap. D Coy and part of C Coy manned the British front line. During this time the Germans started bombing down one of their communication trenches towards the British in their advanced positions. 2/Lt A.B. Turner of the 3rd Bn, 1/Royal Berks, was attached to the 1st Bn and, as the Germans bombed toward them, Turner volunteered to lead a fresh attack when the regiment's bombers could make no headway against the enemy grenade-throwers down Slag Alley. Turner, virtually single-handedly, drove the German bombers back 150 yards, throwing his bombs incessantly

with 'dash and determination'. The Germans, driven back by
Turner's fusillade of bombs, replied in kind; however, he was
not hit by bombs but by a rifle bullet that struck him in the
abdomen. Capt. Frizell, temporary commander of the 1/Royal
Berks, wrote to Turner's father explaining how his son was
helped back to the dressing-station but as it was impossible
for him to stay there he was sent back to the collecting station
on a stretcher. Sadly Turner died of his wounds at No.1
Casualty Clearing Station at Chocques, near Béthune, on 1
October 1915. The notification of the circumstances for which
Turner was awarded a posthumous Victoria Cross appeared
in the *London Gazette* on 18 November 1915. It ended: 'His
action enabled the reserves to advance with very little loss,
and subsequently covered the flank of his regiment in its
retirement, thus averting a loss of some hundreds of men.'

Alexander Buller Turner was born at Thatcham House, which
had been home to generations of Turners, in Thatcham,
near Newbury, Berkshire, on 22 May 1893. His family had
military links and his middle name, 'Buller', indicated that his
mother was descended from Gen. the Rt Hon. Sir Redvers
Henry Buller VC, who gained his award in the Zulu War
in 1879. Turner's father was Maj. Charles Turner of the
Royal Berkshire Regt. Alexander Turner was educated at the
Preparatory School, Parkside, East Horsley, and joined the
1st Bn, Royal Berkshire Regt, as a second lieutenant on 22
June 1915. He was wounded two months later on 15 August.
Having recovered from his injury, he rejoined his regiment, but
going back to the 1st Bn, rather than to the 3rd Bn to whom
he had originally been commissioned. On 28 September, in the
Battle of Loos, 2/Lt Turner gained his VC.

His VC was originally sent by post to his father, Maj.
Charles Turner, but subsequently it was presented to Maj.
Turner personally by King George V at Buckingham Palace
on 16 November 1916. Retained by his family for many
years, his Victoria Cross is now displayed at The Royal
Gloucestershire, Berkshire and Wiltshire Regiment (Salisbury)
Museum, Salisbury, Wiltshire. His brother, Lt-Col. Victor

Buller Turner, who was only 15 years old when his older brother died, won a VC himself twenty-seven years later, on 27 October 1942, while serving in the Western Desert with the Rifle Bde. Later he became the Clerk of the Court and Adjutant of the Queen's Bodyguard of the Yeoman of the Guard. He lived with his two brothers, Capt. C.B. Turner RN (Retd), and Brig. Mark Turner RA (Retd), and their sister, Miss Turner, at Ditchingham, near Bungay, Norfolk.

Alexander Buller Turner's name appears on the War Memorial at Thatcham, Berkshire. He is buried at Chocques Military Cemetery, France, Plot 1, Row B, Grave 2.

A.J.T. FLEMING-SANDES

Hohenzollern Redoubt, France, 29 September

The fighting in and around the Hohenzollern Redoubt was continuous. The Germans were in control of some parts of the strongpoint, while other parts were held by the British. The 2/East Surreys were given the task of clearing up the confusion at the redoubt and attacking 'Little Willie' (see map on page 186), which threatened any British consolidation in the redoubt.

The 2/East Surreys were threatened by German bombers moving up 'Little Willie', and the battalion bombers were forced back behind a new barrier (marked 'Y' on the map) which they had erected behind the original barrier (at X). The German progress was halted by men of the 2nd Bn, led by 2/Lt Jannson, who led his men out of the trenches and, lying in the open, poured enfilade fire at the Germans in their trench, inflicting heavy casualties on the enemy but suffering badly themselves.

At this critical point some troops on the right of the redoubt began to retire, thus leaving exposed the right flank.

The 2/East Surreys had fought hard in the redoubt for some thirty-six hours and by the afternoon of 29 September their trenches were crowded with dead and wounded and they were running short of bombs. The hard-pressed men in the redoubt were themselves faltering when 2/Lt A.J.T. Fleming-Sandes and a party of 2/East Surreys arrived, having been sent up with a supply of bombs. At this point the Germans launched a fresh attack and Fleming-Sandes scrambled on to the parapet and began to hurl bomb after bomb at the Germans, by now just 20 yards away. The enemy withdrew from his furious onslaught and bullets and hand-grenade fragments flew around Fleming-Sandes. His right arm was broken by a rifle shot but he continued to throw bombs with his left until he was again shot, this time in the face. He was soon evacuated to hospital. The defenders had been inspired by his courage and recovered their spirits; they successfully held the redoubt and the neighbouring trenches until they were relieved at 07.00 hours on 1 October. Fleming-Sandes had, by his example, steadied the men around him and saved the situation. His Victoria Cross was gazetted on 18 November 1915.

Alfred and Grace Fleming-Sandes' son, Alfred James Terence (known to his friends as 'Sandy'), was born on 24 June 1894 at their home in Northstead Road, Tulse Hill Park, London. His education began at Dulwich College Preparatory School, and continued at King's School, Canterbury, where he was monitor and house-captain. When war broke out he enlisted as a private in the Artists' Rifles on 5 August 1914, sailing for France with the 1st Bn on 26 October that year. He received a commission in France on 9 May 1915 and served with his new unit, the 2/East Surreys, until he was wounded in action on 29 September at Loos when winning the VC.

He received a great reception when he visited his old school after recovering from his wounds. He was decorated by King George V at Buckingham Palace on 15 January 1916. He was not passed fit for active service again until 1918 when he returned as a lieutenant and was Mentioned in Despatches. After being demobilized in 1919 he received an appointment in the education department of the Sudan Government. Fleming-Sandes was then seconded to the political service in 1924, becoming Assistant District Commissioner at El Nahud. He was called to the Bar at Grays Inn in 1927 and was next a district judge in the Sudan Civil Service. He gained rapid promotion and was awarded the Order of the Nile 4th Class in 1932, the year he became a Provincial Judge. He also married Dorothea May, daughter of Mr and Mrs William Weeks of Sandown, Isle of Wight, in the same year. The ceremony took place on 27 August at Newchurch, Isle of Wight. In 1935 he became a judge in the Sudan High Court.

During the Second World War he was given a commission as 'Bimbashi' (major) in the Sudan Auxiliary Defence Force, a kind of Sudanese 'Home Guard', which he accepted on 23 July 1941. From 1942 to 1944 Fleming-Sandes was Judge Advocate General of the Sudan Defence Force and was Acting Chief Justice of the Sudan on occasions. He retired in 1944 and from 1945 to 1958 was chairman of the Pensions Appeal Tribunal for England and Wales.

Fleming-Sandes was on parade at the VC Centenary Review held by Queen Elizabeth II in Hyde Park on 26 June 1956 and he attended the first and second dinners of the VC and GC Association, held at the Café Royal, London, on 24 July 1958 and 7th July 1960 respectively.

'Sandy' Fleming-Sandes of Redway, Dawlish Road, Teignmouth, Devon, died suddenly of natural causes at 23.20 hours on Wednesday 24 May 1961, at the White Horse Hotel, Romsey, Hampshire, aged sixty-six years and eleven months. He was cremated privately at Torquay crematorium on the 30th. He bequeathed his VC and medals to his wife for her lifetime, and directed his trustees to offer them, after her death, to the East Surrey section of The Queen's Royal Surrey Regiment. This was duly done and his Victoria Cross is now displayed at the Queen's Royal Surrey Regiment Museum, Clandon Park, Surrey. A friend, Mr G.R.F. Bredin, in a letter to *The Times*, described Fleming-Sandes as, 'modest and self-effacing almost to a fault, his life was one of complete devotion to the task in hand. His standards remained inflexible, were they those of professional performance or personal conduct.' He closed by referring to Sandy's 'unostentatious devotion to duty and personal example', qualities that earned him the VC in 1915.

S. HARVEY

'Big Willie' Trench, France, 29 September

The men of the 1st Bn, York and Lancaster Regt (83rd Bde, 28th Div.) moved towards Loos on the 26 September and, like other reinforcements arriving at the front, they were required to relieve the exhausted troops who had made the initial attacks of the Battle of Loos. Orders were received to take up trench positions near the Hohenzollern Redoubt. The trenches were hopelessly congested and the battalion was obliged to occupy some reserve trenches.

A and B Coys, commanded by Capts Forster and Buckley, were sent forward to support British troops in the Hohenzollern Redoubt who were being attacked. The two companies arrived at 'Big Willie' trench at about 05.00 hours on 29 September. The enemy held several sections of trench in the area, which enabled them to launch bombing attacks via communication trenches at the British-held sections. At 06.00 hours the Germans made a major bombing attack just as A Coy was advancing up 'Big Willie' trench to relieve the Buffs (East Kent Regt) in Dump Trench (see map on page 186); the Buffs had already begun to leave their positions. The enemy had observed the progress of the troop relief from slag heaps on the left of Hohenzollern Redoubt and chose this moment to send their bombing parties along every possible approach in an effort to recapture Dump Trench.

The British troops were closely packed in a narrow trench and, aware of the risk to them, Capt. Buckley led B Coy's bombers out of the trench to launch a bombing counter-attack in the open. A Coy and the remnants of the Buffs also attacked, but at high cost to themselves. The shortage of bombs was critical and No. 8273 Pte S. Harvey, of the 1/York and Lancs, volunteered to fetch fresh supplies. The communication trench was blocked with casualties and reinforcements so Pte Harvey ran backwards and forwards across the open from 'Big Willie' trench to the old British front line, under intense fire, to fetch bombs. He succeeded in bringing up thirty boxes of bombs for his comrades in A and B Coys over a period of thirteen hours, before he was wounded in the head. For his courage he was awarded the Victoria Cross which was gazetted on 18 November 1915, the official citation making it clear that it was 'mainly due to Harvey's bravery that the enemy was eventually driven back'.

Samuel Harvey was born at Basford, Bulwell, Nottinghamshire, on 17 September 1881 but soon after his family moved to Vernon Street, Ipswich, Suffolk, close to the docks. He was a small man, only 5 feet tall, but he joined the York and Lancaster Regt in 1905 and sailed to France with the original BEF in 1914. He won his VC near the Hohenzollern Redoubt, and the first his mother heard about it was when he sent her a cigarette card on which his portrait appeared. Pte Harvey was transferred to the 3rd (Home Service) G Bn, Northumberland Fusiliers, as No. 31198 on 7 October 1916. He was decorated by King George V at Buckingham Palace on 24 January 1917. He was wounded in action three times.

After the war Samuel Harvey, nicknamed 'Monkey' because of his sense of humour and love of practical jokes, returned to Ipswich. His post-war years were tragic; he scratched a living as an odd-job man, residing at a series of addresses in the town. He dug people's gardens 'muttering "dig that trench, etc." all the time he was digging'. For a time he was an ostler at the Great White Horse Hotel in Ipswich and was well known to Canon Lummis, then a curate in Ipswich and later a vicar in the nearby parish of Kesgrave. Lummis described Harvey as 'a very rough diamond'.

Harvey married Georgina Brown, a widow from Kesgrave, and lived in Adelphi Place, Ipswich, though she predeceased him and his sisters knew nothing of the marriage. He attended the VC garden party at Buckingham Palace on 26 June 1920 as well as the British Legion VC Dinner at the House of Lords on 9 November 1929. He ended up living at the Salvation Army Hostel in Fore Street, Ipswich, largely forgotten. As he grew older he became absent-minded.

In August 1953 the British Legion took an interest in the 72-year-old VC winner, after a newspaper report described his lucky escape when a length of guttering fell 30 feet from the roof of the Salvation Army Hostel. Two years later he injured his hip in a fall and was left unable to walk. He was taken to London in a wheelchair to meet Queen Elizabeth II at the VC Centenary Review on 26 June 1956, escorted by hospital porter Mr E.J. Crawford of Ipswich. By this time Samuel Harvey had lost his VC. Mr Crawford believed it had been stolen, though the family suspected he had absent-mindedly left it somewhere and it had been 'picked up'.

Samuel Harvey's last sixteen months were spent at a former workhouse, Stow Lodge Hospital, Stowmarket, where he died on 24 September 1960, aged 79 years; a miniature replica of the Victoria Cross was discovered under his pillow. He was given a military burial in Ipswich Old Cemetery, some 200 mourners attending his funeral. The service on 27 September was conducted by the Revd C.P. Newell of St Peter's Church, Ipswich, with television and press cameramen recording the scene. Many old soldiers and members of various Associations attended and a squad of the York and Lancaster Regt was present. Major A.M. Acheston, York and Lancaster Regt, and the Revd Newell made a plea for the return of Harvey's lost VC so that it could be placed in the Regimental Museum. As well as the VC, Harvey was also awarded the Legion of Honour and the Russian Cross of St George 1st Class, and held the 1914 Star and the War and Victory medals.

Originally, he was buried in a pauper's grave in the public communal plot in Plot X, Division 21, Grave 3. Samuel Harvey, thanks to the efforts of author Chris Matson and the Suffolk Branch of The Western Front Association, raised funds for a proper headstone.

On 29 September 2000, Samuel Harvey's resting place was marked with a headstone, 40 years after his death and 85 years to the day, after his heroic VC action.

The ceremony was carried out in the presence of The Worshipful the Mayor of Ipswich and the Mayoress; relatives of Samuel Harvey; representatives of his former regiment, The York & Lancaster Regiment. Members of the Western Front Association, who helped raise funds for the memorial, were also present. The Honour Guard, dressed in First World War uniform, comprised of members of The Association for Military Remembrance 'The Khaki Chums' and music was provided by The Community Wind Band and bugler Bramwell Scott of the Salvation Army sounded The Last Post and Reveille.

O. BROOKS

Near Loos, France, 8 October

The Guards Division was called upon to re-enter the trenches at Loos on the night of 3/4 October. By this time the 21st and 24th Divs had been withdrawn from the battle for reorganization and refitment, and were replaced by the 12th and 46th Divs. The recalling of the Guards coincided with the first of the more determined German attacks launched near the Quarries and against the Hohenzollern Redoubt on 3 October. The enemy were repulsed at the former but their possession of Fosse 8 exposed the British troops to enfilade fire, forcing them out of part of the Hohenzollern Redoubt. The expected German attack came on 8 October after a heavy bombardment lasting three hours, the enemy infantry assaulting the front held by 2nd Guards Bde at about 15.15 hours. The main thrust was aimed against a narrow salient in the line just south of 'Big Willie' trench, where the track leading from Le Rutoire to the Loos–Haisnes road crossed the trenches (see map on page 187). The German intention was to drive the British out of these trenches, thus straightening the line south of 'Big Willie'.

The 3rd Bn, Grenadier Guards, was holding an advanced trench and were almost surrounded by the attacking German battalions (from the *97th*, *55th* and the *77th Infantry Regiments*); two of the 3rd Gren. Guards companies were bombed out of their position, their own bombers having exhausted their bomb supply, and were forced to retreat to a second position in the rear. This could have resulted in an enemy lodgement in the British line. However, the 3rd Bn, Coldstream Guards, who were on their immediate right, managed to save the situation. Despite being hard-pressed themselves, with some Germans having gained a brief foothold in one of their advanced saps before being bombed out by No. 3 Coy, supported by No. 1 Coy, they came to the aid of their fellow Guardsmen. On his own initiative, No. 6738 L/Sgt O. Brooks, 3rd Coldstream Guards, followed by six bombers and a section of rifles, began bombing down the captured trench lost by the Grenadiers. Fierce fighting ensued, lasting some three-quarters of an hour, and ended with L/Sgt Brooks and his men regaining possession of the 200 yards of trench lost earlier. The estimated expenditure of bombs by the battalion during the afternoon was 5,000. The Germans made a last attempt to gain advantage from the fight, assaulting the trenches of the 3rd Coldstreamers, but were repulsed. L/Sgt Brooks was awarded the Victoria Cross for his swift action, the citation praising 'his absolute fearlessness, presence of mind and promptitude'.

Oliver Brooks, 'Olly' to his friends, was born towards the end of 1889 at Bloomfield, Paulton near Midsomer Norton, a mining village in Somerset. He was the youngest of six sons born to Joseph and Mercy Brooks who, by the time of the 1891 census were living in Gladstone Street, Welton, a hamlet adjoining Midsomer Norton. He worked in the Somerset coal pits where, as a boy, he drew coal-trucks harnessed by a chain around his waist. He joined the Coldstream Guards on 17 April 1906, serving for seven years before being released to the Reserve on 17 April 1913. He was a manager of a cinema/theatre at Peasedown, a mining village near his home. He was mobilized at the outbreak of war in 1914, and went to France with the 3rd Coldstream Guards as part of the BEF. In July 1915 he was promoted to lance-sergeant and then to sergeant the day after the action which won him the VC. The award was gazetted on 28 October and on 1 November 1915 Brooks was taken to meet the King on a hospital train at Aire Station, France, on which King George V was being treated after a bad fall from his horse. Despite being confined to bed, the King was determined to invest Brooks himself. Brooks knelt on the floor of the saloon and bent over the prostrate monarch but the King could not manage to get the pin through the thick khaki. A week later Brooks appeared in an advertisement exhorting the virtues of Fry's chocolate.

Sgt Brooks was also wounded in the head and shoulder at Guinchy in September 1916.

At a later stage in the war, Brooks was a bombing instructor, having among his pupils the Prince of Wales who, Brooks said, 'became very proficient' at the art.

Oliver Brooks married Marion Loveday on 17 August 1918, and they had two sons and two daughters. The eldest son was baptised at Windsor on 4 August 1919 and was named Oliver Victor Loos Brooks (see Laidlaw, page 188). Brooks was discharged from the Coldstream Guards on 27 February 1919 and became a commissionaire at the White Hart Hotel, Windsor. He was present at the garden party given by King George V at Buckingham Palace on 26 June 1920 and at the ceremony at the Cenotaph on 11 November that same year. Brooks was also an inaugural member of the Windsor Branch of the Coldstreamers' Association. He acted as wreath-bearer for the Ypres League commemoration ceremony at the Cenotaph on 31 October 1929, handing the wreath to Field-Marshal Lord Plumer, the president of the Ypres League. Brooks took an active interest in the various remembrance ceremonies and attended the British Legion Dinner for VCs at the House of Lords on 9 November 1929.

At about this time he left the White Hart Hotel, Windsor, taking up a similar appointment at the Dorchester Hotel, Park Lane, London, where, in April 1933, the ex-Kaiser's grandson shook his hand saying 'Every nation can recognise a brave man.' Brooks attended a Ball in aid of Disabled Officers' Garden Homes in June 1933 and was present with Michael O'Leary VC at the Ypres Day service at Horse Guards Parade at the end of October that year. In November he laid a wreath at the War Memorial in Bath at the Armistice Day service.

Oliver Brooks died on Friday 25 October 1940, aged 51, at 47 Clewer Avenue, Windsor, where he and his wife had lived for thirty-five years. He was buried in Windsor Borough Cemetery in grave space GN 352: 2 down, 5 across. Mrs Marion Brooks gave her husband's VC and four other medals to the Coldstream Guards regimental museum on 9 August 1967; the medals were accepted by Gen. Sir George Burns, the colonel of the regiment, at a ceremony conducted at Wellington Barracks, Westminster, watched by her grandson, 19-year-old Coldstream Guardsman Brian Lucas-Carter. On Thursday 8 October 1987 Gen. Sir George Burns was at the dedication of a memorial stone to Oliver Brooks VC at Windsor Borough Cemetery, the stone having been presented by the regiment of the Coldstream Guards.

An oval stone tablet dedicated to Sgt Oliver Brooks VC is to be found in Holy Trinity Church, Windsor and on 27 May 1998 the Royal Borough of Windsor and Maidenhead unveiled a blue plaque at 47 Clewer Avenue.

J.C. RAYNES
Fosse 7 de Béthune, France, 11 October

A/Sgt Raynes won his VC on 11 October by saving the lives of fellow members of A Bty (71st Bde RFA, 15th Div.), including that of his best friend Sgt Ayres. The fighting at

Loos carried on into early October, with the Germans determined to wrest back the ground they had lost in September. Fosse 7 de Béthune spoilheap stood near the point where the trenches crossed the Lens–Béthune road (see map on page 187). A Bty had been shelling the enemy from this position and when the infantry assault began, the battery moved into the captured town of Loos. From there they opened fire again but were soon subjected to a counter-battery bombardment which forced them to move out on to a plain near some dug-outs. The battery was heavily shelled with both armour-piercing and gas shells. When the 'cease fire' was ordered, Raynes soon learned that his friend Sgt Ayres had been hit. He ran to where Ayres was lying, some 40 yards away, bandaged his wounds and moved him a little way to greater safety before returning to his gun which was ordered back into action. The German shell-fire became so intense that a 'cease-fire' was again ordered and Raynes, with the help of two gunners who were killed very shortly afterwards, took advantage of the lull to carry Sgt Ayres back to the battery's dug-out. As they arrived at the dug-out, gas-shells began to burst around them and, being unable to find Ayres's 'smoke-helmet', Raynes fetched his own from his gun position and gave it to his wounded friend. Raynes then ventured out in search of another smoke-helmet but caught the full force of the gas and lay unconscious out in the open for a short while before coming round. He returned to the dug-out to find it had been blown in. Despite suffering severely from gas he began digging the men out; sadly he found only two survivors, Ayres and the others having been killed. (They are buried together in Fosse 7 Military Cemetary [Quality Street], Mazingarbe.) Raynes then staggered back to serve his gun.

On 12 October the battery moved to a house in Quality Street. A Bty's commander later reported that 'a huge projectile landed on the house used as our [A Bty] cook-house and completely wrecked it . . . burying sixteen of my men'. Raynes was among the men buried but managed to dig himself out and, although 'bleeding freely in the head and wounded in the leg . . . he then dug out Sgt-Maj. Austin, severely wounded; he carried him across the road to a dressing station and returned to help others who were buried.' After having his own wounds dressed Raynes reported for duty with his battery which was again being heavily shelled. His commander recommended him for his bravery and although Raynes knew before the official announcement on 18 November that he was to receive the VC, he did not let his relatives know. The severity of the enemy shelling endured by A Bty during these two days may be appreciated by the fact that on the 12th the battery commander 'was obliged to send away to the dressing-station the whole of the personnel at that time with the firing battery. Only seven men survived to the end of the engagement'.

John Crawshaw Raynes, son of Stephen and Hannah Raynes, was born in June 1887 in Eccleshall, Sheffield, Yorkshire. He was the eldest of four children, having two sisters and one brother. His early years were spent at Abbeydale Road and Gleadless Road and he was educated at the Heeley National School. He worked for Mr T.W. Wood, a local coal merchant, and also for Mr S.H. Raynes, a decorator in Abbeydale Road. He entered the Army on 10 October 1904, joining the Royal Horse and Royal Field Artillery, and served eight years with the Colours. During this time he married Miss Mabel Dawson on 24 April 1907, at the Leeds Registry Office; she later bore him two sons, John Kenneth, born on 30 January 1912, the year Raynes left the Army, and Tom Crawshaw, born on 6 February 1920. After leaving the Army, Raynes joined the Leeds City police where he worked until the outbreak of war when he was recalled for military service as a reservist. He became an army instructor at Preston and was offered a commission which he declined. He volunteered five times for active service before being sent to the front with a Kitchener's Army draft as a corporal. He became acting-sergeant and after winning the VC was promoted to battery sergeant-major. According to Rev. W. Odom:

. . . an old scholar of our Day and Sunday Schools, a member of our Boys' Brigade – Sergeant-Major J.C. Raynes, who, on his recovery, visited his old school, received a warm welcome from the vicar, teachers, and scholars, and in a simple, unassuming manner, after handing round his VC to the scholars, offered a few words of advice to the lads.

His former police colleagues presented him with a gold watch and chain to mark the honour he had brought to their force. Later he unveiled a local war memorial. His courageous acts took their toll on him, however, and he was discharged from the Army in December 1918 as 'physically unfit'. A fund of £500 raised locally was used to buy him a house.

Returning to civilian life he rejoined the Leeds City police as a sergeant but struggled to continue with his duties, eventually being forced to take a desk job. His condition continued to deteriorate and he was compelled to retire in March 1926 as he was no longer able to do duty as he was suffering from spinal problems which paralysed his legs. He became bedridden, and was nursed by his wife. In 1929, to his deep regret, he was unable to attend the VC Dinner at the House of Lords on 9 November; he wondered if his 18-year-old son might be allowed to go as his representative. Raynes received a telegram on Armistice Day from the other Yorkshire VCs in London, conveying their greetings and expressing their regret that he could not complete the party. They promised him a memento of the dinner. On the day of the VC Dinner the newspaper the *Sheffield Telegraph* launched an appeal fund for Raynes, to raise £600 to buy him and his family 'a convenient bungalow in pleasant and healthy surroundings'.

It seems that Raynes was depressed by his inability to join the 500 VCs in London and suffered a relapse, dying at his home at Grange Crescent, Chapeltown, near Leeds, on Wednesday 12 November 1929, aged 43 years and 7 months. The funeral took place on Saturday 16 November at Leeds. Eleven VCs were present, with the other eight Yorkshire VCs – Capt. G. Sanders, Lt W. Edwards, Sgt F. McNess, Sgt Hull, Sgt Mountain, L/Cpl F.W. Dobson, Pte A. Poulter and Pte W.B. Butler – acting as his pallbearers.

Raynes's coffin rested on a gun-carriage provided by the 71st Field Bde RA, and was followed by Capt. W.E. Gage, chairman of the Leeds 'Old Contemptibles Association', who bore a purple cushion on which rested Raynes' medals, his VC, 1914–15 Star, General Service Medal and Victory Medal. Lt Edwards VC carried a wreath of Flanders poppies and evergreen in the shape of the Victoria Cross, which had been intended to serve as a souvenir of the House of Lords Dinner. It now bore the message: 'In affectionate memory from brother VCs of Leeds, who sorely missed their comrade at the Prince of Wales's dinner, whence this emblem was brought for him.'

The service was held at St Clement's and was attended by the Lord Mayor and Lady Mayoress of Leeds, the Chief Constable and a squad of police. Raynes was buried at Harehills Cemetery, Leeds (Section H, Grave 11). A firing party was provided by the West Yorks Regt and the Last Post was sounded. The cemetery gates had to be closed because of the crowd of an estimated 25,000 to 30,000 people who had come to pay their respects.

The fund begun by the *Sheffield Telegraph* was kept open to the end of the week in which it was begun, and had reached £300 by the day after Raynes's death. The proceeds were handed over to his widow and two sons. Raynes's story appeared in the *Yorkshire Evening Post* in August 1972 following the discovery of an unknown VC portrait. It was finally established that it was of Sgt-Maj. Raynes. His daughter-in-law, who held his VC at that time, asked that the picture be forwarded to the regimental museum. His VC is now held by the Royal Artillery Museum, Woolwich.

While researching the First World War, West Yorkshire Policeman PC Anthony Child discovered that Raynes' grave had fallen into disrepair. Following a complete refurbishment of the impressive headstone over the plot, a ceremony of rededication was held on the 13 November 2008, officiated by the West Yorkshire Police Chaplain.

The name of Battery Sergeant-Major Raynes appears on the VC Memorial plaque in Leeds.

J.L. DAWSON
Hohenzollern Redoubt, France, 13 October

No. 91608 Cpl J.L. Dawson of the 187th Field Company RE won his VC during the second gas attack to retake the Hohenzollern Redoubt by the 46th. Div. The British trenches were full of men but regardless of very heavy fire Dawson climbed up onto the parados, and walked to and fro along the top of the trench in order to be better able to give directions to his own sappers who were preparing gas cylinders for the attack, and also to clear the infantry out of the sections of trench that were choked with gas. He found three leaking gas cylinders, which he rolled away to a distance of some 16 yards and then fired bullets into them in order to release the gas. All this was conducted under heavy fire from the enemy and the fumes from the gas. It was evident that but for his courage and presence of mind many British troops in the trench would have been gassed. His action earned him a Victoria Cross which was gazetted on 7 December 1915.

James Lennox Dawson was born on Christmas Day 1891 at Tillycoultry, Clackmannanshire, Scotland, home of his cousin James Dalgleish Pollock who also won a VC a little over a fortnight before Dawson (see page 214). James Dawson was educated at Alloa Academy and Glasgow University, eventually gaining a BSc degree in chemistry. He became a teacher and was teaching at a school in Govan when war broke out. He joined the 5th Bn, Scottish Rifles (the Cameronians), on 5 November 1914. He trained with the 2/5th Bn, Scottish Rifles, until early spring 1915 when he joined the 1/5th Bn, Scottish Rifles (19th Bde, 6th Div.)

in trenches at Bois Grenier near Armentières. In May 1915 Dawson, on the strength of his degree in chemistry, was ordered to join the Special Brigade RE, then being formed near St Omer, to conduct gas warfare against the Germans. He was compulsorily transferred to the RE, much against his will.

After winning the VC at the Hohenzollern Redoubt on 13 October 1915, he continued to serve in France. He was made a temporary second lieutenant in the RE, and in 1916 was wounded on the Somme, after which he served at home and in the USA. He was promoted to temporary lieutenant on 27 August 1917.

Dawson remained in the Army after the war, becoming a lieutenant in the Royal Army Education Corps in 1920. He was present at the garden party given for VCs at Buckingham Palace on 26 June that year and attended the ceremony at the Cenotaph on 11 November. On 1 April 1921 Dawson was promoted to captain, and later became staff captain on 1 October 1924. In the same year he left for India aboard the SS *Marglen*, landing at Bombay in January 1925. He transferred to the Indian Army Ordnance Corps in 1929 and was Deputy Assistant Director, Ordnance Services, Army Headquarters, India, from 1938 to 1940, Assistant Director from 1940 to 1941 and Liaison Officer with the India Supply Mission in the USA from 1941 to 1946. He retired with the rank of colonel in 1948, and moved to Eastbourne.

He attended the VC Centenary Review on 26 June 1956 and was present at the first and second dinners of the VC and GC Association at the Café Royal, London, on 24 July 1958 and 7 July 1960. In 1962 he attended the Lord Mayor's banquet at Mansion House and Queen Elizabeth II's garden party for VCs, both given on 17 July. The following day he joined fellow VCs at the third dinner of the VC and GC Association.

James Lennox Dawson died at his home, 9 Hartfield Road, Eastbourne, on 15 February 1967, aged 75 years, and he was cremated at Eastbourne Crematorium. His VC was bequeathed to Glasgow University.

C.G. VICKERS

Hohenzollern Redoubt, France, 14 October

The fighting for the Hohenzollern Redoubt had been fierce since the start of the Battle of Loos and although the British gained sections of it they never had full control of the strongpoint and were ousted on 3 October. Lt (Temp. Capt.) C.G. Vickers was in the 1/7th (Robin Hood) Bn, Notts and Derby Regt (the Sherwood Foresters). His battalion was moved forward to the British front line as part of the 139th Bde's supporting role in the 46th (North Midland) Div.'s attack to recapture the Hohenzollern Redoubt, which was launched on 13 October.

On 14 October at 17.30 hours Capt. Vickers and fifty men of D Coy, 1/7th Sherwood Foresters, were ordered forward to the redoubt to relieve the exhausted bombers under Capt. Warren, also of the 1/7th, in 'Little Willie' Trench. This was accomplished and Vickers took charge of the bomb-fighting at the barricade at the north-west end of the redoubt. He had only a few bombers among his men, nearly all of whom were soon killed or wounded. With only two men left to hand him bombs, Vickers held the barricade for several hours against heavy German bombing attacks. During this time Vickers ordered a second barrier to be built 30 yards down the trench behind him. This effectively cut him off from support but his courageous stand enabled his men to complete the second barricade. He held the first position for a considerable time on his own before eventually falling, severely wounded, when the barricade was blown in. For this retention of the British hold on the Hohenzollern Redoubt, for which 'he was, during his occupancy, personally and solely responsible', Capt. Vickers was awarded the VC, the details of the action appearing in the *London Gazette* on 19 November.

Charles Geoffrey Vickers, the son of Charles Henry Vickers, a Nottingham lace manufacturer, and Jessie Ann (née Lomas) of Leicester, was born in Nottingham on 13 October 1894. He was educated at Bramcote preparatory school, Sidney House, Oundle School, and Merton College, Oxford. Prior to going to university, Vickers spent January to April 1913 in Germany, studying the language. He entered Merton College in October 1913 reading for Honour Moderations and 'Greats' having won a Classical Exhibition. He played rugby football for both Oundle School and Merton College. He served five years in the OTC, gaining Certificate A, and was promoted to sergeant. He received a commission as a second lieutenant in the 1/7th (Robin Hood) Bn, the Sherwood Foresters, from Oxford University OTC.

He left for France with the battalion on 25 February 1915, seeing action in Belgium, mostly at Ypres, until September when he was involved in the Battle of Loos where he won the VC on 14 October, the day after his 21st birthday. He was hospitalized in England and was decorated by the King at Buckingham Palace on 15 January 1916.

Later, on 1 June 1916, he joined the Reserve Bn for light duty, and was promoted to captain on 29 August 1916, but he was not passed fit until 15 September. Vickers left England on 23 September to rejoin his former unit, but was recalled from France on 20 February 1917 as an instructor, and later as company commander, in the 19th Officer Cadet Bn.

He married Miss Helen Tregoning Newton, daughter of Mr and Mrs A.H. Newton, of Harpenden, Herts, at St Andrew's Church, Malden Road, London, on 21 March 1918. The following month, on the 5th, he returned to France for a third time. He was promoted to major and became second in command of the 1/Lincolns, a role which he held until the end of the war. He was again wounded, and was Mentioned in Despatches and won the Belgian Croix de Guerre while commanding a composite battalion in the defence of the Marne in June. He also saw action at Kemmel, on the Aisne and throughout the advance of the Third Army from August to

November 1918. He was demobilized with the rank of captain (acting major).

After the war Vickers qualified as a solicitor and attended the VC garden party given by the King on 26 June 1920 and the House of Lords dinner on 9 November 1929. He was a partner in the firm of Slaughter & May from 1926 to 1945. His wife bore him a son and a daughter though the marriage was dissolved in 1934. In 1935 he married Ethel Ellen, youngest daughter of H.R.B Tweed; she bore him a son.

In the Second World War he was recommissioned in the Sherwood Foresters in 1940. From 1941 to 1945 he was seconded from the Army with the rank of colonel as Deputy Director-General of the Ministry of Economic Warfare, in which role he was in charge of economic intelligence; he was also a member of the Joint Intelligence Committee of the Chiefs of Staff.

He spent the years 1945 to 1947 as legal adviser to the National Coal Board and in 1948 became a board member in charge of manpower, education, health and welfare until 1955. He was involved in a variety of public and professional bodies including the London Passenger Transport Board, the council of the Law Society and the Medical Research Council. He was chairman of the research committee of the Mental Health Research Fund which he had helped to found, from 1951 to 1967. He was also an honorary fellow of the Royal College of Psychiatrists. His involvement with important bodies led to the publication of several papers and half a dozen books which explored the institutional frame of modern society.

Vickers enjoyed tennis and literary pursuits, and he was a keen sailor, owning several boats over the years. Shortly before the Second World War he had sailed competitively, coming second in the Fastnet Race. He was knighted for his services in 1946. Lady Vickers, his second wife, died in October 1972. He held the VC, the Croix de Guerre (Belgium), the US Medal of Freedom, the 1914–15 Star, General Service Medals for both world wars, and two Coronation Medals. Sir Geoffrey Vickers died at his home, The Grange, Goring-on-Thames, on 16 March 1982.

The funeral was at Goring Free Church on 23 March and he was later cremated at Oxford Road Crematorium, Oxford. His military medals, including the Victoria Cross, are on display in the Sherwood Foresters Collection in Nottingham Castle. In the grounds of the Castle is the Nottingham and Nottinghamshire Memorial to twenty Victoria Cross Winners where Charles Vickers' name appears along with nineteen other VC winners.

KULBIR THAPA

South of Fauquissart, France, 25 September

The third, and last, Indian soldier to win the VC on the Western Front in 1915 was Rfn Kulbir Thapa, of the 2/3rd Gurkha Rifles; he won his award when his battalion fought at Piètre on 25 September. Part of Garhwal Bde, Meerut Div., the battalion was on the right of the line with the 2nd Leicesters on its left. The ground over which the attack took place was less than half a mile away from where both battalions had fought in the battle of Neuve Chapelle in March.

A four day artillery bombardment preceded the attack, supplemented by a gas attack. As this was the first time the British had used gas, two alternative plans of attack were in force: Plan A would involve the use of the gas while Plan B would not, instead relying on a concentrated artillery bombardment. During the course of the night orders changed from Plan A to Plan B and back again a number of times before Plan A was finally selected. At 04.45 hours a strong smell of gas was apparent among the British troops, and it was first thought that German gas shells were responsible; later it was reported that an enemy trench mortar shell had hit some gas cylinders in the Duck's Bill, a section of trench projecting forwards from the British line some 400 yards to the right of the battalion. This gas discharge put out of action a number of the 3rd Londons who were holding the Duck's Bill (see map on page 25) and also affected many of the battalion's men in the support trenches.

When the British gas and smoke was released, most of the gas drifted along in front of the assaulting battalions, and did not affect the enemy. However, it hampered the assaulting troops and consequently the Gurkhas attacked wearing respirators. The battalion's attack was led by No. 4 Double Coy, commanded by Lts Bagot-Chester and Wood. The two front lines were about 200 yards apart, and almost half of the Gurkhas' advance was obscured by the gas and brown smoke through which they stumbled, but the moment the men emerged from this cover they were met by 'a blizzard of bullets'. Very few of the double company gained the German trench. Lt Bagot-Chester was among the wounded.

However, Lt Wood and four men reached the German wire, which was uncut except for a small section on the left front of the battalion; these five men entered the enemy trench where, with the exception of one man, No. 2129 Rfn Kulbir Thapa, they were killed in hand-to-hand fighting. Kulbir, although wounded, managed to get past the German front line and still moving forward found a wounded private of the 2nd Leics between the first and second lines. He stayed with this man all that day and throughout the night, despite the man's urging him to retreat and save himself.

Early the following morning there was a thick fog which enabled Kulbir to carry the wounded man back through the German front line unseen. Leaving the man in the shelter of a shell hole, he then returned to the German wire to rescue two injured Gurkhas, one after another. By now the fog had lifted and it was daylight. Kulbir went back to the British private and brought him back, carrying him most of the way, to the safety of the trenches held by the 39th Garhwal Rifles. Many of the wounded men managed to crawl back during the night and under cover of the fog, and they reported that the German soldiers had left their trenches early in the morning to go out and shoot and bayonet wounded men. This behaviour was confirmed by Lt Bagot-Chester, who himself was shot more than once as he lay wounded less than 20 yards from the German wire. Kulbir Thapa was recommended for the VC by the battalion's commanding officer, and the recommendation was strongly supported by officers of the 39th Garhwal Rifles and the 2nd Leicesters. The *London Gazette* of 18 November 1915 published the VC citation.

Kulbir Thapa was born on 15 December 1888 at Nigalpani, Palpa, Nepal; he was a Thapa of the Magar clan. He enlisted in 1/3rd Gurkha Rifles, transferring to the 2/3rd Bn at the outbreak of war to complete its war establishment and arrived in France in September 1914. The battalion fought at Givenchy, 1914; Neuve Chapelle and Festubert in 1915 before the action of Piètre.

Once he had recovered from his wounds, Kulbir rejoined his battalion, then stationed near the Suez Canal in Egypt, on 4 January 1916, together with a draft of 203 men from France, many of whom were unfit for further active service. He was promoted Naik (corporal) on parade the next day. He served with his battalion for the remainder of the war, then returned to India and with the rank of Havildar (sergeant) was discharged from the Army in 1929. With another VC winner, Kulbir was photographed in native dress standing in front of the Gurkha Memorial at Gorakhpur, some time after the war. Kulbir Thapa died in Nepal on 3 October 1956; his Victoria Cross is displayed at the Gurkha Museum, Winchester. His name appears on the inside of the Chatri roof at the Commonwealth Memorial Gates near Hyde Park Corner

A great, great nephew of Kulbir Thapa, Surrenda Thapa, a chef in Jersey, CI has been fundraising towards the planning and construction of a High School with facilities for 100 students at Sulka Gandarki in the Seti River valley near Pokhara.

On 17 November 2010 in Pokhara, a residential home for ex-Gurkha soldiers or their widows was officially opened. The home, officially named after Kulbir Thapa by Lt-Gen. Sir Philip Trousdell, can accommodate twenty-six octogenerians and was funded by UK donors in conjunction with the Gurkha Welfare Trust.

G.A. MALING

Near Fauquissart, France, 25 September

The only Victoria Cross to be awarded to a member of the RAMC on the Western Front in 1915 was won by Temp. Lt George Maling, attached to 12th Rifle Brigade (RB), 60th Bde, 20 Div., when the battalion took part in one of the diversionary attacks for the Battle of Loos, known as the action of Piètre.

The main attack on the morning of 25 September was by Garhwal and Bareilly Bdes, Meerut Div., with covering fire from the left flank. 12th RB, the nearest battalion to the left flank of Bareilly Bde, was in a position about 200 yards north-east of Winchester Road, which ran from Fauquissart to Mauquissart.

Parties of 2nd Black Watch (Bareilly Bde) advanced as far as the German second line and by 11.00 hours a company of 12th RB moved into the enemy front line and took over trench blocks previously established by 2nd Black Watch. A German counter-attack about thirty minutes later forced the company out of the trench-block owing to shortage of bombs and bombers; their withdrawal left exposed the flank of Bareilly Bde who, along with other parties of the brigade, were forced back to their original line.

Many casualties were inflicted during this counter-attack, adding to those suffered in the initial attack when the release of gas by the British had been a disaster, most of the gas blowing back into the British lines and causing heavy casualties. Maling was busy tending the wounded from early in the morning of 25 September and continued his work, often in very exposed positions, for over twenty-four hours. The citation for his VC, published in the *London Gazette* of 18 November, gave the details:

For most conspicuous bravery and devotion to duty during the heavy fighting near Fauquissart on 25 September 1915. Lieut. Maling worked incessantly with untiring energy from 6.25 am on the 25th until 8.00 am on the 26th collecting and treating in the open, under heavy shell fire, more than 300 men. At about 11 am on the 25th he was flung down and temporarily stunned by the bursting of a large high explosive shell which wounded his only assistant and killed several of his patients. A second shell soon covered him and his assistants with debris, but his high courage and zeal never failed him, and he continued his gallant work single-handed.

He received his VC from the King at Buckingham Palace on 15 January 1916.

George Allan Maling was born in Sunderland on 6 October 1888, the son of Edwin Allan Maling JP, MRCS, and Maria Jane Maling. He was educated at Uppingham School and Exeter College, Oxford, where he gained an honours degree in Natural Sciences. He continued his studies at St Thomas's Hospital where in 1914 he qualified as MB, BCh, and in 1915 MRCS, LRCP. Maling was commissioned into the RAMC on 18 January 1915 and joined the 12th Rifle Brigade as medical officer, landing in France on 22 July 1915. After his award, he returned to France and was promoted to captain and Mentioned in Despatches during 1916 before working for a time in the Military Hospital, Grantham, Lincs.

On 5 May 1917 he married Daisy Mabel Wollmer, of Winnipeg, at Sutton, Surrey, and during this year he joined 34th Field Ambulance (11 Div.) and served with this unit during 1917 and 1918. After leaving the Army, Maling was appointed Resident Medical Officer at Victoria Hospital for Children, Chelsea, and later surgeon for outpatients at St John's Hospital, Lewisham. Some time later he went into medical partnership, the practice based at Micheldever Road, Lee, South London, where he practised until his death, aged only 40, on 9 July 1929. Maling was buried in Chiselhurst Cemetery, Beaverwood Road, on 12 July, grave A 2017; a boulder forms part of the memorial. He is also commemorated on his parent's grave in Bishopwearmouth Cemetery, County Durham. Maling's Victoria Cross is displayed at the Army Medical Services Museum, Aldershot.

A.F.G. KILBY
Near Cuinchy, France, 25 September

On the opening day of the Battle of Loos the 2nd South Staffs Regt, 6th Bde, 2nd Div., was in the front line at Cuinchy, immediately south of the La Bassée Canal. It was on the tow-path, between the canal and the railway embankment, some 200 yards from where Cpl O'Leary won the first VC of the year (see page 15), that Capt. Kilby led his men with such gallantry, resulting in his posthumous award.

The area was all too familiar to the battalion who had held positions near Cuinchy on a number of occasions before September. The battalion's front of attack was from the brickstacks on its right to the La Bassée Canal on its left. A and B Coys were detailed for the right sector against the German-held brickstacks (which were not shelled by heavy guns in the preceding bombardment for fear of damaging the gas cylinders in the British front line), while C Coy's advance was along the tow-path towards Embankment Redoubt, a strongly fortified position on the western edge of the Railway Triangle.

The British artillery bombardment began at dawn on 21 September in preparation for the assault. The men of 6th Bde were ordered to attack at 06.30 hours on 25 September, after the release of the poison gas. At 04.00 hours on the 25th the battalion received verbal orders from 6th Bde for the gas to be released at 05.50 hours, forty minutes before zero hour. At about 05.30 hours an RE officer in charge of the gas cylinders advised 6th Bde HQ that the wind was blowing in the wrong direction and he was unwilling to take responsibility for the release. After some delay 6th Bde sent orders for the gas to be released as per the original instructions; the gas cylinders were opened and it blew back into the battalion's trenches; all the men were affected to some degree and many were rendered incapable of attacking.

The attack began. On the right A and B Coys attempted to go forward on the narrow paths between the many mine craters but were held up by fierce machine-gun and rifle fire and advanced no further than the nearer edge of the mine craters. D Coy, in support, managed to get a small party under 2/Lt Hall to the German line twenty minutes after the assault started. The left attack, by C Coy under Capt. Kilby, went forward along the tow-path at 06.30 hours, despite most of the men being badly gassed, and came under machine-gun fire from both sides of the canal. Kilby was hit in the hand almost immediately but still went on, urging his men on to the German wire where he was again wounded and his company now bombed continuously. Kilby's foot had been blown off, but despite the pain he continued to fire at the enemy with his rifle. The attack failed and none of the men entered the enemy defences; at 08.00 hours orders were received to withdraw all assaulting men prior to an artillery attack on the enemy front line. This shelling, by heavy guns, did not trouble the front line defenders as the shells landed on the German second line. No subsequent attack was made.

After nightfall volunteers were sought to search no-man's-land for wounded and when men of Kilby's company were asked to search for their captain, forty out of forty-seven available men volunteered. Kilby's body was not found and he was posted missing, presumed killed. He was recommended for the VC by Brig. Daly, 6th Bde, and the citation was published in the *London Gazette* on 30 March 1916. In a letter to Kilby's parents, Brig. Daly wrote that Kilby had previously asked to be allowed to lead any future attack on the Embankment Redoubt as he was convinced the redoubt could be taken. In the brigadier's opinion, when the attack began on 25 September, Kilby was very aware that the problems with the gas would prevent any success but he was determined to lead his men although this meant almost certain death.

During late October, in the same trenches, a white cross was seen in front of the Railway Embankment and the battalion who relieved the S. Staffs later sent a message which advised of the inscription on the cross. It read 'For King and Fatherland. In memory of Lieut. King and Lieut. Hall and eight men of the South Staffordshire Regiment who died like heroes. Erected by OSPAR.' Other accounts record that a cross was also erected to Capt. Kilby, Lt D.M. Williams and thirteen men of his company. It was apparently inscribed 'For King and Country – died like heroes'. The existence of this cross has not been verified.

Kilby's VC was presented to his father by the King at Buckingham Palace on 11 July 1916.

Arthur Forbes Gordon Kilby was born at East Hayes, Cheltenham, on 3 February 1885. The only son of Sandford James Kilby, Bengal Police, Customs and Salt Dept, and his wife Alice, of Skelton House, Leamington, he was educated at Bilton Grange near Rugby and Winchester College and entered Sandhurst after preparation at Frankfurt, Germany. He was commissioned into 1st Bn South Staffs in August 1905, promoted to lieutenant in October 1907 and to captain on 1 April 1910 when aged only 25. Kilby was transferred to the 2nd Bn in December 1910. A keen ornithologist and an accomplished linguist, he was fluent in Hungarian and German and when war began was learning Spanish. With his battalion he landed in France on 13 August 1914 and went into action shortly afterwards at Maroilles on 25/26 August where he was badly concussed by a shell. He was separated from his unit for some time and was later hospitalized with shell-shock, not returning to his battalion until 24 September when it was fighting in the Battle of the Aisne. Here he went out on a number of solo sniping forays and more than once got behind enemy lines to bring back valuable information.

The battalion moved north to the Ypres sector in October and on 1 November, when north-west of Becelaere, he led a counter-attack which earned him fulsome praise from his commanding officer. On 12 November Kilby was recommended for the MC when he, with Capt. Johnson, commanded a number of men who held a stretch of trenches all day after French troops on their left had retired and exposed the battalion's flank. He was wounded in the right arm and lung by a bullet and sent to hospital in England and, although he did not fully recover the use of his right hand, rejoined his battalion in May 1915.

Kilby received his MC on 24 September 1915 and was then recommended for the DSO for 'consistent good work, making some very useful reconnaissances'. The report cited one example: on the night of 5/6 September Kilby went along the tow-path towards Embankment Redoubt with another officer and obtained valuable information about the German defences. However, the DSO recommendation was overtaken by the events of 25 September.

Kilby is commemorated on the Loos Memorial to the Missing at Dud Corner Cemetery. In 1919 a memorial designed by Sir W.J. Tapper was placed in St Nicholas's Chapel, York Minster; it was inscribed with details of Kilby's deeds and awards and contained a bust of him surmounted by the family coat-of-arms. It was an appropriate place for a memorial as Kilby had been stationed at nearby Strenshall earlier in his career and had made frequent visits to the cathedral in his study of architecture; his family has also provided two Lord Mayors of York. A memorial to Kilby is also to be found in the Garrison Church, Whittington Barracks, Lichfield. His name is also listed on a war memorial in St Cuthbert's Church, Peasholme Green, York.

Captain Kilby was assumed to be a prisoner of war after being wounded and his mother Alice enlisted the help of a family friend (who was a Dutch citizen) in order to communicate with a senior German official about her son's situation. Eventually information was received from Germany that Capt. Kilby had died and had never been a prisoner of war.

On the death of his father, Kilby's VC, the tunic he had been wearing when he won his MC, and a portrait of him were willed to Mrs Kilby for life, then to his daughter, Dorothy Alice Howlett.

Kilby's body was eventually found on 19 February 1929 and interred at Arras Road Cemetery, Roclincourt, Plot III, Row N, Grave 27. His tunic, with an obvious bullet hole, together with a number of other items, was donated to the regiment by his sister and held in the regimental museum. His medals are held by the family.

R.P. HALLOWES
Hooge, Belgium, 25 September–1 October

The 4th Bn, Middlesex Regiment (8th Bde, 3rd Div.) was involved in one of the subsidiary operations that took place simultaneously with the opening of the Battle of Loos on 25 September. The battalion was moved forward into Sanctuary Wood on 18 September. The plan was for the 8th Bde to attack the German positions north of Sanctuary Wood from the Ypres–Menin road at a point opposite 'Stirling Castle'; a single company of the 1st Royal Scots Fusiliers (9th Bde) was to attack on their right to straighten their part of the line, and two battalions from the 7th Bde (3rd Div.) were to attack the area around Hooge Château (see map on page 179); these attacks were an extension of the 14th Div.'s attack on Bellewaarde Farm. The frontage of attack allotted to 8th Bde was 1,500 yards, and the assault was to be made by the 2nd Royal Scots and the 1st and 4th Gordon Highlanders, with the 2nd Suffolks and 4th Middlesex being held in reserve.

The 8th Bde moved into the trenches in preparation for the assault on the night of 23 September. Shortages of material caused serious problems, especially the lack of wire-cutters. The British bombardment began at 03.30 hours, and was followed at 04.19 hours by the exploding of two mines under the German trenches opposite the 2nd Royal Scots. Two further mines were fired thirty seconds later in the same location. At 04.20 hours the attacking troops went forward. The 4th Middlesex *War Diary* states that at about 10.30 hours they were informed 'that the front line was giving way, partly on account of artillery fire and partly from lack of bombs'. The battalion bombers were in the process of assisting in the detonation of the brigade's supply of bombs when orders came to send a party of bombers, with two supporting platoons, to bomb up the communication trenches and relieve the 4th Gordon Highlanders who had been driven out of their earlier gains at Fort 13 in the German lines. Throughout the day successive companies of the 4th Middlesex were sent forward to reinforce or relieve other regiments. All night long the Middlesex men were engaged in repairing and rebuilding trenches in order to maintain a continuous and defensible position just north of Sanctuary Wood.

On the night of 26/27 September 2/Lt Hallowes noticed two wounded men lying out in the open. Regardless of the danger he left the trench and, despite coming under fierce rifle fire, coolly superintended the removal of the two wounded Royal Scots men to a place of safety. He had just returned to the trenches when the Germans began to shell the area heavily; it was one of four severe bombardments the 4th Middlesex were to endure in the six days before 1 October. The enemy had gauged the range very accurately and Hallowes, fearing that some of his men might falter, climbed onto the parapet to shout encouragement and put fresh heart into them. He did this on more than one occasion, as Pte W. Corner of B Coy reported later, saying: 'Lt Hallowes . . . seemed to be everywhere, giving encouragement'. More than once Hallowes also made a daring reconnaissance of the German positions, and when his men's supply of bombs was running short he made his way back under very heavy shell fire and brought up a fresh supply.

For six days Lt Hallowes set a magnificent example to his men, showing an almost total disregard of danger, but on 1 October he was mortally wounded. The Battalion *War Diary* ends its entry for this period with: 'The conduct of Lt R.P. Hallowes was an example to all. He showed great coolness and resolution on this and previous occasions. When mortally wounded he still went on encouraging his men, his last remark being, "Men, we can only die once, if we have to die let us die like men – like diehards".' His death was the more tragic for the fact that he did not die from enemy action but was killed accidentally by a bomb dropped in the trench by one of a carrying party of another regiment. Hallowes was awarded the VC posthumously, for deeds carried out on the 25 September.

Rupert Price Hallowes was born on 5 May 1881, at Redhill, Surrey, the youngest son of Frederic Blackburn Hallowes FRCS and Mary Ann Taylor, daughter of the Revd W. Hutchinson, the rector of Checkly, Staffordshire. Hallowes was educated at Conyngham House School, Ramsgate, and at Haileybury College. He was a keen shot and took part in the Ashburton Shield at Bisley in 1896 and 1897, representing his College. Before the war he was an Instructor for the Boy Scouts at St Peter's, Port Talbot Troop, and was assistant secretary for the Boy Scouts Association for many years.

He was gazetted second lieutenant in the Artists' Rifles on 17 November 1909. When war broke out he was assistant manager of the Mansel Tin-Plate Works at Aberavon. He re-enlisted in the Artists' Rifles as a private on 5 August 1914. He went to France on 27 December, later gaining a commission from the ranks, and trained at the Cadet School at Blendacques near St Omer, before joining the 4th Bn, the Middlesex Regiment, as temporary second lieutenant in April 1915. He won the MC on 19 July at Hooge when, as enemy troops advanced down a communication trench towards his position, he climbed out of the trench and, standing in the open, fired at the enemy, killing and wounding several of them. He also assisted in making a block dug-out in a communication trench and helped rebuild a demolished parapet that had been blown in by shells, all the time under heavy bombardment, and during the night he kept in touch with supporting troops and brought up supplies of bombs. His MC was gazetted on 6 September 1915 and he showed modesty about the whole affair. Later, Hallowes' gallantry at Hooge from 25 September until his death on

1 October earned him the VC, which was gazetted on 18 November.

The Mansel Tin-Plate Works paid the full cost (£400) of a new receiving ward and X-ray room at the Aberavon General Hospital in his memory, the money being raised by the Works' staff and employees; the Boy Scouts Association installed complete x-ray apparatus in the new purpose-built room. Hallowes' was the first VC to be awarded to the Middlesex Regt in the First World War; it was also the second VC to be awarded to an officer who had been trained for his commission at the Cadet School at Blendacques. He is buried at Bedford House Military Cemetery, Zillebeeke, Plot XIV, Row B, Grave 36. His Victoria Cross is displayed at the National Army Museum, Chelsea.

A.A. BURT

Cuinchy, France, 27 September

The 1/1st Herts Regt, 6th Bde, 2nd Div., was not in action on 25 September, the opening day of the battle of Loos, but the following day were brought in to relieve half of the line held by 1st King's (Liverpool) Regt astride the Cambrin–La Bassée Road. On 25 September an attack was ordered for 17.00 hours which was dependent on the effects of a British release of poison gas on the enemy. As machine-gun fire was opened on a patrol of the Herts no attack was launched. The front trenches were crowded with men assembled for the proposed attack when they were subjected to *minenwerfer* (a large high explosive mortar) fire. One of these large projectiles landed in a trench but did not explode: No. 1665 Cpl Burt ran to the bomb, held the fuse with his foot, pulled it out and threw it over the parapet; he probably saved the lives of nearly twenty men in that section of trench. Burt had no way of knowing if the bomb would explode and he could easily have taken cover behind a traverse instead.

For this selfless act of courage he was awarded the VC, which was gazetted on 22 January 1916, and he was invested with his medal by the King at Buckingham Palace on 4 March 1916.

Alfred Alexander Burt was born at Port Vale, Hertford, on 3 March 1895 and was only five months old when the family moved to 19 Nelson Street. His parents had lived in Hertford for over twenty years. One of a large family, Burt was educated at Cowbridge Road School and when he left there he worked as a gas-fitter for the Hertford Gas Company. Ten days before the war began he obtained another job at Basingstoke but, as a member of 1/1st Herts, a Territorial battalion, he was mobilized on 4 August 1914.

With his battalion he trained at Stowlangtoft and Rougham Park, near Bury St Edmunds, Suffolk, as part of the East Midland Bde, East Anglian Div. In November the battalion went to France and joined 4th (Guards) Bde, 2nd Div., with whom Burt saw action at Cuinchy in February and Festubert in May 1915. The battalion was attached to 6th Bde, also in 2nd Div., on 19 August 1915 and before the battle of Loos Burt was promoted to L/Cpl.

Pupils of his old school, Cowbridge County Council School, made a collection and presented Burt with an inscribed silver cigarette case. They then gave three cheers and sang 'For he's a jolly good fellow.' On Easter Monday 1916, some 3000 people gathered in the grounds of Hertford Castle to witness the presentation of an illuminated address, gold watch and chain, and a voucher for £100, gifts from the townspeople of Hertford. Burt graciously accepted the gifts and told the audience, 'I only did what many other British soldiers have done, but I was very fortunate to be recognized.' At that time two of his brothers were in the armed forces and no fewer than forty of his mother's relatives were also serving their country. He re-enlisted with his battalion as his initial period of service was completed and served on the Western

Front for the remainder of the war, being discharged from the Army in 1919 with the rank of sergeant.

In 1925 Burt moved to Chesham, Bucks., and was the licensee of the New Inn, Waterside, where he stayed until just before the Second World War when he moved to 175 Chartridge Lane, Chesham. He attended many of the VC gatherings through the years and met Canon Lummis on 27 June 1956 on the occasion of the VC Centenary Review when, Lummis noted, Burt was in a wheelchair. Burt was reported to be an invalid from the early 1950s and in a letter to Canon Lummis in April 1957, he wrote that he was recovering from a serious illness.

On 8 May 1962 Alfred Burt was admitted to Tindal General Hospital, where he died on 9 June. Shortly before, he had received a letter from the Queen's private secretary expressing the Queen's sorrow at not having been able to meet him on her visit to Buckinghamshire on 6 April. He was cremated at a private ceremony at Garston West Herts Cemetery, Watford, on Thursday 14 June and his plot was marked by a small iron plate under a cherry tree. Burt left a wife, son and daughter. Mrs Jenny Newton, Burt's daughter, presented her father's medals to the Hertfordshire Museum in August 1979.

H. CHRISTIAN

Cuinchy, France, 18 October

Among the brickstacks in the area to the south of the La Bassée Canal, a 23-year-old regular soldier, Pte Harry Christian, won the VC.

His battalion, the 2nd Bn, King's Own Royal Lancaster Regt, 83rd Bde, 28 Div., had completed a tour of duty at the Hohenzollern Redoubt on 6 October, and moved out to a rest area. But on 15 October the 83rd Bde returned to the line in the Cuinchy sector and the 2nd King's Own took over a stretch of front line trenches from Hanover Street north to the La Bassée Canal (see map on page 18). The Regimental History states, 'the whole area was a maze of trenches, shell craters, communication trenches, saps and sidings. Several large craters in front of the lines had been occupied and connected with trenches.' Two companies held the firing line and in one of these, holding a mine crater with a small party of men, was No. 10210 Pte Christian. On 19 October the Battalion *War Diary* records that the enemy destroyed about 50 yards of parapet on the left of the line, 'killing 4 ORs and wounding or injuring by burying 6 ORs'. Much of this damage was caused by *minenwerfers*, a very large type of enemy trench mortar. The bombardment forced Christian and the men with him to withdraw from the crater. During their withdrawal he realized that three of his party were missing and he returned to the crater even though it was still under fire, to look for them. He found the missing men, all of whom had been buried by the explosions; one at a time he dug them out and carried them back for medical attention. He then found himself a vantage point from where he could see the flight of the *minenwerfer* projectiles and could warn his comrades of their approach, giving the troops a chance to find cover.

Christian was awarded the VC for most conspicuous bravery although the award was not gazetted until 3 March 1916; the citation states 18 October as the date of the action but the Battalion *War Diary* specifies 19 October. He received his medal from the King on 18 September 1917.

Harry Christian was born at Wall Thwaite, Pennington, near Ulverston in Lancashire on 17 January 1892 and received his education at the National Schools, Ulverston. After a number of farming jobs he enlisted in the Army at Lancaster in November 1909 and was serving with 2nd Bn, King's Own, at Lebong, India, at the outbreak of war. He arrived in France on 16 January 1915. He was wounded and briefly returned to England on 17 July 1915.

His battalion left France and sailed to Egypt, landing in Salonika in December 1915. In September 1917 Christian went home on leave and an investiture was held at Ibrox Park, Glasgow, where some 80,000 people assembled inside the football ground to give the King a rousing welcome. Following a mixture of decorations and awards – the loudest applause being reserved for a female munitions worker who received the OBE – it was Christian's turn; he was carried on a invalid chair from a tunnel beneath the main stand by two St Andrew's ambulancemen, one of whom held open Christian's greatcoat while the King pinned on the medal. The applause was reported as 'deafening' as Christian was carried away from the dais. He had contracted malaria in Salonika and an attack had struck him down minutes before the ceremony.

Christian later returned to his battalion in Salonika and served with it for the rest of the war, being stationed north of Lake Doiran in Macedonia when the war ended. He was discharged from the Army on 4 April 1922 and for forty years was the landlord of the Park Hotel, Egremont, Cumberland, where he was described as 'a model landlord'. He retired in 1963 and lived at 1 Dent Road, Thornhill, near Egremont, where in later years he was looked after by his niece, Mrs Farran. Harry Christian died in West Cumberland Hospital on 2 September 1974 at the age of 82 and was buried at Egremont Cemetery. A memorial plaque positioned on a private house bearing the names of men who served from the hamlet of New Mill, not far from Egremont, includes the name of Harry Christian. His medals were purchased by the King's Own Regt in 1974.

T. KENNY

Near La Houssoie, France, 4 November

No. 17424 Pte Thomas Kenny of the 13th Durham Light Infantry (DLI), 68th Bde, won the 23rd Div's first VC at the age of thirty-three, while attempting to save his officer near La Houssoie in the vicinity of Erquinghem.

On 2 November, in very wet weather, the 13th DLI relieved the 12th DLI in trenches near La Houssoie; the trenches were inundated and the parapets and dug-outs were caving in. On the night of 4 November Lt P.A. Brown was superintending a working party engaged in improving the wire defences. Thick fog covered no-man's-land and at 21.15 hours Brown, accompanied by Pte Kenny, went towards the enemy parapet. They lost their direction in the fog and found themselves close to the enemy lines; some Germans, who were lying in a ditch in front of their parapet, opened fire, shooting Brown through both thighs. Despite being heavily fired upon Pte Kenny crawled through the mud for more than an hour, carrying his wounded officer on his back, searching desperately in the fog for the way back to his lines. He refused to go on alone although repeatedly told to do so by Lt Brown. Nearly exhausted, he came upon a ditch which he recognized and making his officer as comfortable as he could, he went to fetch help. Finding an officer and a few men of the 13th DLI in a listening post, he guided them to where Lt Brown lay. A hostile party then attacked the rescuers, opening heavy rifle and machine-gun fire and throwing bombs from a range of 30 yards. The officer from the listening post, Capt. White, ordered the rescue party to go on with the wounded Lt Brown, while he held the enemy off with a rifle. With some assistance Pte Kenny had succeeded in bringing his officer safely to the British lines, but tragically Lt Brown died before he could be carried to the dressing station. Nevertheless Kenny's selfless courage earned him the highest award for valour. His VC was gazetted on 7 December 1915, the citation stating that 'Kenny's pluck, endurance, and devotion to duty were beyond praise'.

Thomas Kenny was born at South Wingate, Durham on 4 April 1882. After he left St Mary's Roman Catholic School at Wingate he worked as a quarryman and, later as a miner at Wheatley Hill Colliery. He enlisted in August 1914 on the outbreak of war with the 13th (Service) Bn DLI, and on 16 September 1914 the recruits entrained at Newcastle upon Tyne, their destination being Bullswater Camp, near Pirbright in Surrey. Despite the rain, mud and cold the men lived in tents until the end of November before completing their training and receiving one week's leave in late July 1915. Private Thomas Kenny, 'B' Company, 13th (Service) Battalion DLI, landed at Boulogne with his battalion on 26 August 1915. Initially the battalion was supplying many working parties as many of the men were miners, but in early October the DLI went into the line at Bois Grenier, which, although thought of as a 'quiet' section, casualties occurred on a daily basis. This is illustrated by the following letter written home by a DLI officer, Lieutenant Philip Anthony Brown:

> About 12.30am, a man came and said he could hear moaning over the parapet. I was afraid that this meant that some of my men, who had just started on a listening patrol, had been hit . . . . I went down with my observer, a very nice Irishman frm County Durham, who goes with me everywhere, and crept along . . . a very shallow trench. We soon came on one man down in the bottom of the ditch. It was difficult to move him, but finally my observer got him on his back. Poor fellow had a bad wound in the side.

This was the first night of the battalion's first tour of duty in the trenches and the observer was Private Thomas Kenny.

He was married with seven children, five girls and two boys; the eldest was ten and the youngest just two months old when he came home on leave in December 1915 for the first time since winning the VC a month earlier on 4 November. He was decorated by King George V at Buckingham Palace on Saturday 4 March 1916. Mrs Brown, the mother of Philip Brown, was there to meet the man who had tried so hard to save her son's life. A few days later, Thomas Kenny returned home to his wife and family. At the Palace Picture Theatre, with the local Boy Scouts and Prize Band as escort and before a capacity audience, he was presented by the manager of Wingate Colliery with £50 in War Bonds, a gift from local people. The next morning, 11 March, Thomas Kenny went to his old school to be presented with a marble clock, pipe and tobacco and to listen to a poem specially composed for the occasion and read by one of the children. Kenny returned to his battalion in France as a lance-sergeant, saving one Sgt Moody's life during the Battle of the Somme; Moody lost a leg during the fighting, but was carried to safety by Kenny. The unit left for Italy in November 1917 but returned to France in March 1918 in time for the German offensive; by then Kenny was CSM. He was discharged in 1919 and returned home to Wingate. He attended the garden party for VC winners held at Buckingham Palace on 26 June 1920.

In 1927 Kenny moved to Darlington Street, Wheatley Hill, and was employed at this time as a 'stone hand' at the nearby Wheatley Hill Colliery. Despite financial difficulties he was able to go the British Legion's dinner held at the House of Lords on 9 November 1929. During his stay in London he met Mrs Brown, the mother of Lt P.A. Brown. He and his wife had met Mrs Brown more than once, and one of Kenny's daughters was in domestic service with the officer's brother. The following month he was present at the first annual dinner and reunion of the 13th Bn DLI, at which he met again Sgt Moody, whose life he had saved on the Somme. Thomas Kenny died in Durham on 29 November 1948, aged sixty-six, and was buried at Wheatley Hill Cemetery, County Durham on 2 December. Following an appeal by members of The 'Faithful' Inkerman Club, his unmarked grave was finally given a headstone in August 1994. The stone was unveiled by Captain Richard Annand VC, during a simple ceremony.

A bronze statue of Captain Annand VC stands at South Shields Town Hall. The statue along with that of Pte Thomas Kenny VC was unveiled in May 2007. Capt. Annand, who died in 2004, ignored enemy fire to rescue his badly wounded batman, using a wheelbarrow, during the retreat to Dunkirk in May 1940.

J. CAFFREY

La Brique, Belgium, 16 November

The 2nd York and Lancaster Regt (16th Bde, 6th Div.) moved into the Ypres salient on the night of 31 May/ 1 June, at which point 'trench casualties almost doubled immediately'. On 30 July 16th Bde was prepared for immediate movement, and the next day was located around 'Goldfish Château', half a mile north-west of Ypres, as a precautionary measure, to support the 14th Div. positions at Hooge which had been severely attacked the previous day. On the night of 5/6 August the 2 York and Lancasters relieved the 9th King's Royal Rifles (42nd Bde, 14th Div.) in the Hooge trenches. The following three days were used to prepare for an attack to be launched on 9 August to restore the line at Hooge. The battalion remained on duty in the salient though changes took place to the composition of units of the 6th Div. during November. Maj.-Gen. W.N. Congreve, the commander of 6th Div., was promoted to command XIII Corps on 14 November and was replaced by Maj.-Gen. C. Ross. By the end of August the battalion had received four drafts of replacements numbering 340 men, bringing it back up to strength after the attack at Hooge.

On 13 November the 2nd York and Lancasters returned to the trenches, this time at La Brique. HQ and A and B Coys were driven by motor bus to Brielen, while D Coy and two platoons of C Coy went by train to the track crossing at 'Goldfish Château'. The relief was completed by 22.50 hours that night and the situation was described as 'quiet'.

The next day, 16 November, was fine and bright, and as the light grew Pte John Caffrey spotted a badly wounded man lying between 300 and 400 yards in front of the German trench, totally exposed to the Germans' view. At about 09.00 hours, in broad daylight, Caffrey, together with Cpl Stirk of the RAMC, set out from their trench in a rescue attempt but

they were beaten back by shrapnel fire. Within a short time
they made a second bid to reach the wounded man, all the
while under close rifle and machine-gun fire. They successfully
reached the man, who was from the West Yorkshire Regt,
and bandaged his wounds, but just as Cpl Stirk lifted the
wounded man on to Caffrey's back for the return to their
lines, Stirk was shot in the head. Caffrey lowered the soldier
to the ground and bandaged Stirk's wound and helped him
back to safety. He then went out for a third time to bring in
the casualty. He had shown the 'utmost coolness and bravery'
throughout the rescue. The battalion *War Diary* notes that
they suffered 'a good deal of hostile shelling throughout the
afternoon'. The battalion was relieved by the 8th King's Royal
Rifles on the night of 18/19 November.

Caffrey's Victoria Cross was awarded for this rescue
and was gazetted on 22 January 1916. It was the first to
be awarded to a member of the 6th Div. and he was
decorated by King George V at Buckingham Palace on
23 February 1916. It appears that Cpl Stirk received no
official recognition for his part in the rescue, beyond being
mentioned in the citation of Caffrey's award. In a way
Caffrey's deed was a repeat of an earlier act of heroism
which earned him the Russian Order of St George 4th Class,
awarded on 25 August 1915 when he brought in a seriously
wounded officer under heavy fire.

John Caffrey bore the same name as his father and he was
born at Birr, King's County (later Offaly), Ireland, on 23
October 1891, though some sources suggest he was born on
21 December that year. He left Ireland at an early age and
settled in England and was educated at St Mary's Catholic
School, Derby Road, Nottingham. He joined the 12th
Nottingham Company of the Boys Brigade, and appears to
have been popular.

He enlisted in the army in 1910 and joined the 7th Bn, the
Nottinghamshire and Derbyshire Regt. At his own request he
transferred to the 2nd York and Lancasters, in which his father
had served. With the coming of war he was mobilized on

4 August 1914. The battalion moved by train from Limerick, where it was stationed, to Queenstown, embarking on the SS *Sleive Bawn* on 14 August, bound for Holyhead. They sailed for France on the SS *Minneapolis* on 8 September 1914, arriving at St Nazaire at 05.15 hours on 9 September. Caffrey went into action with his battalion on 21 September east of Vailly on the Aisne. He served with the 2nd Bn, York and Lancaster Regt, throughout the war. Shortly after winning the VC Caffrey was promoted to corporal and later, while on leave, he married Florence, daughter of Mr and Mrs Avery, on 24 March 1917 at St Barnabas Church, Cambridge.

Caffrey was discharged from the Army in 1919 with the rank of sergeant. In addition to his VC he held the 1914 Mons Star with clasp (5 August– 22 November 1914), the War Medal, the Victory Medal, and the Russian Order of St George 4th class. He also received the King George VI Coronation Medal, 1937 and held two medals for the cross-country championships of the Irish Army, and one medal for the Aldershot cross-country championship. He was present at the garden party for VC winners given by the King at Buckingham Palace on 26 June 1920.

Following his discharge Caffrey became a member of the Sunderland fire brigade, afterwards working with Messrs Cammell Laird at the 'Metropolitan Carriage and Wagon Company's Works' until 1931. On Armistice Day, 11 November 1929, Caffrey was photographed selling poppies in London.

On 26 June 1931 Caffrey found himself 'on the dole' owing to the closure of Cammell Laird's works. He spent the next three months seeking work but found that not even his VC could help; he was reported in a newspaper dated 19 October 1931: 'What do they say when you tell them you are a VC?' 'Very sorry.' Caffrey told the interviewer that he found the trauma of trying to find work 'a heart-breaking job'. During the interview the reporter found that Caffrey was drawing 15s 3d each week. Of that sum 15s went on rent and other 'pressing items', leaving Caffrey with a mere 3d. Beyond this sum his wife earned 10s a week at office cleaning and he drew £2 10s a quarter as a VC. This penury seemed a world away from the reception he and other Victoria Cross holders had received at the British Legion Dinner at the House of Lords on 9 November 1929.

The local newspaper drew Caffrey's plight to the attention of Mr Norman Birkett KC, the Liberal candidate for East Nottingham. Outraged that such a situation should befall one of Nottingham's 'bravest war heroes' he immediately engaged Caffrey as one of his staff for the duration of the election, promising to use all means to find him more permanent employment later. The result of all this was that the reporter could write on 27 November 1931 that John Caffrey would be given 'a responsible post at Shakespeare Street under the Public Assistance Administration'.

In 1933 'Mr Jack Caffrey VC was the marker' for the November parade of The Nottingham Catholic Ex-Servicemen's Association on Armistice Day. A year later he was one of five VCs attending the ceremony at the Cenotaph on Armistice Day. According to newspaper reports the men – Messrs O'Leary, Caffrey, Moffitt, O'Neill and Wilkinson – found the battery of cameras nerve-wracking. Sgt John Caffrey VC attended the funeral of an old friend, RSM Frank Parr MC, DCM, who was buried with full military honours, at Wilford Hill Cemetery, Nottingham, on 2 April 1936. In November that year he was selling poppies for Armistice Day, being photographed in Nottingham with the local Mayor, who bought a poppy from him. He had been one of two representatives of his regiment, the 2nd York and Lancasters, invited to witness the royal procession from a first-class position in The Mall, London, which Caffrey stated 'was a wonderful sight and I shall never forget it'. This was the second coronation procession he had seen. He had been among the soldiers who had lined the route of George V's coronation procession in 1911.

Soon after the outbreak of the Second World War Caffrey rejoined the Army, enlisting in Nottingham. He was appointed CSM in the Home Guard in November 1939. After the war he attended the Victory Parade on 8 June 1946 and the dinner at the Dorchester Hotel that followed.

After the war John Caffrey became a 'sergeant' at one of Butlin's holiday camps. On 28 September 1952 he was on parade with five other VCs at the annual rally of the

Distinguished Conduct Medal League held at Horse Guards Parade, London.

John Caffrey died on 26 February 1953, aged 62 years, at Derby. A bearer party from the regimental depot was present at his funeral service which was held at St Patrick's Church, London Road, Nottingham. He was buried in Wilford Hill Cemetery, and his VC is held by the regimental museum, the York and Lancaster Regt, in Rotherham.

On 23 May 2007, after fund-raising by two local men, Sean Westerby and Ron Booth, a new headstone was unveiled in Wilford Hill Cemetery, Nottingham, the previous headstone recognised Caffrey's parents but did not display his name. John Caffrey's name also appears on the Memorial to Nottingham's VCs at Nottingham Castle.

S. MEEKOSHA

Near the Yser, France, 19 November

From 1 October two of the four battalions forming the 146th Bde, 49th Div., were from the West Yorkshire Regt. They were the 1/6th and 1/8th West Yorks and had been in the line north and north-west of Ypres between Norteldje Estaminet and Wyatts Lane. After the Battle of Loos and subsequent actions at the Hohenzollern Redoubt the general situation was one of preparation for the next assault. During this period of relative inactivity No. 1147 Cpl Samuel Meekosha was to win the West Yorkshire Regt its first Victoria Cross.

Cpl. Meekosha was with a platoon of about twenty NCOs and men of the 1/6th West Yorks, holding an isolated section of trench at 'the Pump Room', about 2 miles north-north-east of Ypres (see map on page 264). The trench was held for forty-eight hours at a time. All movement had to be carried out in the hours of darkness owing to the fact that the positions were visible from the German line. On the 1/6th's second day the Germans laid down a bombardment with heavy artillery. The *War Diary* notes that 6 men were killed and 7 wounded, and that all were more or less buried by the debris. Cpl Meekosha immediately took command as the only uninjured NCO. He first sent 'three of the fellows who were only recruits back to headquarters' to apprise them of the situation. The few remaining men helped dig the buried and wounded men out. As Meekosha told a reporter in 1929: 'We had to dig in full view of the German trenches, and they machine-gunned us from about 2 o'clock to 4.30.' The citation also notes that 'no less than ten more big shells [fell] within twenty yards of him' during his efforts to dig the wounded and dead out. Three privates, Johnson, Sayers and Wilkinson, who remained and helped Cpl Meekosha, were each rewarded with the DCM. Meekosha is reported as having said that they got 'four of the chaps out'; the citation for his VC is more generous in stating he had saved 'at least four lives'. He had certainly shown scant regard for his personal safety during the rescue of his fellow platoon members. The battalion was relieved by 1/5th West Yorkshire Regt that night and went into Divisional Reserve near Poperinghe.

Samuel Meekosha was born on 16 September 1893 at 3 High Street, Leeds, Yorkshire. His mother, Mary (née Cunningham) was of Irish descent and had married Alexander Meekosha in Leeds, late in 1892. Alexander was a Russian-Polish immigrant from Warsaw and a tailor by trade. It seems the family moved to Bradford in about 1895 as Samuel's brother Martin was born there in the latter part of that year. When the 1911 Census was taken his surviving siblings; Martin, Joseph, Mary and Eleanor (his sister Elizabeth and brother Bernard both died very young in 1897 and 1907 respectively) were at home with their mother at 7 Bramby Street, Bradford.

Mrs Meekosha is not recorded in the Electoral Register for the period 1914–15, nor in the Bradford Directory for 1916. However, there are records stating that his brother Joseph

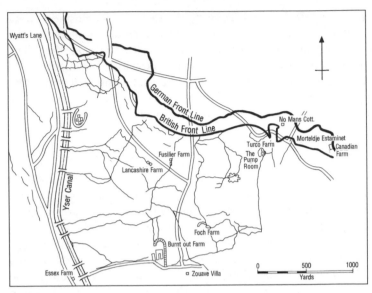

La Brique area

became a private in the 2nd Bradford Pals and his brother
Martin was preparing for the Catholic priesthood in Belgium.

Samuel went to St Joseph's Roman Catholic School in
Bradford, the family residing at this time at 91 Tennant
Street, West Bowling, Bradford. He also attended
Bradford Technical College. Before enlisting in the Army
Samuel Meekosha was an office worker for a Bradford
manufacturing company. On 20 February 1911 he enlisted
in the 1/6th West Yorkshire Territorial Regt. No. 1147
Pte Samuel Meekosha was mobilized on 5 August 1914.
At this time the 1/6th, together with the 1/5th, 1/7th and
1/8th battalions of the West Yorks Regt formed the 1st West
Riding Bde of the 1st West Riding (Territorial) Div. On 10
August 1914 the brigade was concentrated at Strensall and
York, followed by duty on the Lincolnshire coast until 9
April 1915 when it was moved to Gainsborough where the
men were prepared for service overseas.

Samuel Meekosha served with the 1/6th West Yorks in
France and Belgium throughout the war. He arrived in

France on 15 April 1915, his first twenty-four hours in trenches being spent on 27 April, 1 mile east of Laventie; the 1st Bn enjoyed the dubious distinction of being the first of the 1st West Riding Bde to assume sole responsibility for a section of the line. Meekosha was promoted to the rank of corporal on 13 February 1915. It seems that he re-signed on 15 December 1915.

Meekosha's VC was gazetted on 22 January 1916 and he was decorated by King George V at Buckingham Palace on 4 March 1916. During 1916 Samuel Meekosha married Bertha Elizabeth Charlotte, the youngest daughter of Mr and Mrs G.F. Duval of Bradford, who was later to bear him three children; the eldest son, Felix, was born in 1919, and the younger son Sidney and daughter Mary followed.

Returning to his regiment Meekosha took part in the Battle of the Somme. Later, on 26 June 1917, he was commissioned second lieutenant and served again in France and Belgium from 15 August 1917 to 19 December 1917. He was promoted to lieutenant on 27 December 1918 and to captain on 15 May 1919. He remained in the Army, transferring to the Corps of Military Accountants on 19 November 1919. He was ranked captain and account officer 6th class on 31 January 1920. A few months later he attended the garden party given for VC recipients at Buckingham Palace on 20 June 1920. He eventually retired from the Army on 17 March 1926.

Upon returning to civilian life Samuel Meekosha bought a wholesale tobacconist's business in Bradford. His wife helped to finance the concern. It seems to have begun well though when the expenses of town premises proved too heavy, Mrs Meekosha turned their home into a place of business. Initially, the venture seemed promising, though 'bad debts and ill-luck' forced him to sell out in about April 1929. For a while Meekosha was out of work, then, leaving his family in Bradford, he moved to Birmingham for a temporary job that paid only on commission. This was at the beginning of September 1929. Six weeks later the *Bradford Telegraph and Argus* contacted the Meekosha family, then residing at 288 Great Horton Road, Bradford, extending an offer of paying 'the expenses incurred by Bradford's VC during the reunion in London'. The offer was made after they had heard about

Capt. Meekosha's financial difficulties following the failure of his business. Mrs Meekosha considered the offer 'very sporty' and made it clear that without the newspaper's assistance 'it would have been impossible for my husband to attend the VCs dinner'. Capt. Meekosha was very grateful for the financial support and his attendance at the reunion dinner was assured by the fact that the railway companies had agreed 'to allow the VCs to travel to London free'. Meekosha was then living at 21 Beaufort Road, Edgbaston, Birmingham, but hoping to return to Bradford as soon as suitable permanent work could be found.

The VC reunion, though a pleasant occasion for Meekosha, proved also to be a source of great upset for him. Upon his return from London he told a reporter, 'I am ashamed of my city. The treatment of me from the day I won the VC . . . has been more than scurvy. I have felt it greatly and have been hurt.' Meekosha felt that his city did not care. This seemed to be reflected in the fact that, apart from one personal friend, there was no one to see him off at the train station. His return was equally unmarked. In contrast, other VCs from the Leeds area whom he met on the train were 'full of talk about the glorious send-off which had been given them'. They were disgusted by the poor treatment meted out to their fellow VC. His 'send-off' also contrasted with the VCs' reception in the south where they were mobbed by enthusiastic well-wishers. The other thing that rankled, as Meekosha told the *Bradford Telegraph and Argus*, was that he was unemployed and despite his efforts had been unsuccessful in securing a post in Bradford, yet total strangers he met in London had offered him a job. He made it clear that he did not wish people to think him conceited but that he was 'concerned about the principle involved'. A letter appeared in the *Bradford Daily Telegraph* on Armistice Day 1929 suggesting that the city officials should invite Capt. Meekosha 'to the functions in connection with the Prince of Wales's visit'. This seems to have been arranged, for Meekosha's 'champion', the *Bradford Telegraph and Argus*, reported on 13 November that 'Captain Sam Meekosha, Bradford's VC, to-day sent [the following] telegram . . . to the Prince of Wales' who was staying at the Midland Hotel, Bradford: 'Bradford's VC respectfully reciprocates your London welcome. – Captain S Meekosha.'

The job offer that he showed the reporter on 13 November is unspecified, but in early 1930 he became a sales representative for John Player & Sons, covering South Wales. He lived for a time in Penarth, Glamorgan, later moving to Penrhiw Villas, Oakdale, Monmouthshire. Meekosha seems to have done well in his role within the John Player organization. An article in the trade magazine *Tobacco*, dated 1 February 1937, described the annual dinner and dance on 15 January of the South Wales and Monmouthshire branch of the Tobacco Trade Travellers' Association presided over by 'Captain S. Meekosha VC, chairman of the [above] branch'. His wife was with him and a representative of the Cardiff branch of the TTTA made a presentation to her. The affair was held at the Park Hotel, Cardiff. The article makes it clear that Capt. Samuel Meekosha's branch was a newcomer, being referred to as 'our baby of the Tobacco Travellers' Association'.

With the coming of the Second World War Capt. Samuel Meekosha was commissioned in the Royal Army Ordnance Corps on 15 January 1940. A year later he changed his surname, by deed poll, to Ingham. Speculation continues as to whether he changed his instantly recognisable name to Ingham to acknowledge his mother's shortened maiden name Cunningham, or to take on his second wife's name, Mary Constance Ingham. Either way, he was a very modest man. On 6 October 1944, as Maj. Ingham, he transferred to the Regular Army Reserve of Officers. He was finally discharged from the Reserve of Officers on 6 October 1948.

Maj. Samuel Ingham died on 8 December 1950 at Blackwood, Monmouthshire. He was cremated at Pontypridd Crematorium. No other memorial to him is known. Besides the VC, Meekosha's other medals included the 1914–15 Star and the British War and Victory Medals. He later received the George VI Coronation Medal of 1937 and the Defence Medal and the British War Medal (1939–45). His Victoria Cross was sold at auction in London on 3 May 2001 for a hammer price of £92,000 to an unknown buyer. The Second World War medals of his son Felix, who served in the Royal Engineers, were also sold at the same auction.

A.G. DRAKE

Near La Brique, Belgium 23 November

No. 8/107 Cpl Alfred George Drake of the 8th Bn, the Rifle Brigade, was part of a four-man patrol sent out into no-man's-land on the night of 23 November to reconnoitre close to the German lines. When the enemy sent up a Very light, the small group was discovered, and subjected to a heavy burst of rifle and machine-gun fire; Lt Tryon, the patrol leader, and one rifleman were immediately hit. Drake ordered the surviving rifleman to help his fellow back to the British trenches. Lt Tryon would have died without immediate medical attention so Drake remained beside his officer, tending his wounds. As the official citation recounts, Drake 'was last seen kneeling beside him and bandaging his [Tryon's] wounds, regardless of the enemy's fire'. A rescue party was sent out a little later and found Lt Tryon and Cpl Drake close to the German lines. The officer was unconscious, but his wound had been bandaged with skill and care; close by lay the dead body of Cpl Drake, riddled with bullets.

Alfred George Drake was born on 10 December 1893 at 19 Skidmore Street, Mile End, in Stepney, East London. The 1901 and 1911 Census show the family living at 42 Bale Street, St Dunstan, Stepney, Parish of Mile End Old Town. Alfred had five siblings but by 1911 only four children were still living in the four-roomed house with their father, Robert, a dock worker for The Port of London Authority, and mother Mary Ann. Bale Street was rated as 'poor' in the survey conducted by Booth in 1899, with family income of between 18 to 21 shillings per week. By 1911 Alfred, who had attended Ben Jonson County Council School until he was fourteen, was working as a Dock Messenger, now aged seventeen. On the outbreak of war he wanted to join up straight away; however, due to family illness, he joined up on 3 September 1914 and went into the Rifle Brigade, arriving in France in May 1915. He was promoted to corporal within nine weeks.

Alfred George Drake was born on 10 December 1893 at 19 Skidmore Street, Mile End, in Stepney, East London. The 1901 and 1911 Census show the family living at 42 Bale Street, St Dunstan, Stepney, Parish of Mile End Old Town. Alfred had five siblings but by 1911 only four children were still living in the four-roomed house with their father, Robert, a dock worker for The Port of London Authority, and mother Mary Ann. Bale Street was rated as 'poor' in the survey conducted by Booth in 1899, with family income of between 18 to 21 shillings per week. By 1911 Alfred, who had attended Ben Jonson County Council School until he was fourteen, was working as a Dock Messenger, now aged seventeen. On the outbreak of war he wanted to join up straight away; however, due to family illness, he joined up on 3 September 1914 and went into the Rifle Brigade, arriving in France in May 1915. He was promoted to corporal within nine weeks.

After giving his life to save his officer he was gazetted for a posthumous VC on 22 January 1916. The award was presented to his father, Mr Robert Drake, on 16 November 1916. He is buried at La Brique Military Cemetery, Plot I, Row C, Grave 2. In April 1923 a memorial was unveiled at the Ben Jonson London County Council School by the Earl of Cavan. Dame Clara Butt was present and sang 'O Rest in the Lord'. Maj. Tryon MP, a cousin of Lt Henry Tryon who's life Drake had saved, was also at the ceremony. Unfortunately Henry Tryon, after recovering from his wounds and rejoining his regiment, was killed on 15 September 1916 and the name of Captain H. Tryon (as he then was), appears on the Thiepval Memorial to the Missing.

In April 1923 a lectern was dedicated to Arthur George Drake at St Thomas Church, Arbour Square, Stepney, but in 1941 the church was hit by incendiary bombs and had to be closed. During the 1950s the ruins of the church were demolished and flats erected on the site.

W. YOUNG

Near 'Little Z', East of Foncquevillers, France, 22 December

During the winter of 1915 (and, indeed, until the following summer) the 8th (Service) Bn, East Lancashire Regt, occupied one part of the British 37th Div.'s front along the Foncquevillers–Monchy au Bois line, 700 yards east of Foncquevillers and about 1,800 yards north of Gommecourt. The trenches were virtually impassable in late December because of the constant wet weather which made them waterlogged. The trench conditions were so miserable that platoon reliefs were carried out every twenty-four hours. In these conditions, action was limited to bombing raids, wire-cutting and night patrols. No. 17742 Sgt Allan of the 8th East Lancs was wounded in the thigh while on patrol. As the light increased on the morning of 22 December, No. 5938 Pte W. Young of the 8th East Lancs looked across no-man's-land and saw a company NCO lying in front of the wire, wounded. On his own initiative Young climbed over the parapet and, disregarding the enemy's fire, went into no-man's-land to aid Sgt Allan.

The NCO told Young to get under cover but his advice was ignored. While attempting to get Sgt Allan to a place of safety Pte Young was almost immediately hit by two bullets; one shattered his jaw, the other struck him in the chest. Despite his severe wounds Young, now joined by Pte Green, managed to bring in their wounded NCO. Young walked back to the dressing station in the village of Foncquevillers to have his wounds treated. Pte Green was given a green card which resulted in the award of a DCM, and with remarks to the effect that his conduct had been reported to higher authority. Young's VC was gazetted on 30 March 1916.

❖ ❖ ❖

William Young was born at Maryhill, Glasgow, on 1 January 1876. He was the son of Samuel Young, a contractors' labourer, and of his wife Mary Ellen. William was educated at a local elementary school and joined the Army at the age of 15 years. After serving as a regular soldier he was put on the Reserve. Returning to civilian life he was employed in a variety of labouring jobs and at the outbreak of war he was working at the Preston Gas Company's gas works. He and his wife had eight children at this time, and a ninth was born later, the family residing at 7 Heysham Street, Preston, Lancashire.

Upon mobilization he rejoined the Army, sailing to France on 14 September 1914. He was involved in some of the early fighting and suffered a bullet wound in the thigh in November. He returned to duty and was gassed in the spring of 1915. His eyesight was affected and he did not return to the front until the winter, when he won the VC on almost his first time back in the trenches.

Young was brought to England for treatment of the wounds he received in his VC action, being moved from the Military Hospital at Rouen where his initial medical care began, to hospitals in Exeter, London and Aldershot. He appeared to be making good progress in his recovery and on 19 April 1916 he returned to Preston to a hero's welcome and a civic reception. A fund was started for the benefit of his family by local people. After further hospital treatment Young returned home for ten days' leave at the end of June and early July. Afterwards he went back to the Cambridge Hospital, Aldershot, for a final operation. He did not recover consciousness after the operation – apparently the chloroform had affected his heart. He died at 08.55 hours on 27 August 1916, his wife at his bedside. The local fund begun for the Young family then stood at £560 and the money was duly passed on to Mrs Young. Some of the money was invested to give the family a return of about 10 shillings per week.

William Young was given an impressive military funeral and his coffin, draped in a Union Jack, was borne on a gun carriage. He was buried at Preston's old cemetery near to the New Hall Lane entrance on 31 August 1916, and he lies in Plot 5, Row C, Grave 10. His medals were presented to Maj.-Gen. Houston, Colonel of the Queen's Lancashire Regt, on Sunday 7 July 1985 by Pte Young's son, Mr William H. Young.

SOURCES

The sources used in the preparation of this book include the following :

Lummis VC files at the National Army Museum, London
The Victoria Cross files at the Imperial War Museum, London
The National Archives, Kew, Surrey
The Royal Artillery Institution, Woolwich
Regimental Museums and Archives
The *London Gazette* 1914–20 (HMSO)
www.victoriacross.org.uk
www.victoriacross.org.uk
The Scottish War Memorials Project
www.ukniwm.org.uk

M.J. O'Leary
The Sphere 3 July 1915
Daily Telegraph various issues
War Budget 6 March 1915, 22 July 1915
1st Irish Guards *War Diary* (WO95/1342 PRO)

The Times 25 June 1920, 1 November 1937
Daily Mail
Daily Express 17 June 1940
The People 10 March 1940
RCMP Quarterly Vol 27 No 2 October 1961
The Ranger July 1962
Household Brigade Magazine
Madame Tussaud's
RCMP Historical Branch
Gobar Sing Negi
2/39th Garhwal Rifles *War Diary* (WO95/3945 PRO)
New Delhi Evening News 10 June 1970
Journal of the Connaught Rangers Association. No. 3. Vol. 1. January 2006.

W. Buckingham
2nd Leicester Regt *War Diary* (WO95/3945 PRO)
Record Office for Leicestershire, Leicester & Rutland

J. Rivers
Nottingham Guardian 8 April 1937
Derbyshire Advertiser 26 July 1935

Derby Evening Telegraph 5 March 1937 and 7 April 1937
www.nottinghamshire-victoria-cross-memorial.org.uk
Derek Price

W. Anderson
The Green Howards Gazette May 1969

C.C. Foss
2nd Bedfordshire Regt *War Diary* (WO 95/1658 PRO)
Daily Graphic 29 August 1949
Daily Telegraph 11 April 1953
The Statesman (Calcutta)
Times of India
Biggleswade Chronicle
Sid Lindsay

E. Barber
Lloyds Weekly News 18 April 1915
1st Grenadier Guards *War Diary* (WO 95/1658 PRO)

W.D. Fuller
Nottingham Guardian
Sheffield Telegraph 6 May 1935
Western Daily Press 8 July 1935
Bristol Evening Post 26 September 1935
Bath and Wilts Chronicle 29 January 1936
The Times 27 November 1947
Police Review 4 December 1987

H. Daniels
Eastern Daily Press various issues
Daily Mail 17 May 1915
Sunday Express

The Aldershot News February 1925
South Wales Echo 19 June 1933
Burnley Express 9 February 1938
Yorkshire Evening News 14 December 1953
Yorkshire Post 21 December 1953
The Caterer
2nd Rifle Brigade *War Diary* (WO 95/1731 PRO)
Local and Family History, Library and Information Service, Leeds City Council
Leeds Grand Theatre
Dave Stowe

C.R. Noble
Bournemouth Evening Echo 13 July 1979
Bournemouth Borough Council

C.G. Martin
56th Field Company R.E. *War Diary* (WO 95/2784 PRO)
Bath Chronicle 1 July 1933
Bath and Wilts Chronicle 8 June 1940
Daily Express 2 May 1915
Daily Telegraph c 24 May 1915
'Sapper' February 1981
The Royal Engineers Journal 1981

R. Morrow
1st Royal Irish Fusiliers *War Diary* (WO 95/1428 PRO)
Courier and News (Ulster) 9 November 1988

G.R.P. Roupell
1st East Surrey Regt *War Diary* (WO/95 1563 PRO)

*The Journal of The East Surrey
Regt* November 1956
Soldier Article – date unknown
*The Journal of The Queen's
Royal Surrey Regt* November
1963
The Old Contemptible April
1970 and October 1973
The Times 21 November 1947
Daily Telegraph 6 March 1974
Who's Who 1960

B.H. Geary
Daily Sketch 1 August 1934
Daily Telegraph 1 August 1934
Montreal Daily Star 15 January
1935
Toronto Globe 19 April 1935
London Gazette 30 September
1927
Crockford's Clergy List 1936
Who's Who 1949
This England Winter 1970

G.H. Woolley
9th London Regt (QVR) *War
Diary* (WO 95/1558 PRO)
Suffolk Chronicle and Mercury
12 July 1915
Daily Telegraph 12 December
1968

E. Dwyer
1st East Surrey Regt *War Diary*
(WO 95/1563 PRO)
The War Budget 8 July 1915
Daily Mail 29 June 1915 and 11
September 1916
Daily Telegraph 10 July 1915
Morning Post 14 July 1915 and
11 September 1916
Fulham Chronicle various issues
Surrey Comet 3 March 1962

*Journal of The Queen's Royal
Surrey Regt* November 1962

F. Fisher
Department of Public Records
and Archives, Historical
Branch, Canada
Victor 14 January 1967
13th Canadian Infantry
Battalion *War Diary* (WO
95/1263 PRO)

F.W. Hall
8th Canadian Infantry Battalion
War Diary (WO 95/3769
PRO)
Sentinel May 1968

E.D. Bellew
The Civilian July 1919
The Daily Sun (Vancouver) 22
September 1919
7th Canadian Infantry Battalion
War Diary (WO 95/3768 PRO)
Toronto Globe 25 October 1929
Winnipeg Evening Tribune 29
October 1929
Winnipeg Free Press 20 October
1934
Victor 10 May 1985

F.A.C. Scrimger
*Canadian Medical Association
Journal* April 1916
Montreal Star
The Legionary March 1937

Mir Dast
The Vivid 30 October 1915
57th Rifles *War Diary* (WO
95/3923 PRO)
58th Rifles *War Diary* (WO
95/3948 PRO)

I. Smith
Weekly Dispatch 5 September 1915
The Sphere 12 August 1922
Gunfire No 30
The Age 23 April 1991
Independent 11 October 1995
Australian Dictionary of Biography Vol II
1st Manchester Regt *War Diary* (WO 95/3927 PRO)
Maurice Smith
Dr Judy Landau
VAJEX Australia Inc.
Jullundur Brigade Association

J. Lynn
The Lancashire Fusilier's Annual
War Illustrated 24 July 1915
2nd Lancashire Fusiliers' *War Diary* (WO 95/1507 PRO)

E. Warner
1st Bedfordshire Regt *War Diary* (WO 95/1570 PRO)
The Wasp and the Eagle 1962

J. Upton
Daily Sketch 2 July 1915
Lincolnshire Life January 1994

C.R. Sharpe
Daily Sketch 2 July 1915
Cumberland Star 22 February 1963
British Legion Journal April 1963
Cemeteries and Crematorium Department, City of Lincoln

J. Ripley
Daily Sketch 2 July 1915
The Sphere 12 July 1915
Scotsman 15 August 1933

Montrose Standard 25 August 1933
Red Hackle October 1933
1st Black Watch *War Diary* (WO 95/1263 PRO)

D. Finlay
Soldier May 1967
2nd Black Watch *War Diaries* (WO 95/3948 PRO, WO 95/5138 PRO)
The Scottish War Memorial Project

D.W. Belcher
Sunday Pictorial 18 July 1915
The Times 1 February 1917
Sunday Dispatch 24 May 1931
Tunbridge Wells Advertiser 1933 and 1935
Surrey Advertiser 16 February 1935
Sevenoaks Courier 11 October 1935
Dorking Advertiser 17 June 1938
The People 26 November 1939
Surrey Comet 9 August 1941
1/5th London Regiment *War Diary* (WO 95/1498 PRO)

F. Barter
Daily Sketch 7 July and 9 August 1915
South Wales Daily News 13 July 1915
Daily Chronicle 14 August 1915
South Wales Echo 8 November 1929
Western Mail 28 March 1992
2/3rd Gurkha *War Diary* (WO 95/4689 PRO)

J.H. Tombs
Warrington Guardian July and
    August 1915
Daily Chronicle 13 August 1915
Daily News (Perth) 6 November
    1929
Daily Sketch 4 November 1929
Daily Telegraph 28 August 1954
Toronto Globe and Mail 4 July
    1966
1st Liverpool (King's) Regt *War
    Diary* (WO 95/1359 PRO)
Sid Lindsay
Courtney Finn (Grantham Civic
    Society)

J.G. Smyth
The Times Weekly Edition 30
    July 1920
Daily Telegraph various issues
    1962 to 1983
The Times 27 April 1983
This England Autumn 1983

L.J. Keyworth
Daily Telegraph 12 July 1915
Lincolnshire Echo 20 July 1931
Daily Mail 22 March 1963
Southwark Recorder
Herts Advertiser
*Orders and Medals Research
    Society* No 3 Vol 6 September
    1967
Local Services Library,
    Southwark Education and
    Leisure Services
24th London Regt *War Diary*
    (WO 95/2744 PRO)
www.thelincolnshireregiment.org

W. Mariner
Daily Mirror 13 August 1915
Daily Sketch 13 August 1915

W. Angus
Daily Mail 31 August 1915
Daily Sketch 15 January 1917
    and 5 December 1929
The People 12 November 1939
The Scotsman 30 September 1957
Glasgow Herald 15 June 1959
Victor 31 August 1963
Sunday Express 1 January 1995
The papers of Brig. A.F. Lambert
    (IWM)

F.W. Campbell
Daily Sketch 13 July 1915
Department of Tourism and
    Information (Historical
    Branch), Canada
1st Canadian Infantry Battalion
    War Diary (WO 95/3760
    PRO)

S.C. Woodroffe
8th Rifle Brigade *War Diary*
    (WO 95/1896 PRO)
Medal News

G.A. Boyd-Rochfort
Daily Mirror 2 September and 8
    September 1915
Daily Mail 3 September 1915
The Times 8 August and 2
    September 1940

D. Laidlaw
7th KOSB *War Diary* (WO
    95/1953 PRO)
The Pipes of War Sir Bruce
    Seton and John Gaunt 1920
Morning Post 16 October 1929
North Mail (Newcastle) 30
    October 1931
Weekly Scotsman 21 November
    1931

Alnwick and County Gazette 14 April 1934
Pearson's Weekly 1 October 1938
Answers 12 November 1938
The People 28 January 1940
The Times 3 June 1950
Berwickshire Advertiser 4 June 1950
Medal News April 1994

G.S. Peachment
2nd KRRC *War Diary* (WO 95/1272 PRO)

A.M. Read
1st Northamptonshire Regt *War Diary* (WO95/1271 PRO)

A. Vickers
2nd Royal Warwickshires *War Diary* (WO 95/1664 PRO)
Suffolk Chronicle and Mercury 12 March 1916
Birmingham Mail 28 July 1944

H. Wells
2nd Royal Sussex Regt *War Diary* (WO 95/1269 PRO)
Kentish Gazette/Herne Bay Press/ Whitstable Press 6 September 1974, 14 September 1979

H.E. Kenny
13th Durham Light Infantry *War Diary* (WO 95/2182 PRO)
Newcastle Evening World 9 November 1929
Newcastle Daily Journal 17 October 1929, 9 December 1929 and 24 November 1932
F.H. Johnson

73rd Field Coy R.E. *War Diary* (WO 95/1925 PRO)
Glendining's Sale Catalogue 1 March 1989

A.F. Douglas-Hamilton
6th Cameron Highlanders *War Diary* (WO 95/ ?PRO)
The 79th News September 1958

R. Dunsire
13th Royal Scots *War Diary* (WO 95/1946 PRO)

A.F. Saunders
Ipswich Evening Star 14 November 1932 and 18 November 1935
The Times 5 July 1934
Cambridge Daily News 18 November 1935
The Times 4 August 1947
East Anglian Magazine August 1964
Castle: The Journal of The Royal Anglian Regt Vol 8, No 5, 1989
Britannia and Castle June 1994

J.D. Pollock
5th Cameron Highlanders *War Diary* (WO 95/1767 PRO)
Press and Journal 1 August 1956
The 79th News September 1958
A.B. Turner
1st Royal Berkshire Regt *War Diary* (WO 95/1361 PRO)
News Chronicle 21 November 1942

A.J.T. Fleming-Sandes
2nd East Surrey Regt *War Diary* (WO 95/2279 PRO)

Daily Mail Date unknown
The Times May 1961
Daily Telegraph and Morning Post 26 May 1961
Daily Telegraph 26 May 1961
Teignmouth Post and Gazette 2 June 1961
Illustrated London News 3 June 1961
The Times 4 August 1961

S. Harvey
1st York and Lancaster Regt *War Diary* (WO 95/2275 PRO)
Daily Express 17 August 1953
East Anglian Daily Times 28 January, 25 June and 26 June 1956, 24 September and 28 September 1960
Eastern Daily Press 28 September 1960
Ipswich Evening Star 12 February 1983, 28 February 1986

O. Brooks
3rd Coldstream Guards *War Diary* (WO 95/1358 PRO)
Morning Post 8 November 1915
Various other un-named newspaper cuttings November 1915
The Times 1 November 1929
Daily Sketch 6 April 1933
Bystander 14 June 1933
Daily Herald 30 October 1933
The Star 3 November 1933
Bath Chronicle 18 November 1933
The Household Brigade Magazine
Windsor Express 16 October 1987

J.C. Raynes
71st Brigade RFA *War Diary* (WO 95/1923 PRO)
War Weekly 18 December 1915
Sphere 25 December 1915
Daily Telegraph 14 November 1929
Daily Mail 14 November 1929
The Times 14 November 1929
East Anglian Daily Times 14 November 1929
Sheffield Telegraph 14 November 1929
Yorkshire Telegraph 15 November 1929
Yorkshire Evening Post 16 September 1972

J.L. Dawson
Daily Telegraph 17 February 1967
Evening News 25 July 1967

C.G. Vickers
1/7th Notts and Derby *Regt War Diary* (WO 95/2694 PRO)
The Times 21 October 1972 and 18 March 1982

G.A. Maling
Sunderland Echo 2 March 1940
Cemeteries Services, London Borough of Bromley

A.F.G. Kilby
The Times 8 March 1923
The Stafford Knot October 1969

R.P. Hallowes
4th Middlesex Regt *War Diary* (WO 95/1422 PRO)
Diary of the Great War (typed manuscript) Lt.-Col. Wollscombe, date unknown

A.A. Burt
Herts Mercury 29 January 1916
Daily Mirror 9 November 1929
Bucks Examiner 14/15 June 1962
1st Herts Regt *War Diary* (WO 95/1358 PRO)

H. Christian
The Times 19 September 1917
Glasgow Sunday Mail 12 April 1936
The Lion and the Dragon Vol 5 No 7 Spring 1975
http://1914-1918.invisionzone.com

T. Kenny
1st Loyal North Lancs Regt *War Diary* (WO 95/1270 PRO)
Tobacco 1 December 1929
News of the World 21 July 1940
Lancashire Lad – The Journal of the Lancashire Regiment Winter 1978

J. Caffrey
2nd York and Lancaster Regt *War Diary* (WO 95/1610 PRO)

Nottingham Journal 19 October 1931 and 20 October 1931
Universe 17 November 1933
Nottingham Evening Post 7 November 1936
Daily Graphic 28 September 1952

S. Meekosha
1/6 West Yorkshire Regt *War Diary* (WO 95/2794 PRO)
Bradford Telegraph and Argus Various editions October/ November 1929
South Wales Echo 20 July 1935
Tobacco 1 February 1937

A.G. Drake
8th Rifle Brigade *War Diary* (WO 95/1896 PRO)
Tower Hamlets Local History Library and Archive
Tower Hamlets Local History Library and Archives

W. Young
8th East Lancs Regt *War Diary* (WO 95/2537 PRO)

BIBLIOGRAPHY

The following list is a selection of the published sources used in this book. It does not include regimental, brigade or divisional histories which are too numerous to list.

Bancroft, J.W., *Devotion to Duty: Tribute to a Region's VCs*. 1990
Baynes, J., *Morale*. Leo Cooper. 1987
Bishop, A., *Our Bravest and Our Best*. McGraw-Hill-Ryerson. 1995
The Bond of Sacrifice. The Naval and Military Press. 1993
Brice, B. (comp.), *The Battle Book of Ypres*. Spa Books. 1990
Bristow, A., *A Serious Disappointment*. Leo Cooper. 1995
Canada in the Great War. 6 Vols 1921
Clark, A., *The Donkeys*. Hutchinson. 1961
Coleman, F., *With the Cavalry in 1915*. Sampson Low, Marston. 1916
Creagh, O'Moore and Humphries, E.M., *The VC and DSO*. 3 Vols. Standard Art Co. 1924
Curling, Bill, *The Captain*. Barrie and Jenkins. 1970
Deeds That Thrilled the Empire. Hutchinson. n.d.
Doyle, A. Conan, *The British Campaign in France and Flanders 1915*. Hodder and Stoughton. 1917
Duguid, Col. A. Fortescue, *Official History of the Canadian Forces in the Great War*. Vol 1. 1938
Edmonds, Brig.-Gen. J.E. (ed.), *Military Operations in France and Belgium 1914–18*. 11 vols. Macmillan. 1926–47
Eyre, Giles E.M., *Somme Harvest*. Jarrolds. 1938
Farndale, Gen. Sir Martin, *History of the Royal Regiment of Artillery on the Western Front 1914–18*. RAI, 1986
F.O.O. *With The Guns*. Eveleigh Nash. 1916
Gliddon, G. (ed.), *Norfolk and Suffolk in the Great War*. Gliddon Books. 1988

Graves, Robert, *Goodbye to All That*. Penguin. 1973

Hammerton, Sir J.A. (ed.), *A Popular History of the Great War*. 6 Vols

—— (ed.) *I Was There*. 4 Vols. Waverley. 1938

—— (ed.) *The War Illustrated*. 9 Vols. Amalgamated Press. 1914–19

Higley, D., *History of the Ontario Provincial Police*. Queen's Printer. 1984

Hurst, S.C., *The Silent Cities*. Naval and Military Press. 1993

James, Brig. A.E. *British Regiments 1914–18*. Samson Books. 1978

Johnson, J.H., *Stalemate*. Arms and Armour. 1995

Jones, Nigel H., *The War Walk*. Hale. 1983

Kirby, H.L., Pte. *William Young, VC*. THCL Books. 1985

KRRC Chronicle, 1915. The Wykeham Press. 1916

Leask, G.A., *VC Heroes of the War*. Harrap. 1917

Liddell-Hart, B., *A History of the World War 1914–18*. Faber & Faber. 1938

Location of Hospitals and Casualty Clearing Stations B.E.F. 1914–19. IWM

MacDonald, L., *1915 The Death of Innocence*. Headline. 1993

MacGill, Patrick, *The Great Push*. Caliban. 1984

Mason, P., *A Matter of Honour: An Account of the Indian Army*. 1986

McWilliams, James L. and Steel, R. James, *Gas! The Battle for Ypres 1915*. Vanwell. 1985

The Medical VCs. RAMC

Merewether, J.W.B., and Smith, F.E, *The Indian Corps in France*. John Murray. 1929

Moore, W., *Gas Attack!* Leo Cooper. 1987

Nicholson, Col. G.W.L., *Canadian Expeditionary Force 1914–19*. 1962

The Register of the VC. This England Books. 1988

Richter, D., *Chemical Soldiers*. University Press of Kansas. 1992

The Royal Artillery War Commemoration Book. Bell. 1988

Scott, M., *The Ypres Salient*. Gliddon Books. 1992

Slowe, P. and Woods, R., *Fields of Death*. Robert Wade. 1990

Smyth, J., *The Story of the Victoria Cross*. 1963

——. *The Only Enemy*. 1959

——. *Milestones*. 1979

Swinton, E.D., *Twenty Years After: The Battlefields of 1914–18: Then and Now*. 3 Vols. Newnes. 1936–38

Terraine, J., *The Great War 1914–18*. Arrow. 1967

Trench, Charles Chevenix, *The Indian Army and The King's Enemies*. 1988

The War Budget. Vols 2,3,4. The Daily Chronicle. 1914–18
The War Diary of the Master of Belhaven. Wharncliffe. 1990
War Graves of the Empire. The Times. 1928
Warner, P., *The Battle of Loos.* 1976
Williams, W. Alister, *The VCs of Wales and the Welsh Regiments.* 1984
Wonderful Stories: Winning the VC in the Great War. Hutchinson
Woolley, G.H., *Sometimes A Soldier.* Benn. 1963

INDEX